Date: 9/18/14

741.5 SUP V.1
Soule, Charles,
Superman/Wonder Woman.
Power couple /

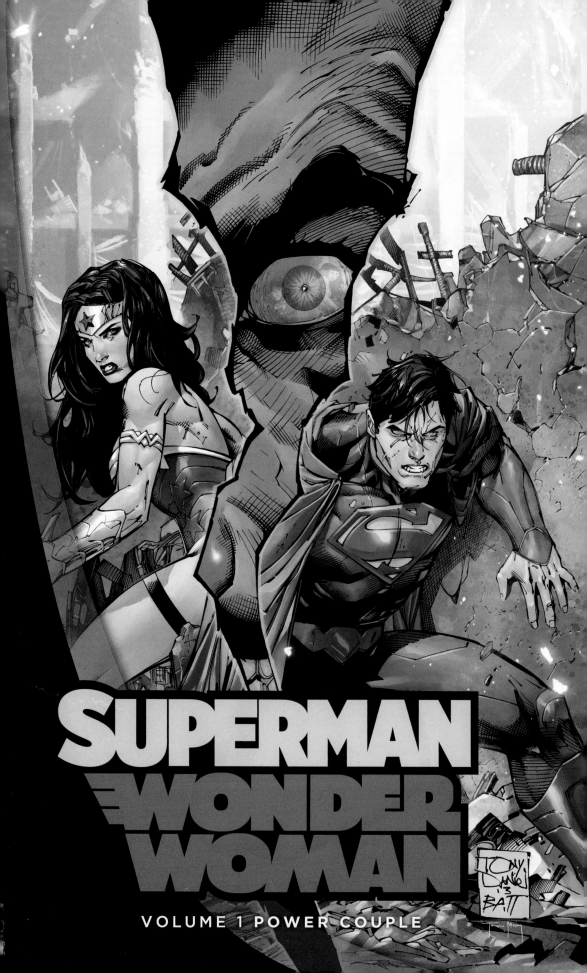

SUPERMAN
WONDER WOMAN

VOLUME 1 POWER COUPLE

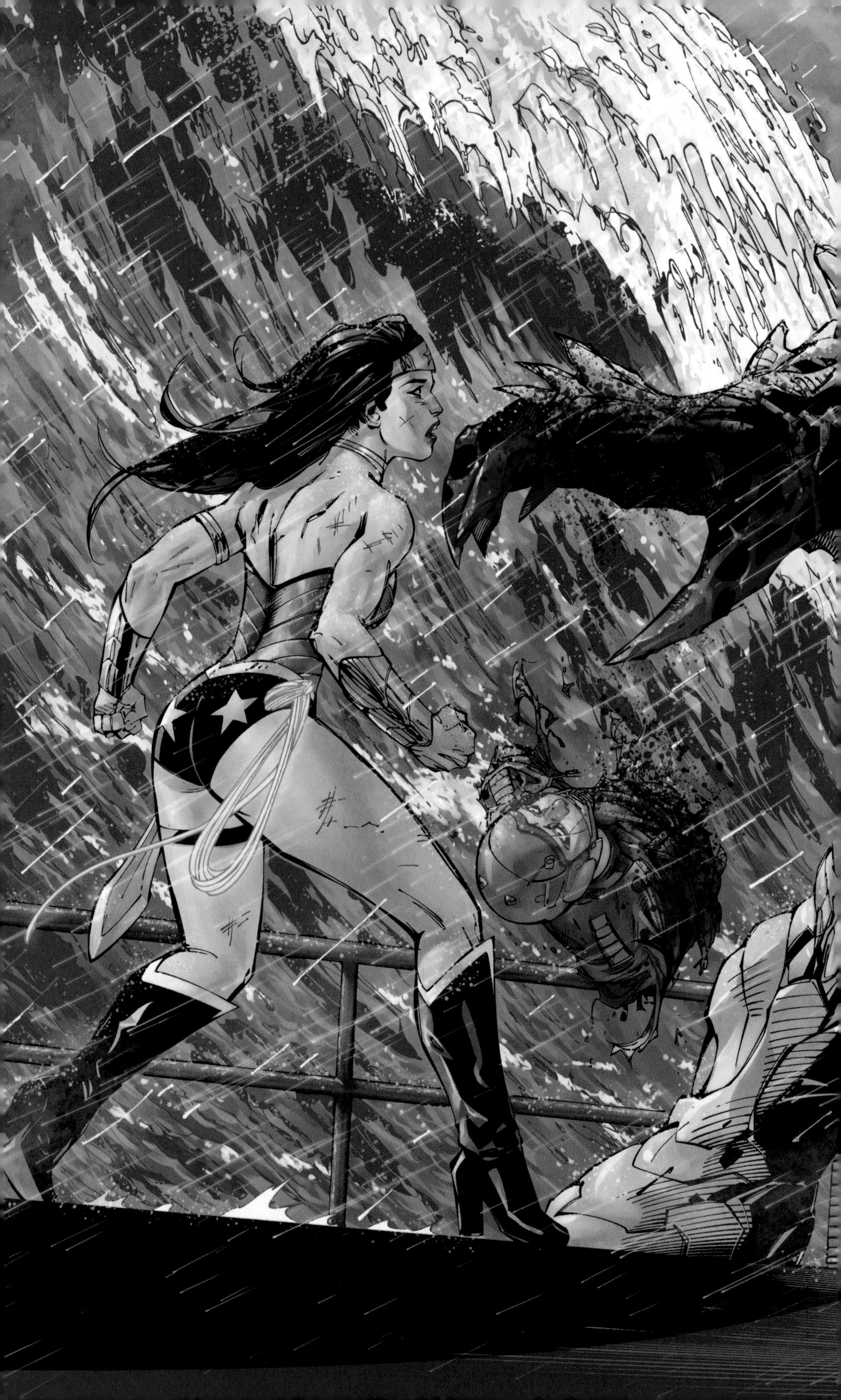

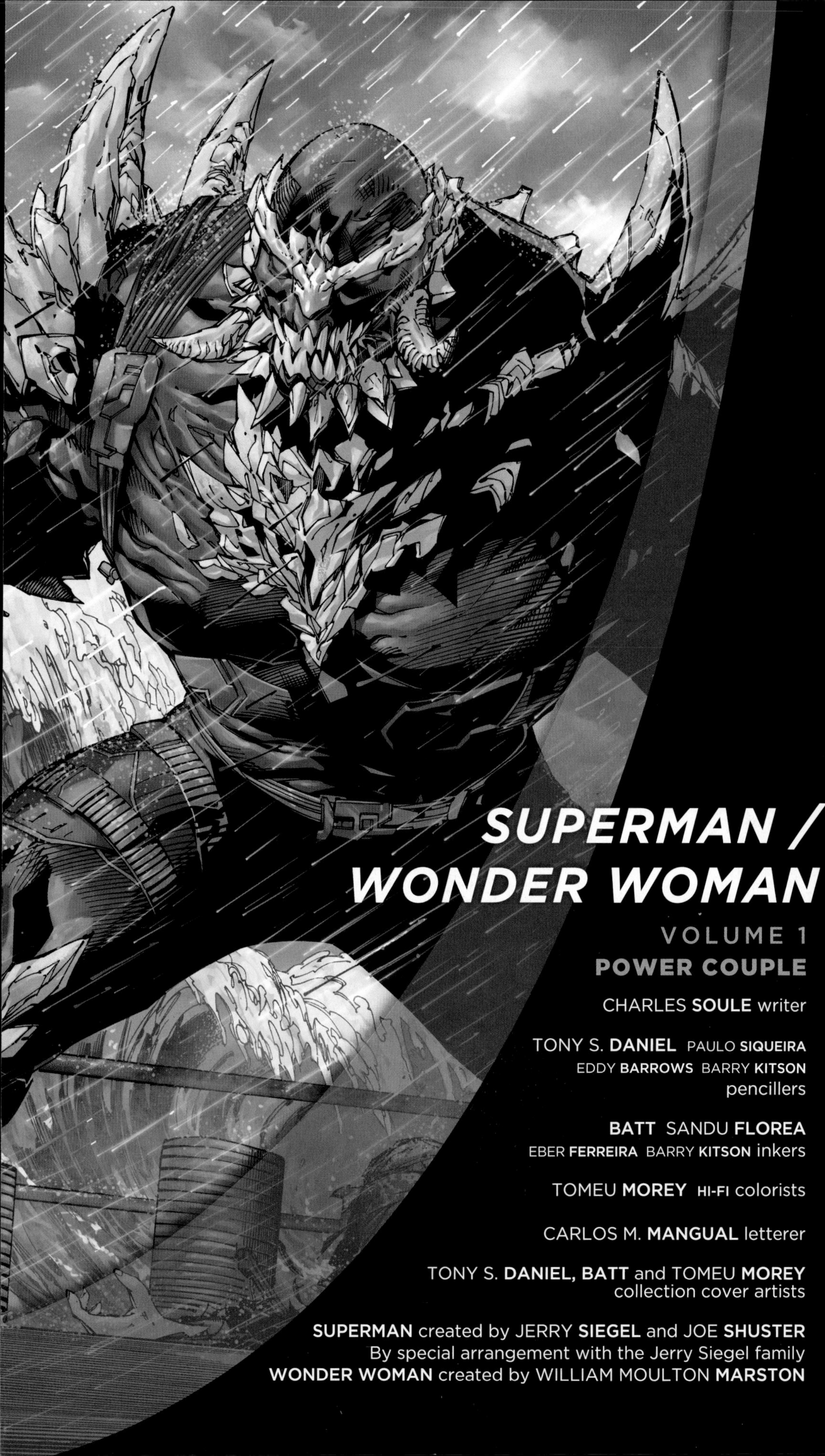

SUPERMAN / WONDER WOMAN

VOLUME 1

POWER COUPLE

CHARLES **SOULE** writer

TONY S. **DANIEL** PAULO **SIQUEIRA** EDDY **BARROWS** BARRY **KITSON** pencillers

BATT SANDU **FLOREA** EBER **FERREIRA** BARRY **KITSON** inkers

TOMEU **MOREY** **HI-FI** colorists

CARLOS M. **MANGUAL** letterer

TONY S. **DANIEL, BATT** and TOMEU **MOREY** collection cover artists

SUPERMAN created by JERRY **SIEGEL** and JOE **SHUSTER**
By special arrangement with the Jerry Siegel family
WONDER WOMAN created by WILLIAM MOULTON **MARSTON**

EDDIE BERGANZA Editor – Original Series RICKEY PURDIN Associate Editor – Original Series
ANTHONY MARQUES Assistant Editor – Original Series   PETER HAMBOUSSI Editor
ROBBIN BROSTERMAN Design Director – Books

BOB HARRAS Senior VP – Editor-in-Chief, DC Comics

DIANE NELSON President DAN DIDIO and JIM LEE Co-Publishers GEOFF JOHNS Chief Creative Officer
AMIT DESAI Senior VP – Marketing and Franchise Management
AMY GENKINS Senior VP – Business and Legal Affairs NAIRI GARDINER Senior VP – Finance
JEFF BOISON VP – Publishing Planning MARK CHIARELLO VP – Art Direction and Design
JOHN CUNNINGHAM VP – Marketing TERRI CUNNINGHAM VP – Editorial Administration
LARRY GANEM VP – Talent Relations and Services ALISON GILL Senior VP – Manufacturing and Operations
HANK KANALZ Senior VP – Vertigo and Integrated Publishing JAY KOGAN VP – Business and Legal Affairs, Publishing
JACK MAHAN VP – Business Affairs, Talent NICK NAPOLITANO VP – Manufacturing Administration SUE POHJA VP – Book Sales
FRED RUIZ VP – Manufacturing Operations COURTNEY SIMMONS Senior VP – Publicity BOB WAYNE Senior VP – Sales

SUPERMAN/WONDER WOMAN VOLUME 1: POWER COUPLE

Published by DC Comics. Copyright © 2014 DC Comics. All Rights Reserved.

Originally published in single magazine form as SUPERMAN/WONDER WOMAN 1-7 © 2013, 2014 DC Comics.
All Rights Reserved. All characters, their distinctive likenesses and related elements featured in this publication are
trademarks of DC Comics. SCRIBBLENAUTS and all related characters and elements are trademarks of and
© Warner Bros. Entertainment Inc. ROBOT CHICKEN, the logo and all related elements are trademarks of and copyright by
Cartoon Network (s2014). MAD and Alfred E. Neuman © and ™ E. C. Publications, Inc.
The stories, characters and incidents featured in this publication are entirely fictional.
DC Comics does not read or accept unsolicited ideas, stories or artwork.

DC Comics, 1700 Broadway, New York, NY 10019
A Warner Bros. Entertainment Company.
Printed by RR Donnelley, Salem, VA, USA. 8/15/14. First Printing.

ISBN: 978-1-4012-4898-7

Library of Congress Cataloging-in-Publication Data

Soule, Charles.
Superman/Wonder Woman. Volume 1, Power Couple / Charles Soule, Tony Daniel.
pages cm. — (The New 52!)
ISBN 978-1-4012-4898-7 (hardback)
1. Graphic novels. I. Daniel, Tony S. (Antonio Salvador) II. Title. III. Title: Power Couple.
PN6728.S9S65 2014
741.5'973—dc23
2014018207

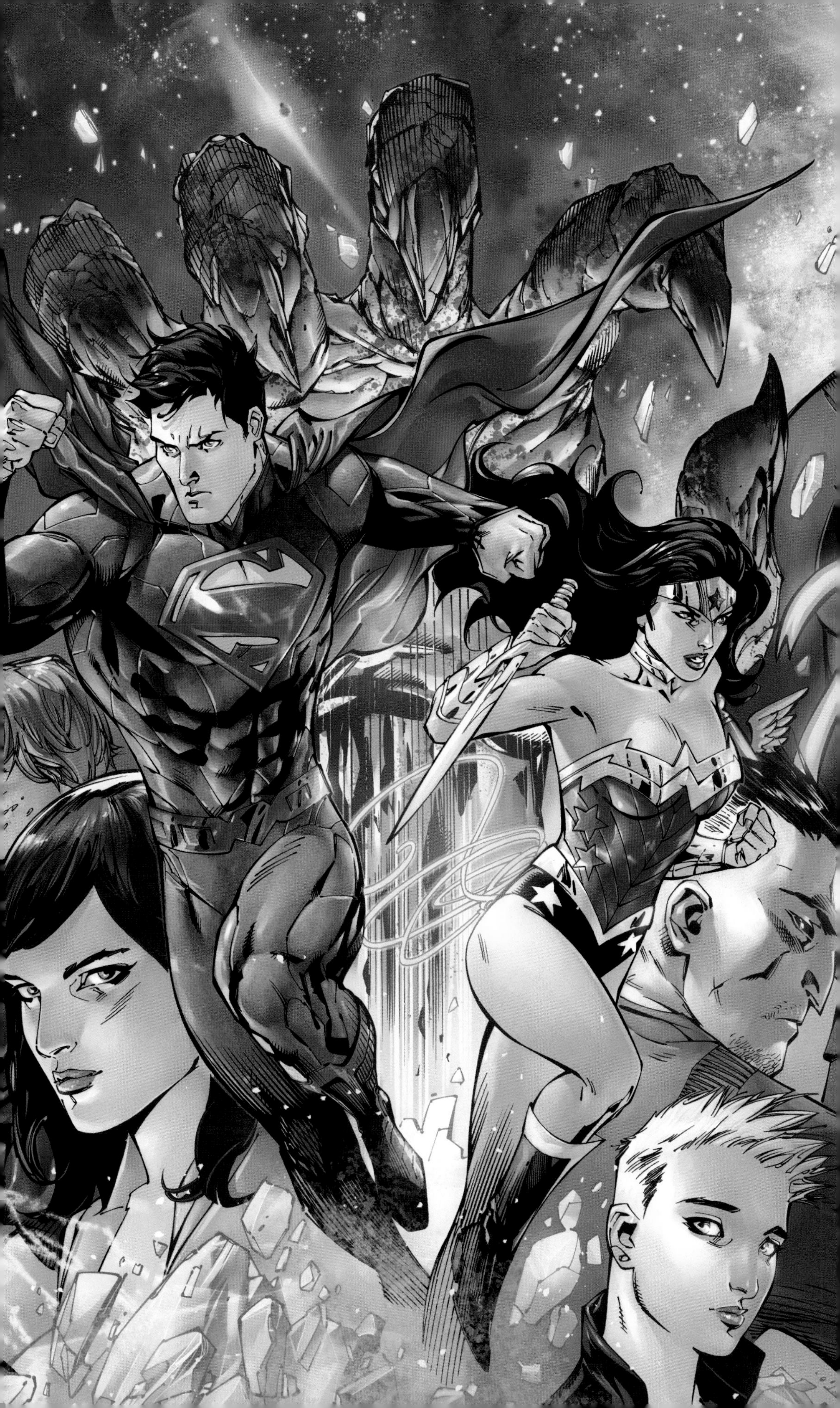

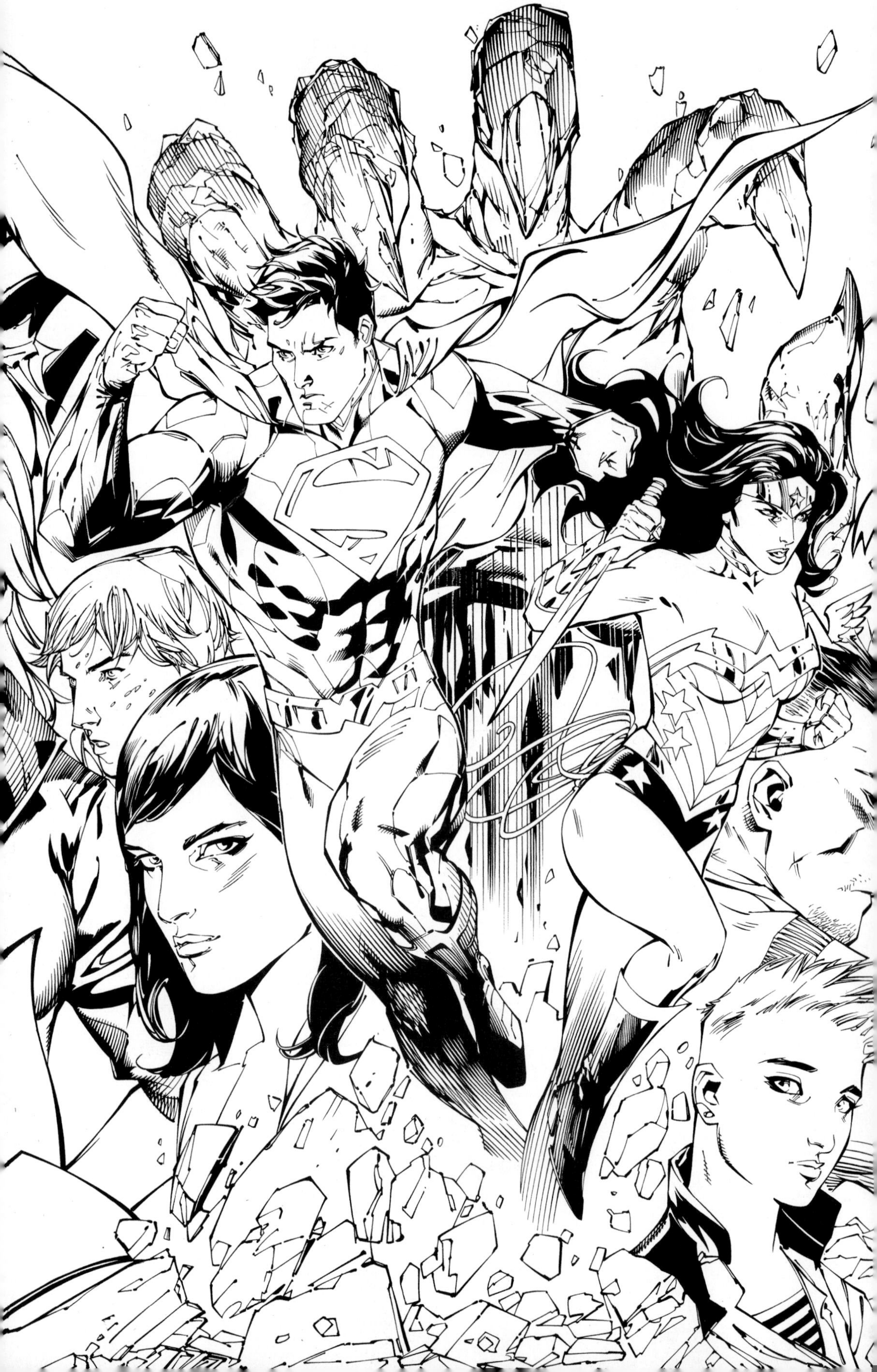

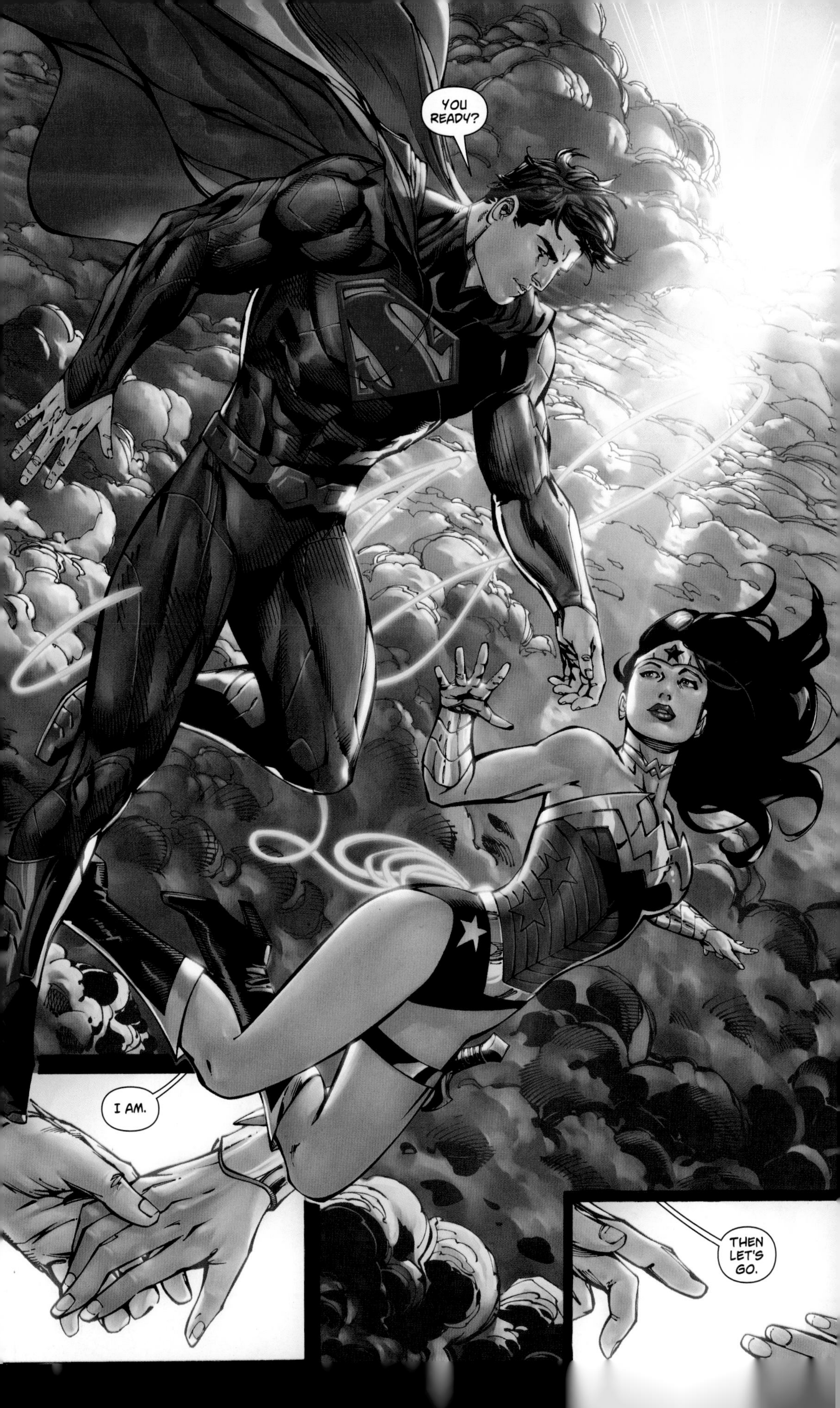
YOU READY?
I AM.
THEN LET'S GO.

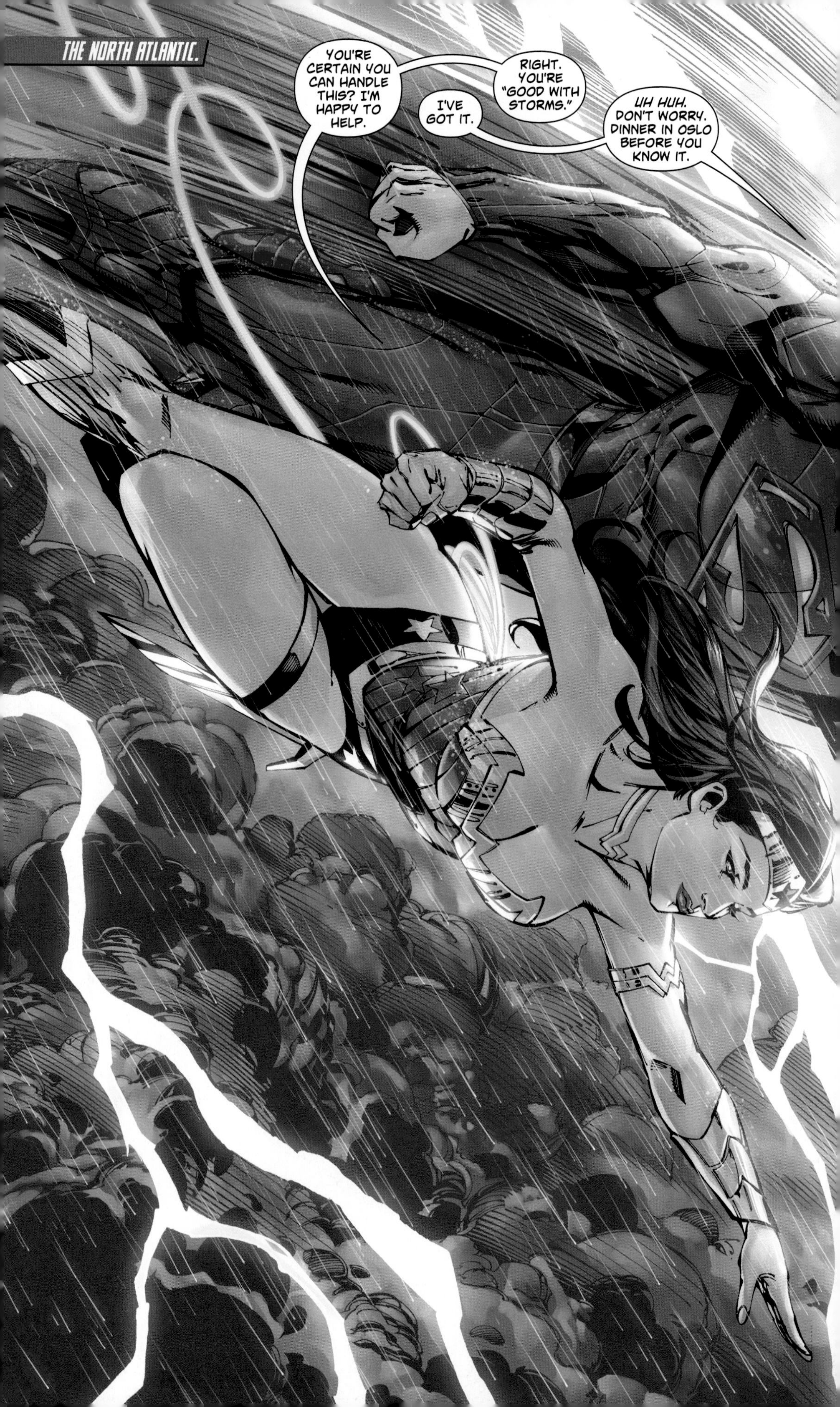
THE NORTH ATLANTIC.
YOU'RE CERTAIN YOU CAN HANDLE THIS? I'M HAPPY TO HELP.
I'VE GOT IT.
RIGHT. YOU'RE "GOOD WITH STORMS."
UH HUH. DON'T WORRY. DINNER IN OSLO BEFORE YOU KNOW IT.

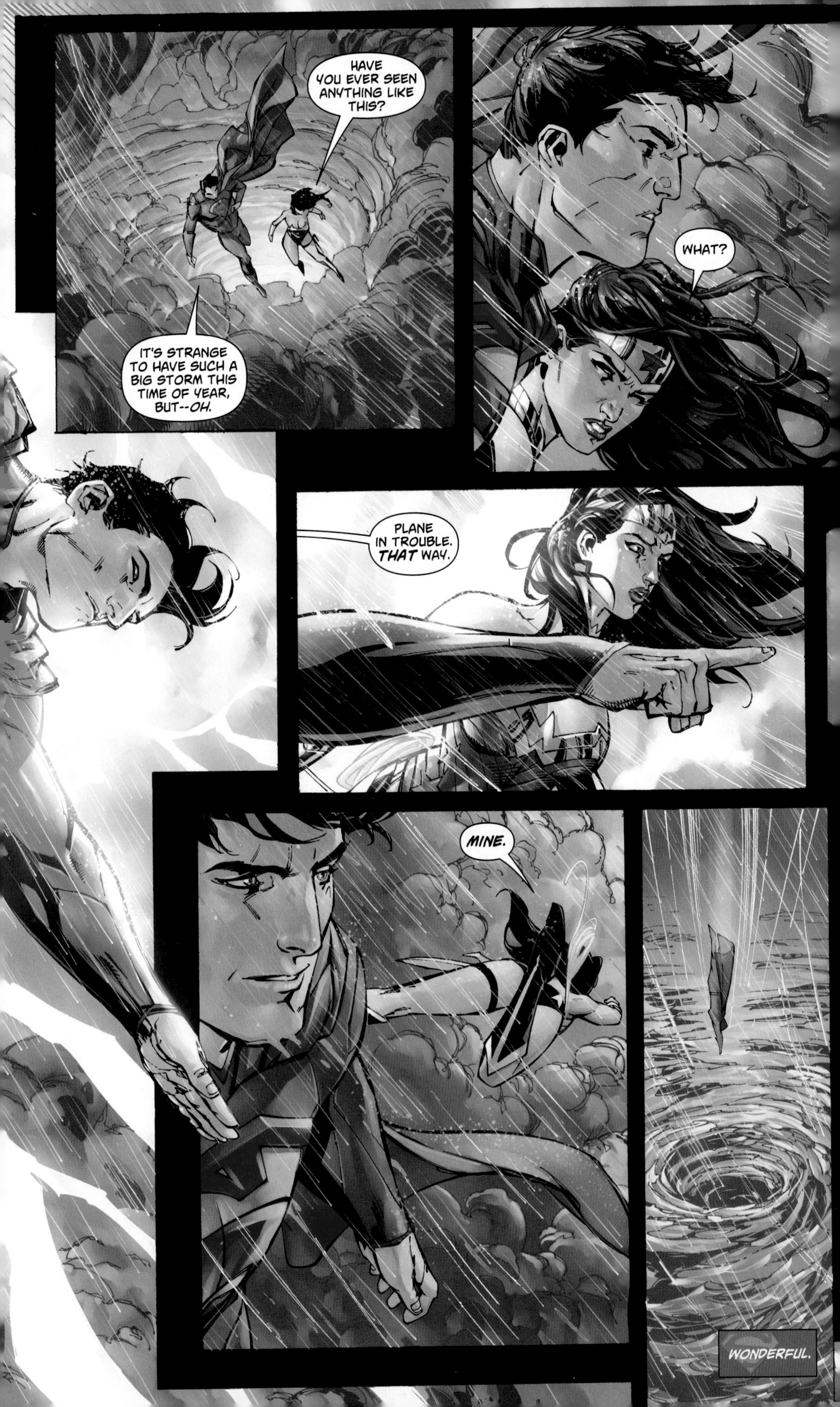
HAVE YOU EVER SEEN ANYTHING LIKE THIS?
IT'S STRANGE TO HAVE SUCH A BIG STORM THIS TIME OF YEAR, BUT--OH.
WHAT?
PLANE IN TROUBLE. THAT WAY.
MINE.
WONDERFUL.

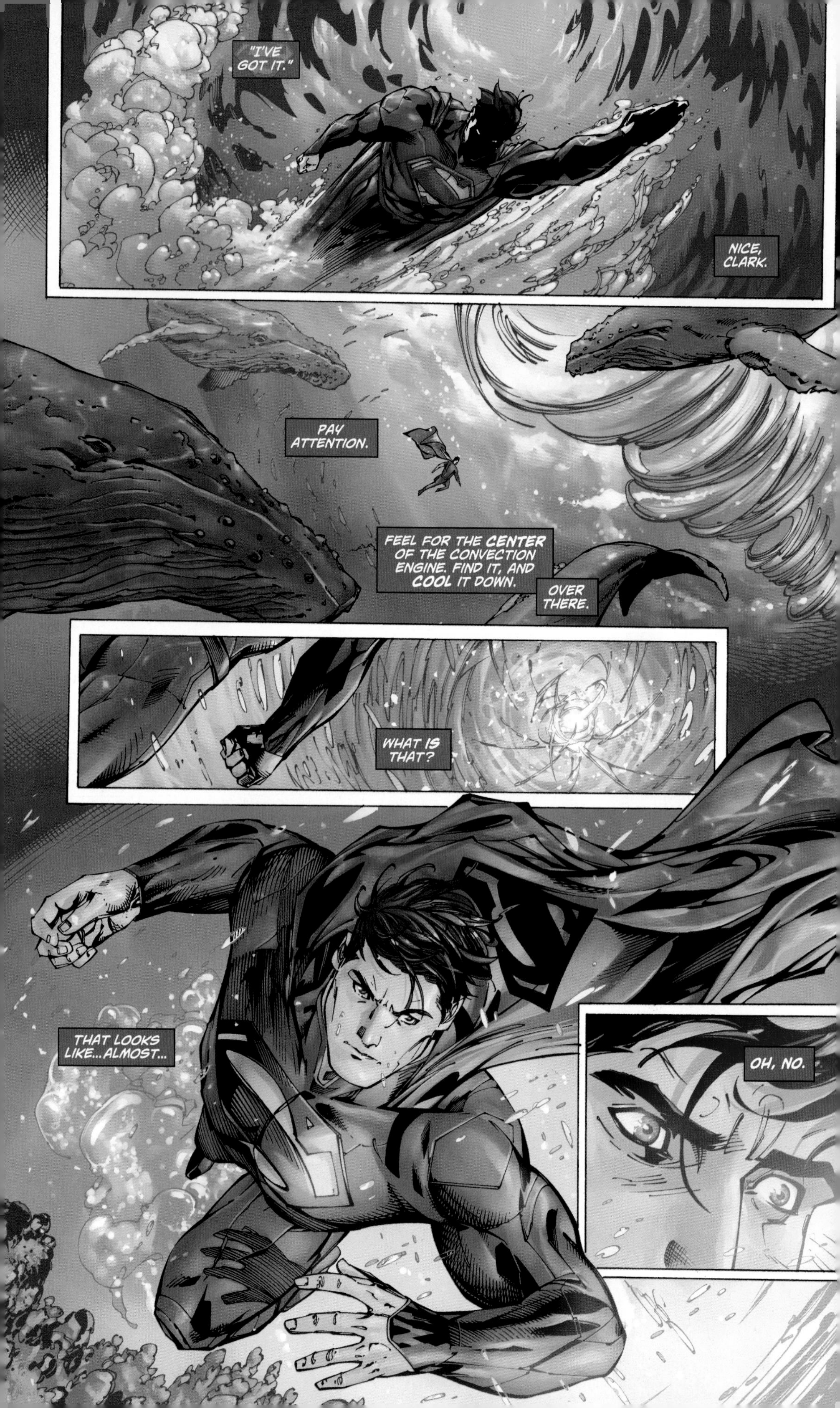
"I'VE GOT IT."
NICE, CLARK.
PAY ATTENTION.
FEEL FOR THE CENTER OF THE CONVECTION ENGINE. FIND IT, AND COOL IT DOWN.
OVER THERE.
WHAT IS THAT?
THAT LOOKS LIKE...ALMOST...
OH, NO.

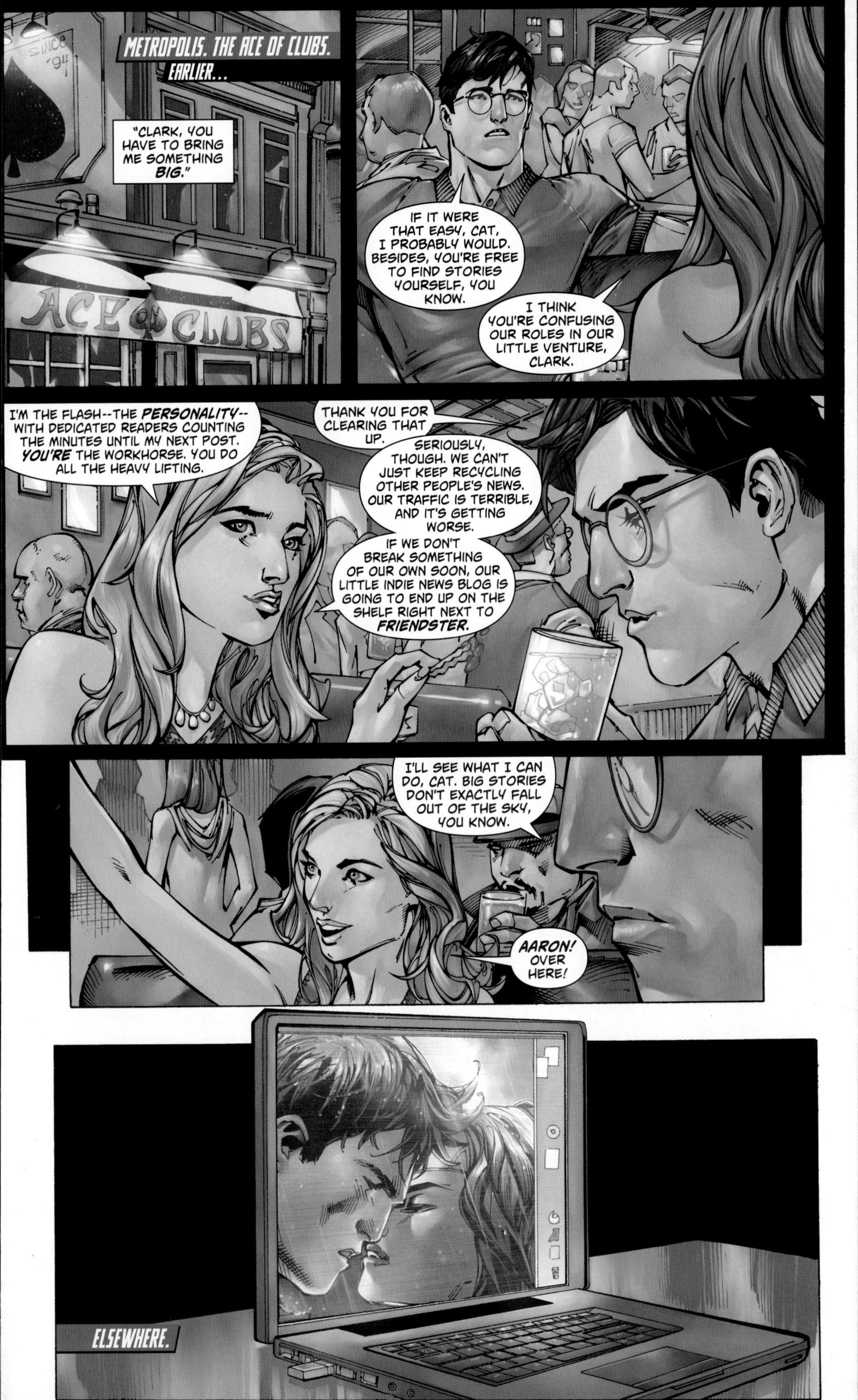
METROPOLIS. THE ACE OF CLUBS.
EARLIER...
SINCE '94
"CLARK, YOU HAVE TO BRING ME SOMETHING BIG."
ACE CLUBS
IF IT WERE THAT EASY, CAT, I PROBABLY WOULD. BESIDES, YOU'RE FREE TO FIND STORIES YOURSELF, YOU KNOW.
I THINK YOU'RE CONFUSING OUR ROLES IN OUR LITTLE VENTURE, CLARK.
I'M THE FLASH--THE PERSONALITY--WITH DEDICATED READERS COUNTING THE MINUTES UNTIL MY NEXT POST. YOU'RE THE WORKHORSE. YOU DO ALL THE HEAVY LIFTING.
THANK YOU FOR CLEARING THAT UP.
SERIOUSLY, THOUGH. WE CAN'T JUST KEEP RECYCLING OTHER PEOPLE'S NEWS. OUR TRAFFIC IS TERRIBLE, AND IT'S GETTING WORSE.
IF WE DON'T BREAK SOMETHING OF OUR OWN SOON, OUR LITTLE INDIE NEWS BLOG IS GOING TO END UP ON THE SHELF RIGHT NEXT TO FRIENDSTER.
I'LL SEE WHAT I CAN DO, CAT. BIG STORIES DON'T EXACTLY FALL OUT OF THE SKY, YOU KNOW.
AARON! OVER HERE!
ELSEWHERE.

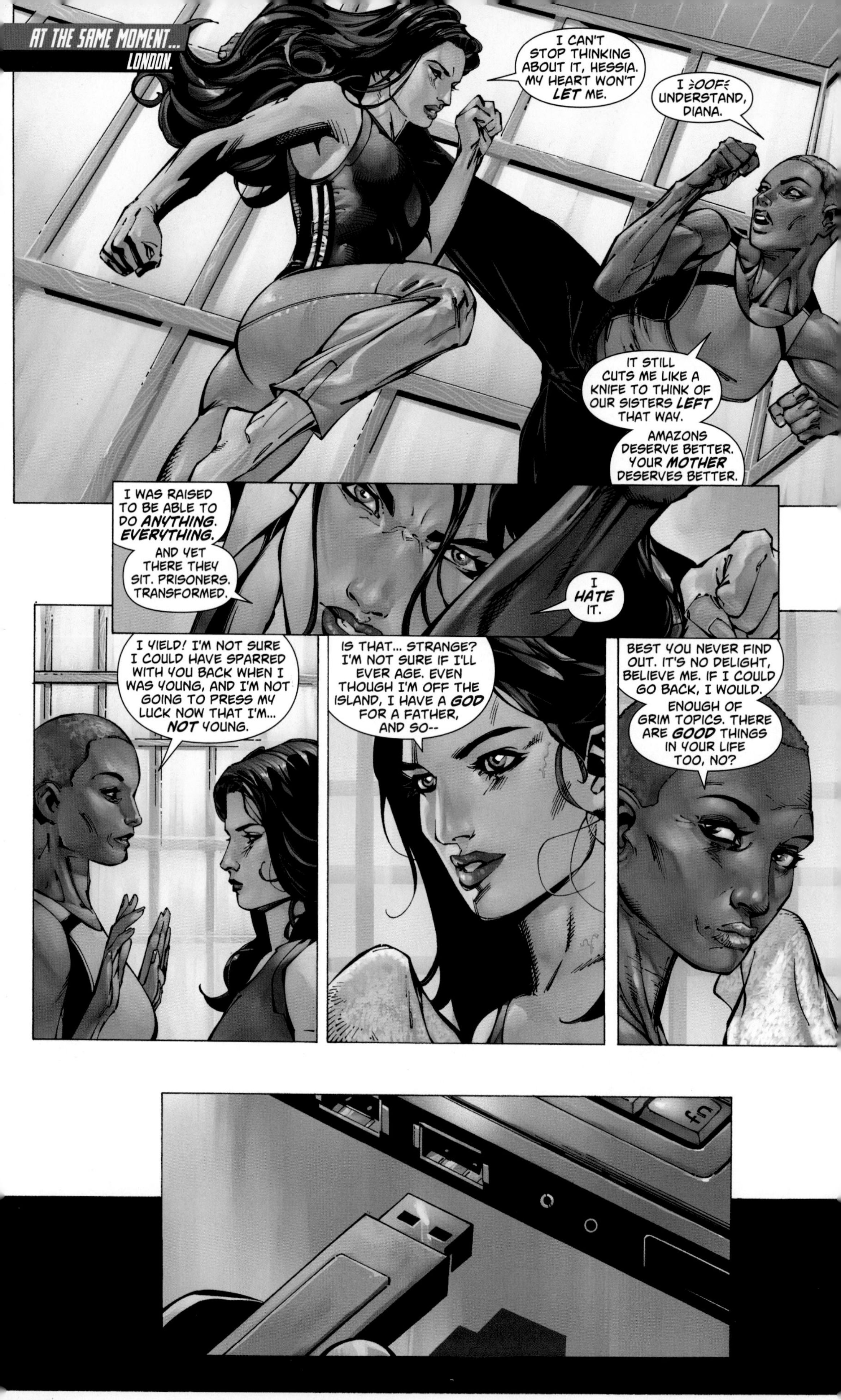

AT THE SAME MOMENT... LONDON.
I CAN'T STOP THINKING ABOUT IT, HESSIA. MY HEART WON'T LET ME.
I ≥OOF≤ UNDERSTAND, DIANA.
IT STILL CUTS ME LIKE A KNIFE TO THINK OF OUR SISTERS LEFT THAT WAY.
AMAZONS DESERVE BETTER. YOUR MOTHER DESERVES BETTER.
I WAS RAISED TO BE ABLE TO DO ANYTHING. EVERYTHING.
AND YET THERE THEY SIT. PRISONERS. TRANSFORMED.
I HATE IT.
I YIELD! I'M NOT SURE I COULD HAVE SPARRED WITH YOU BACK WHEN I WAS YOUNG, AND I'M NOT GOING TO PRESS MY LUCK NOW THAT I'M... NOT YOUNG.
IS THAT... STRANGE? I'M NOT SURE IF I'LL EVER AGE. EVEN THOUGH I'M OFF THE ISLAND, I HAVE A GOD FOR A FATHER, AND SO--
BEST YOU NEVER FIND OUT. IT'S NO DELIGHT, BELIEVE ME. IF I COULD GO BACK, I WOULD.
ENOUGH OF GRIM TOPICS. THERE ARE GOOD THINGS IN YOUR LIFE TOO, NO?
fn

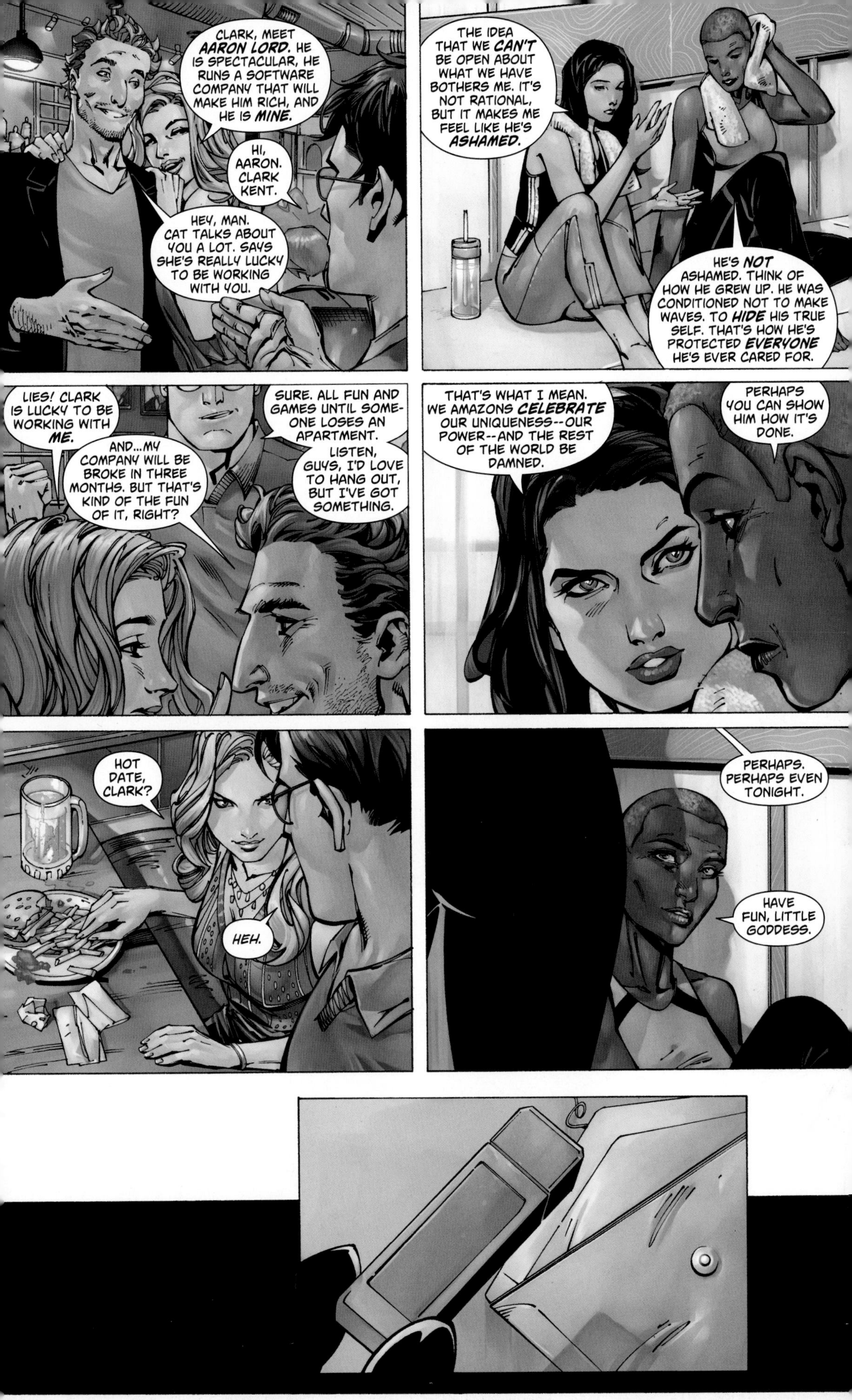
CLARK, MEET AARON LORD. HE IS SPECTACULAR, HE RUNS A SOFTWARE COMPANY THAT WILL MAKE HIM RICH, AND HE IS MINE.
HI, AARON. CLARK KENT.
HEY, MAN. CAT TALKS ABOUT YOU A LOT. SAYS SHE'S REALLY LUCKY TO BE WORKING WITH YOU.
THE IDEA THAT WE CAN'T BE OPEN ABOUT WHAT WE HAVE BOTHERS ME. IT'S NOT RATIONAL, BUT IT MAKES ME FEEL LIKE HE'S ASHAMED.
HE'S NOT ASHAMED. THINK OF HOW HE GREW UP. HE WAS CONDITIONED NOT TO MAKE WAVES. TO HIDE HIS TRUE SELF. THAT'S HOW HE'S PROTECTED EVERYONE HE'S EVER CARED FOR.
LIES! CLARK IS LUCKY TO BE WORKING WITH ME.
AND...MY COMPANY WILL BE BROKE IN THREE MONTHS. BUT THAT'S KIND OF THE FUN OF IT, RIGHT?
SURE. ALL FUN AND GAMES UNTIL SOME-ONE LOSES AN APARTMENT.
LISTEN, GUYS, I'D LOVE TO HANG OUT, BUT I'VE GOT SOMETHING.
THAT'S WHAT I MEAN. WE AMAZONS CELEBRATE OUR UNIQUENESS--OUR POWER--AND THE REST OF THE WORLD BE DAMNED.
PERHAPS YOU CAN SHOW HIM HOW IT'S DONE.
HOT DATE, CLARK?
HEH.
PERHAPS. PERHAPS EVEN TONIGHT.
HAVE FUN, LITTLE GODDESS.

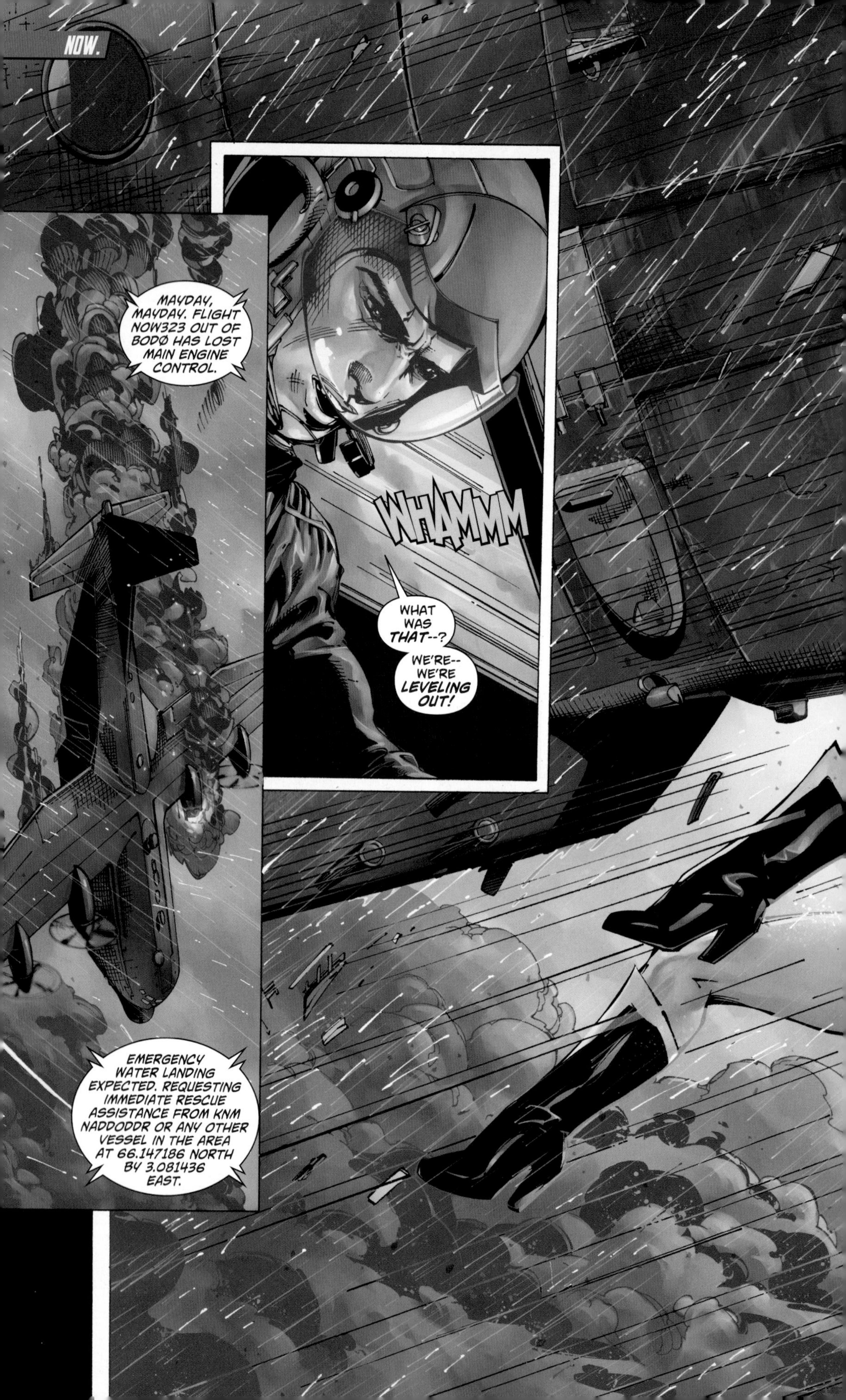
NOW.
MAYDAY, MAYDAY. FLIGHT NOW323 OUT OF BODØ HAS LOST MAIN ENGINE CONTROL.
WHAMMM
WHAT WAS THAT--?
WE'RE-- WE'RE LEVELING OUT!
EMERGENCY WATER LANDING EXPECTED. REQUESTING IMMEDIATE RESCUE ASSISTANCE FROM KNM NADDODDR OR ANY OTHER VESSEL IN THE AREA AT 66.147186 NORTH BY 3.081436 EAST.

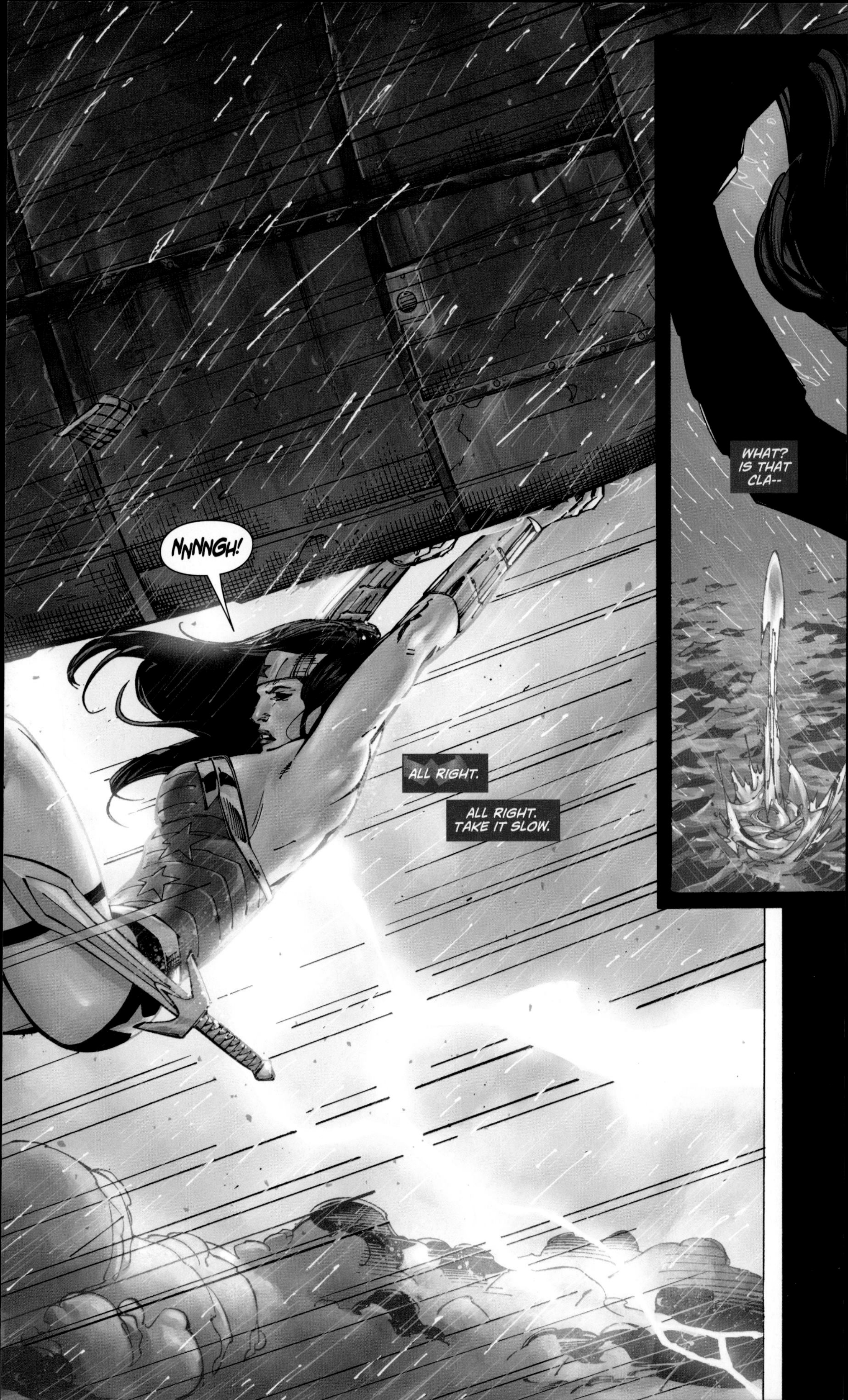
NNNNGH!
ALL RIGHT.
ALL RIGHT. TAKE IT SLOW.
WHAT? IS THAT CLA--

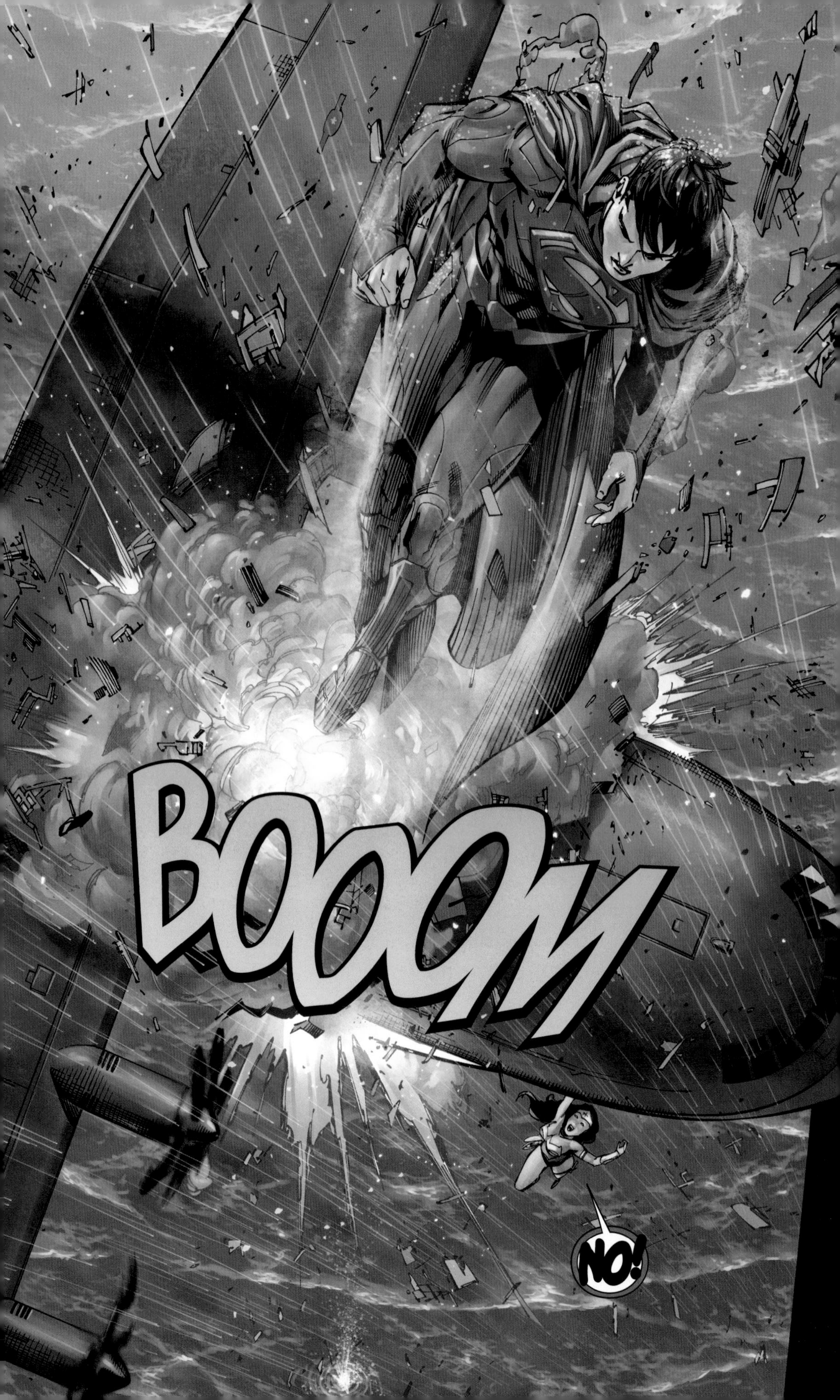
BOOOM
NO!

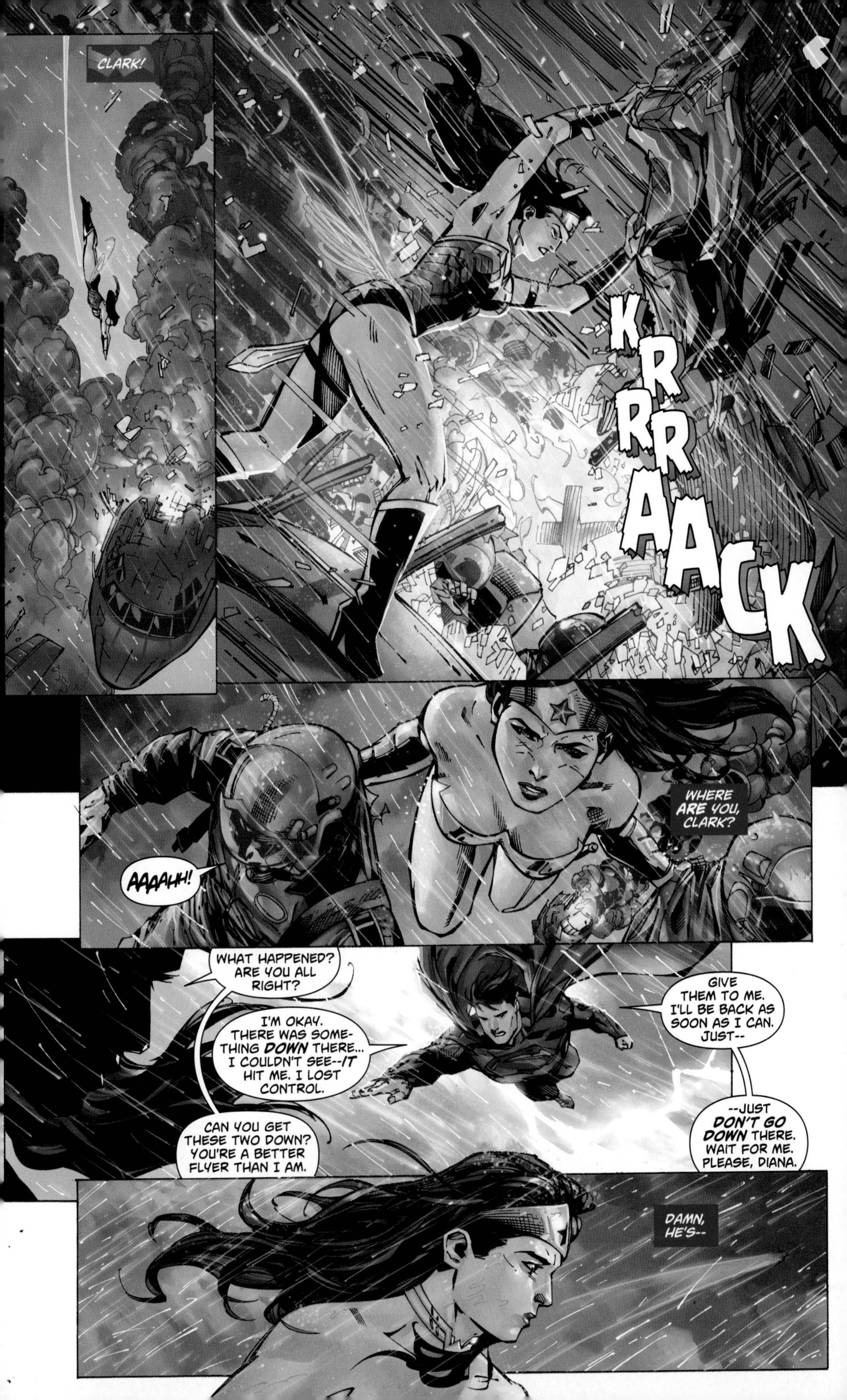
CLARK!
KRRRRAAACK
WHERE ARE YOU, CLARK?
AAAAHH!
WHAT HAPPENED? ARE YOU ALL RIGHT?
I'M OKAY. THERE WAS SOMETHING DOWN THERE... I COULDN'T SEE--IT HIT ME. I LOST CONTROL.
CAN YOU GET THESE TWO DOWN? YOU'RE A BETTER FLYER THAN I AM.
GIVE THEM TO ME. I'LL BE BACK AS SOON AS I CAN. JUST--
--JUST DON'T GO DOWN THERE. WAIT FOR ME. PLEASE, DIANA.
DAMN, HE'S--

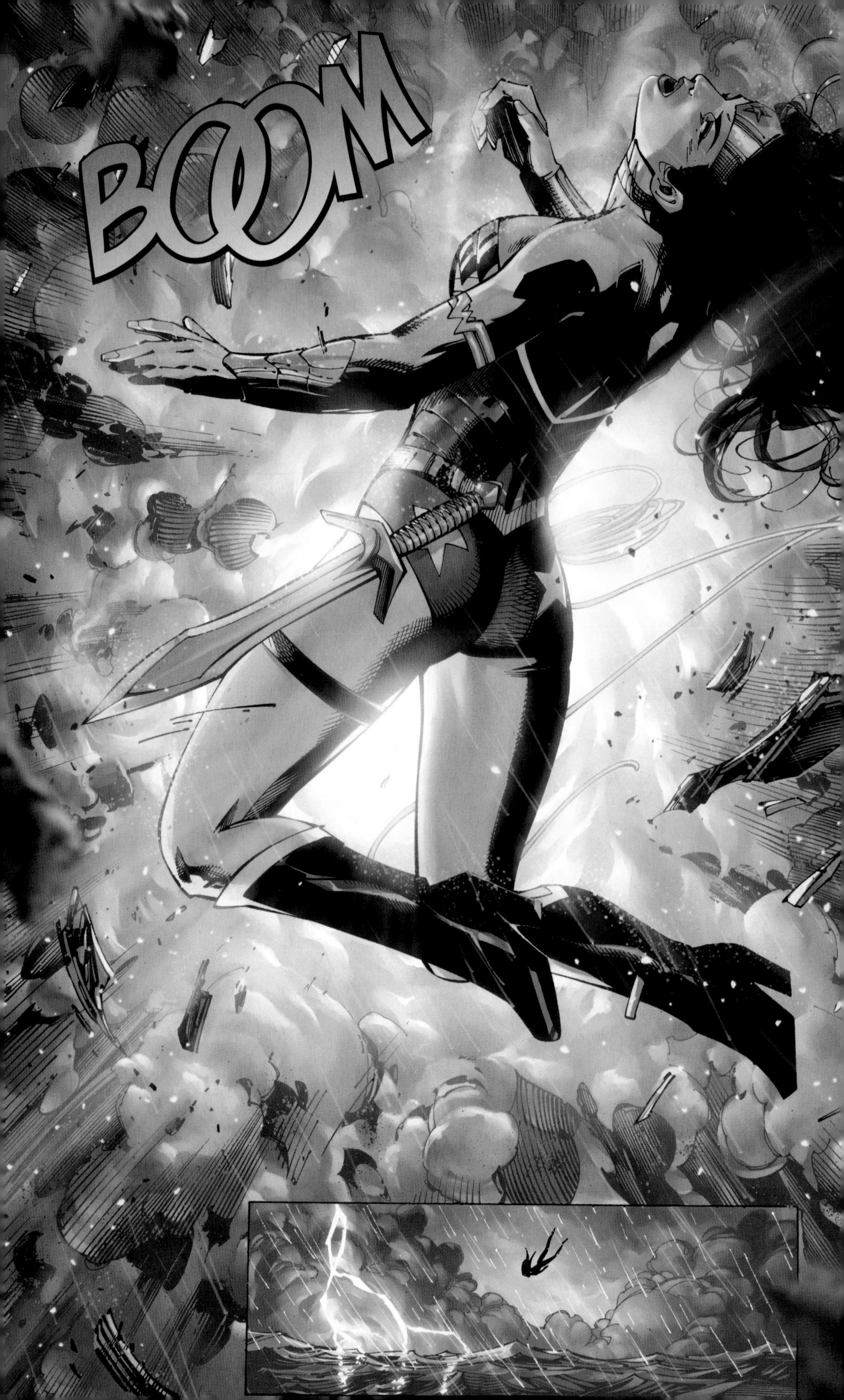
BOOM

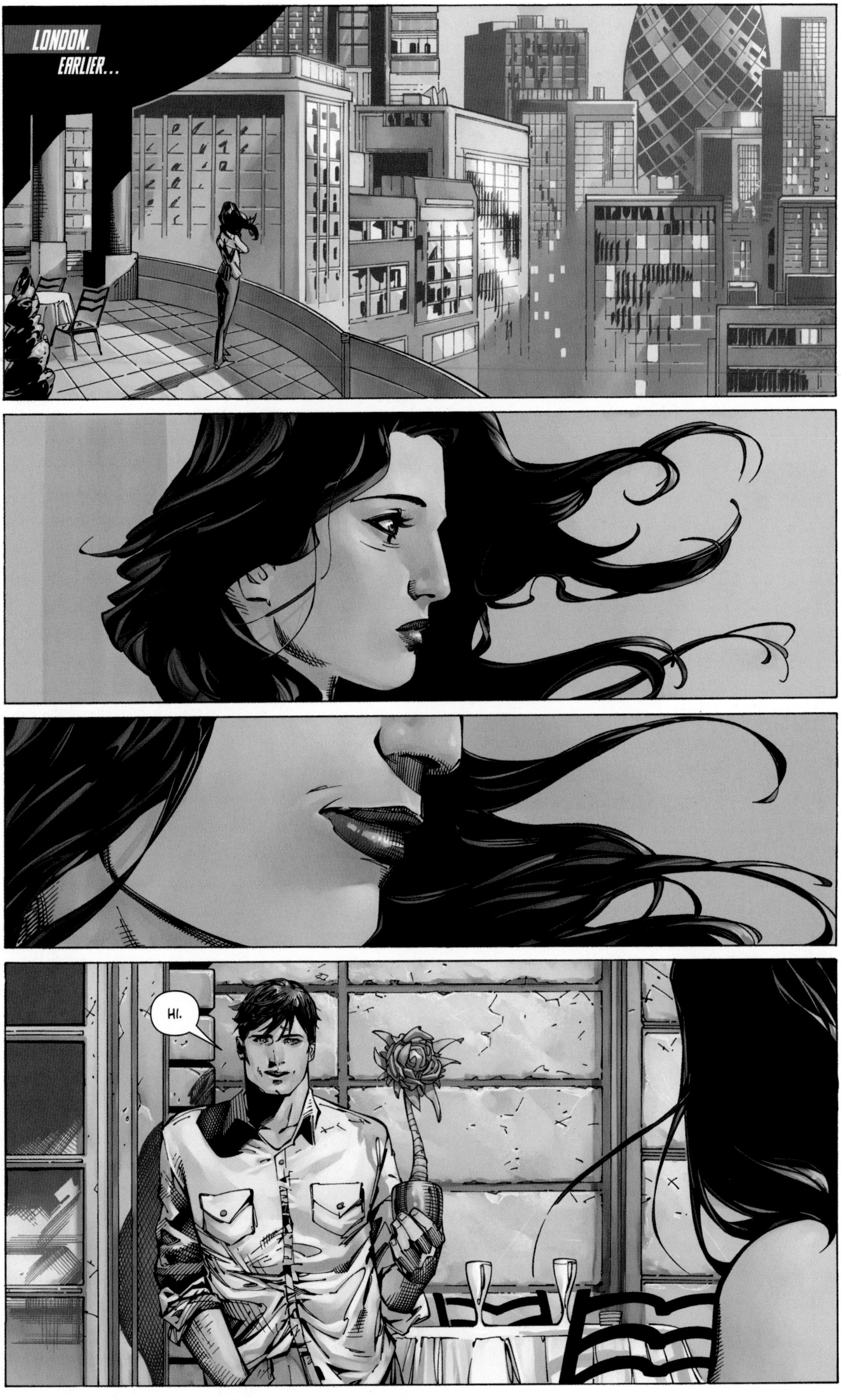

LONDON.
EARLIER...
HI.

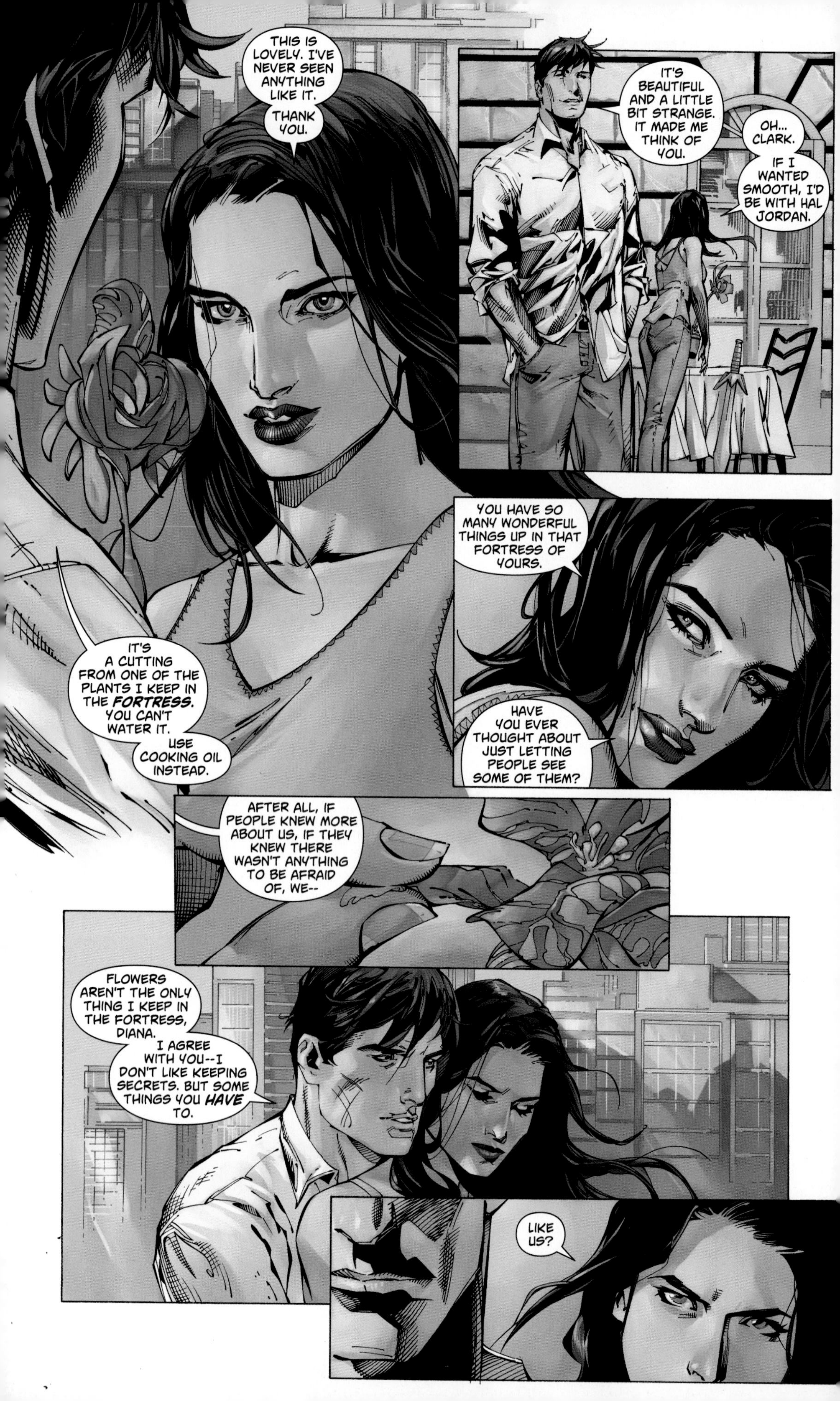
THIS IS LOVELY. I'VE NEVER SEEN ANYTHING LIKE IT.
THANK YOU.
IT'S BEAUTIFUL AND A LITTLE BIT STRANGE. IT MADE ME THINK OF YOU.
OH... CLARK.
IF I WANTED SMOOTH, I'D BE WITH HAL JORDAN.
IT'S A CUTTING FROM ONE OF THE PLANTS I KEEP IN THE FORTRESS. YOU CAN'T WATER IT.
USE COOKING OIL INSTEAD.
YOU HAVE SO MANY WONDERFUL THINGS UP IN THAT FORTRESS OF YOURS.
HAVE YOU EVER THOUGHT ABOUT JUST LETTING PEOPLE SEE SOME OF THEM?
AFTER ALL, IF PEOPLE KNEW MORE ABOUT US, IF THEY KNEW THERE WASN'T ANYTHING TO BE AFRAID OF, WE--
FLOWERS AREN'T THE ONLY THING I KEEP IN THE FORTRESS, DIANA.
I AGREE WITH YOU--I DON'T LIKE KEEPING SECRETS. BUT SOME THINGS YOU HAVE TO.
LIKE US?

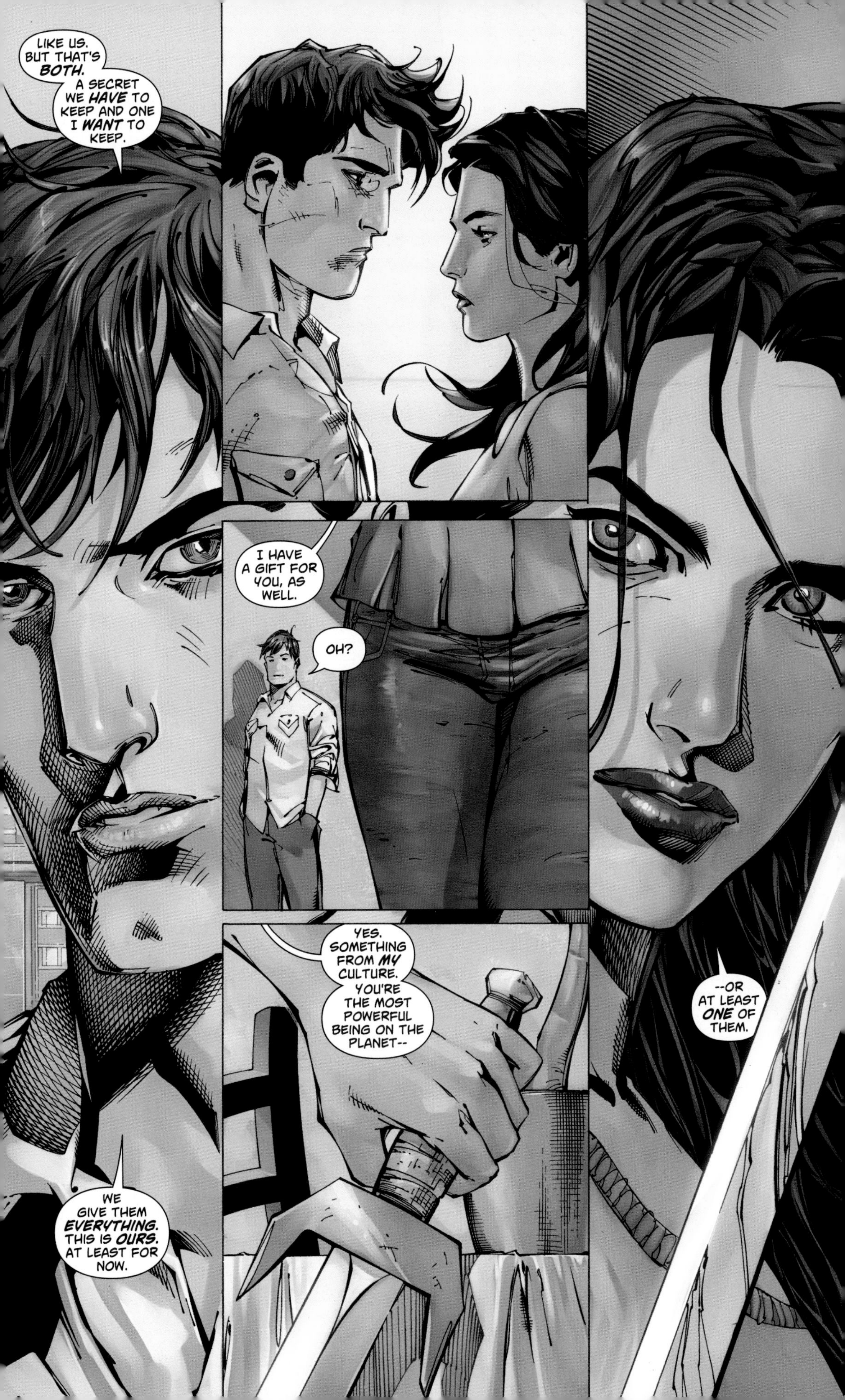
LIKE US. BUT THAT'S BOTH.
A SECRET WE HAVE TO KEEP AND ONE I WANT TO KEEP.
I HAVE A GIFT FOR YOU, AS WELL.
OH?
YES. SOMETHING FROM MY CULTURE.
YOU'RE THE MOST POWERFUL BEING ON THE PLANET--
--OR AT LEAST ONE OF THEM.
WE GIVE THEM EVERYTHING. THIS IS OURS. AT LEAST FOR NOW.

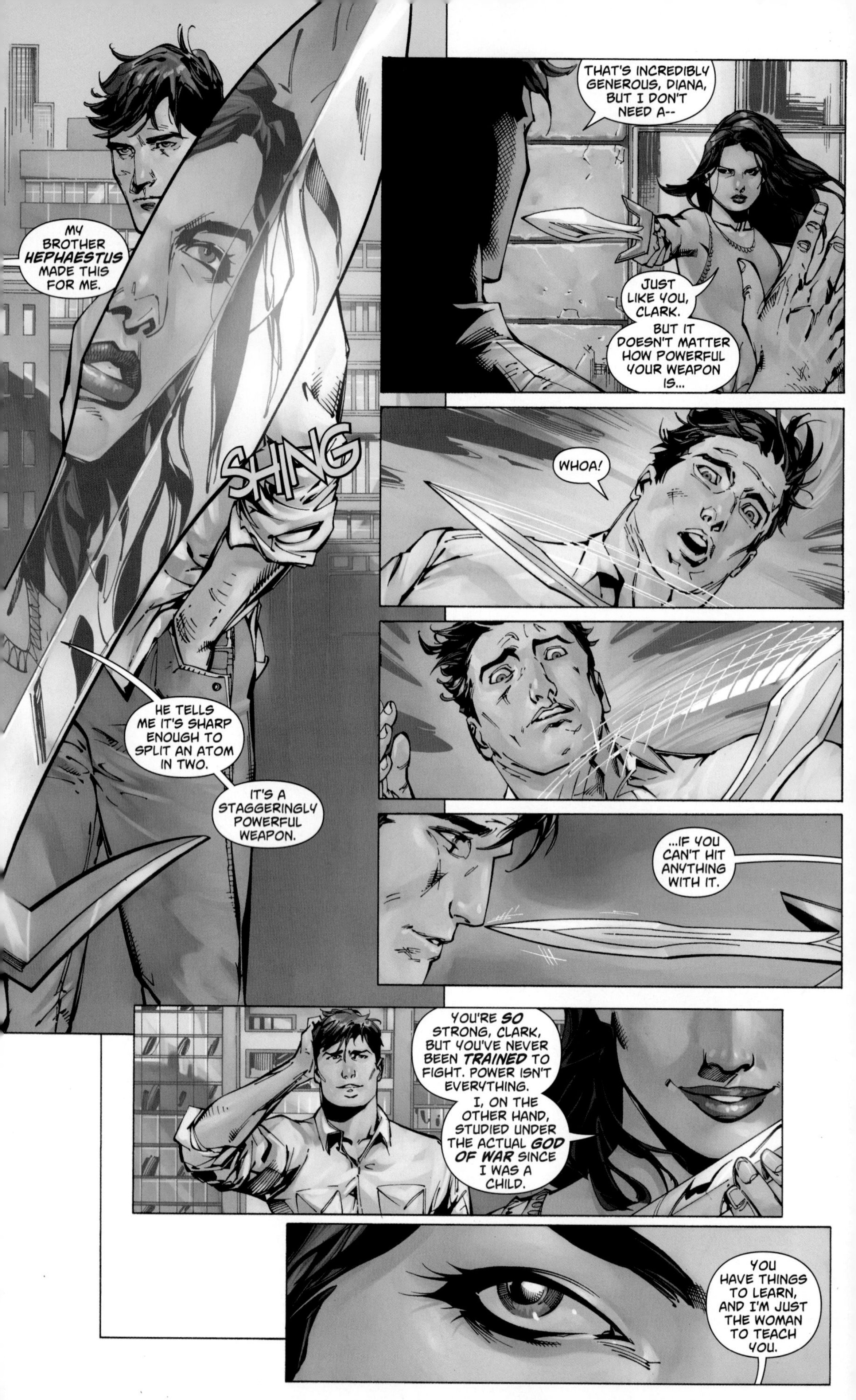
MY BROTHER HEPHAESTUS MADE THIS FOR ME.
SHING
HE TELLS ME IT'S SHARP ENOUGH TO SPLIT AN ATOM IN TWO.
IT'S A STAGGERINGLY POWERFUL WEAPON.
THAT'S INCREDIBLY GENEROUS, DIANA, BUT I DON'T NEED A--
JUST LIKE YOU, CLARK.
BUT IT DOESN'T MATTER HOW POWERFUL YOUR WEAPON IS...
WHOA!
...IF YOU CAN'T HIT ANYTHING WITH IT.
YOU'RE SO STRONG, CLARK, BUT YOU'VE NEVER BEEN TRAINED TO FIGHT. POWER ISN'T EVERYTHING.
I, ON THE OTHER HAND, STUDIED UNDER THE ACTUAL GOD OF WAR SINCE I WAS A CHILD.
YOU HAVE THINGS TO LEARN, AND I'M JUST THE WOMAN TO TEACH YOU.

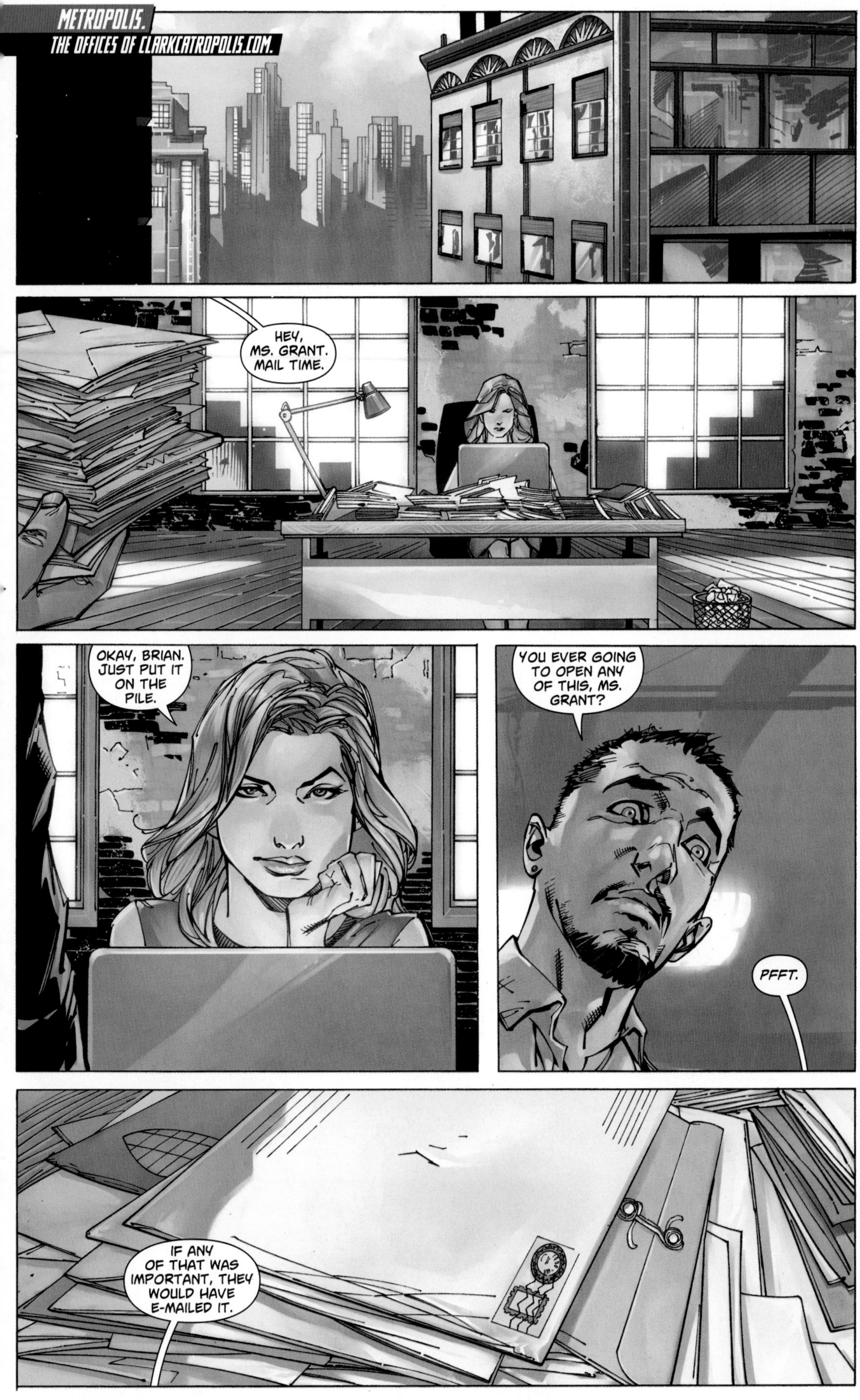
METROPOLIS.
THE OFFICES OF CLARKCATROPOLIS.COM.
HEY, MS. GRANT. MAIL TIME.
OKAY, BRIAN. JUST PUT IT ON THE PILE.
YOU EVER GOING TO OPEN ANY OF THIS, MS. GRANT?
PFFT.
IF ANY OF THAT WAS IMPORTANT, THEY WOULD HAVE E-MAILED IT.

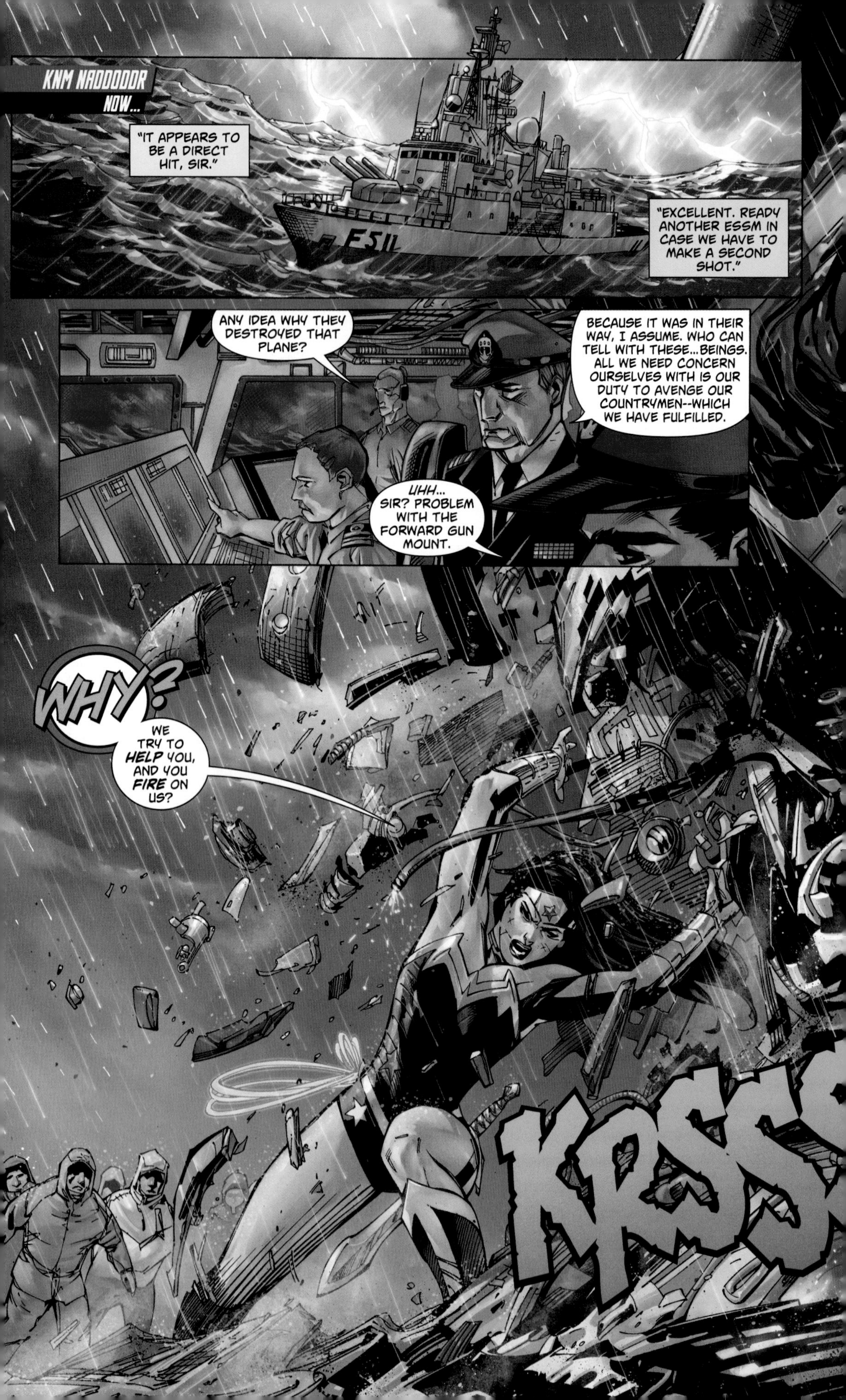
KNM NADDODDR
NOW...
"IT APPEARS TO BE A DIRECT HIT, SIR."
"EXCELLENT. READY ANOTHER ESSM IN CASE WE HAVE TO MAKE A SECOND SHOT."
ANY IDEA WHY THEY DESTROYED THAT PLANE?
BECAUSE IT WAS IN THEIR WAY, I ASSUME. WHO CAN TELL WITH THESE...BEINGS. ALL WE NEED CONCERN OURSELVES WITH IS OUR DUTY TO AVENGE OUR COUNTRYMEN--WHICH WE HAVE FULFILLED.
UHH... SIR? PROBLEM WITH THE FORWARD GUN MOUNT.
WHY?!
WE TRY TO HELP YOU, AND YOU FIRE ON US?
KRSSS

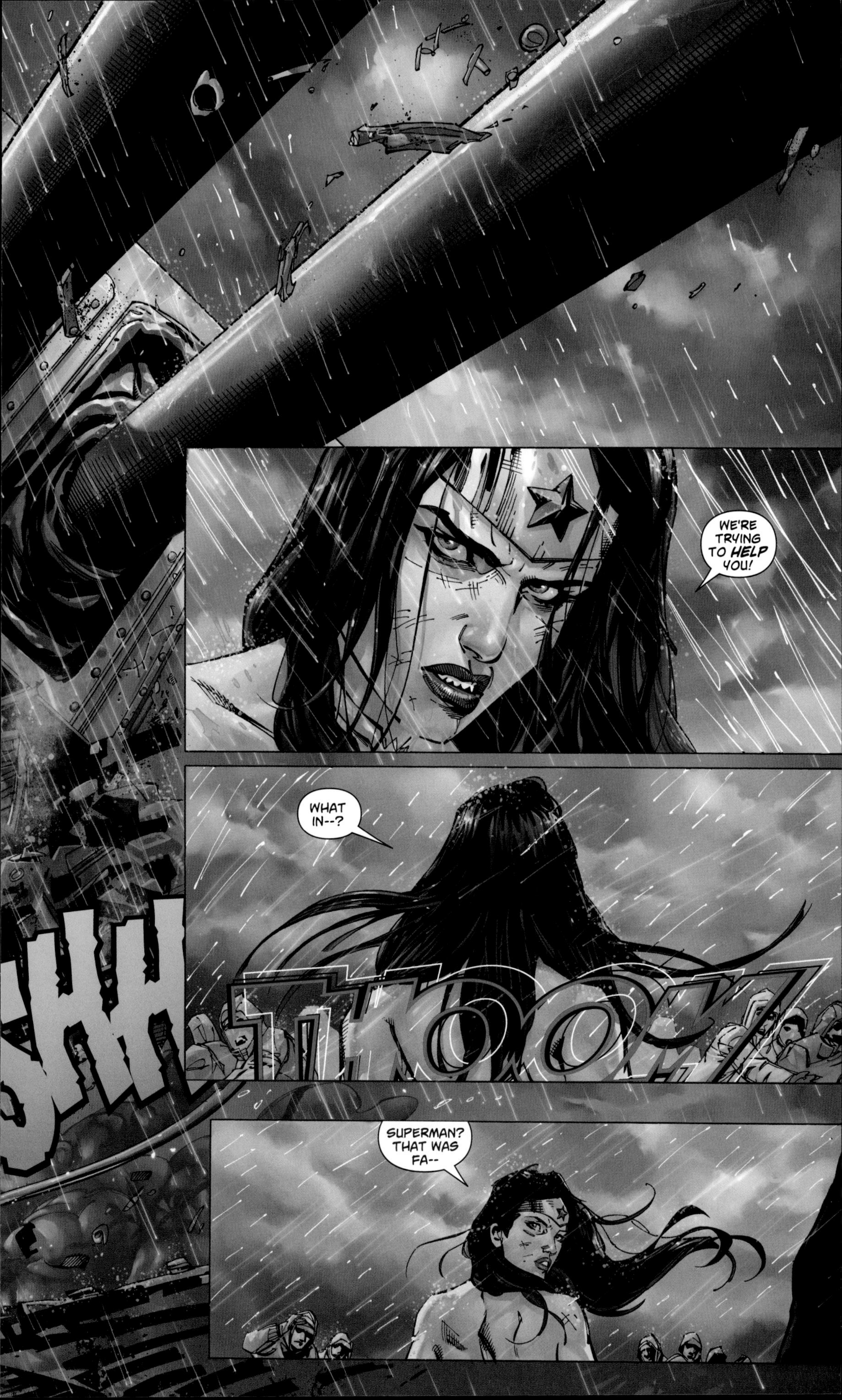

WE'RE TRYING TO HELP YOU!
WHAT IN--?
SHH
THOOM
SUPERMAN? THAT WAS FA--

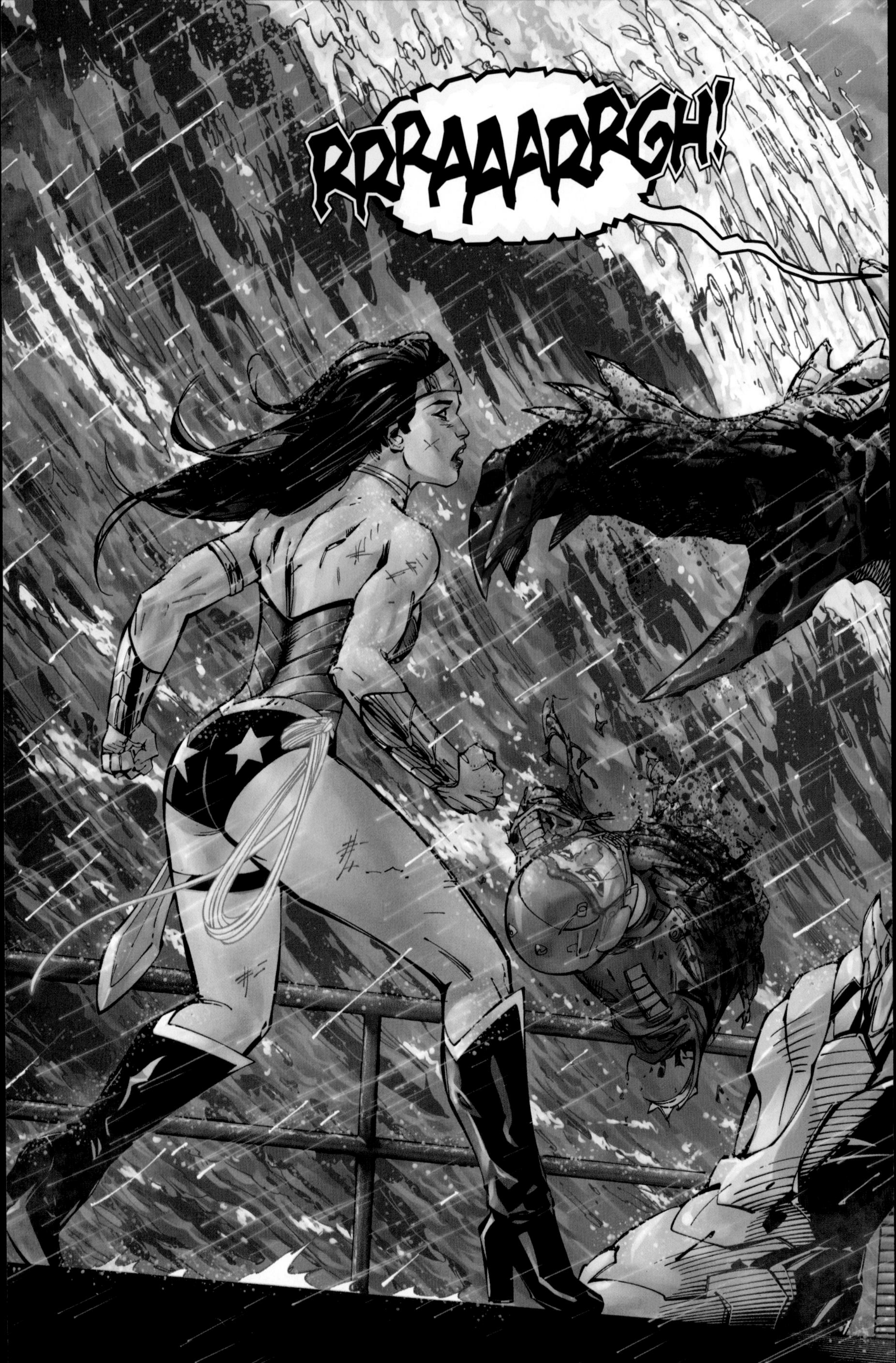
RRRAAAARRGH!

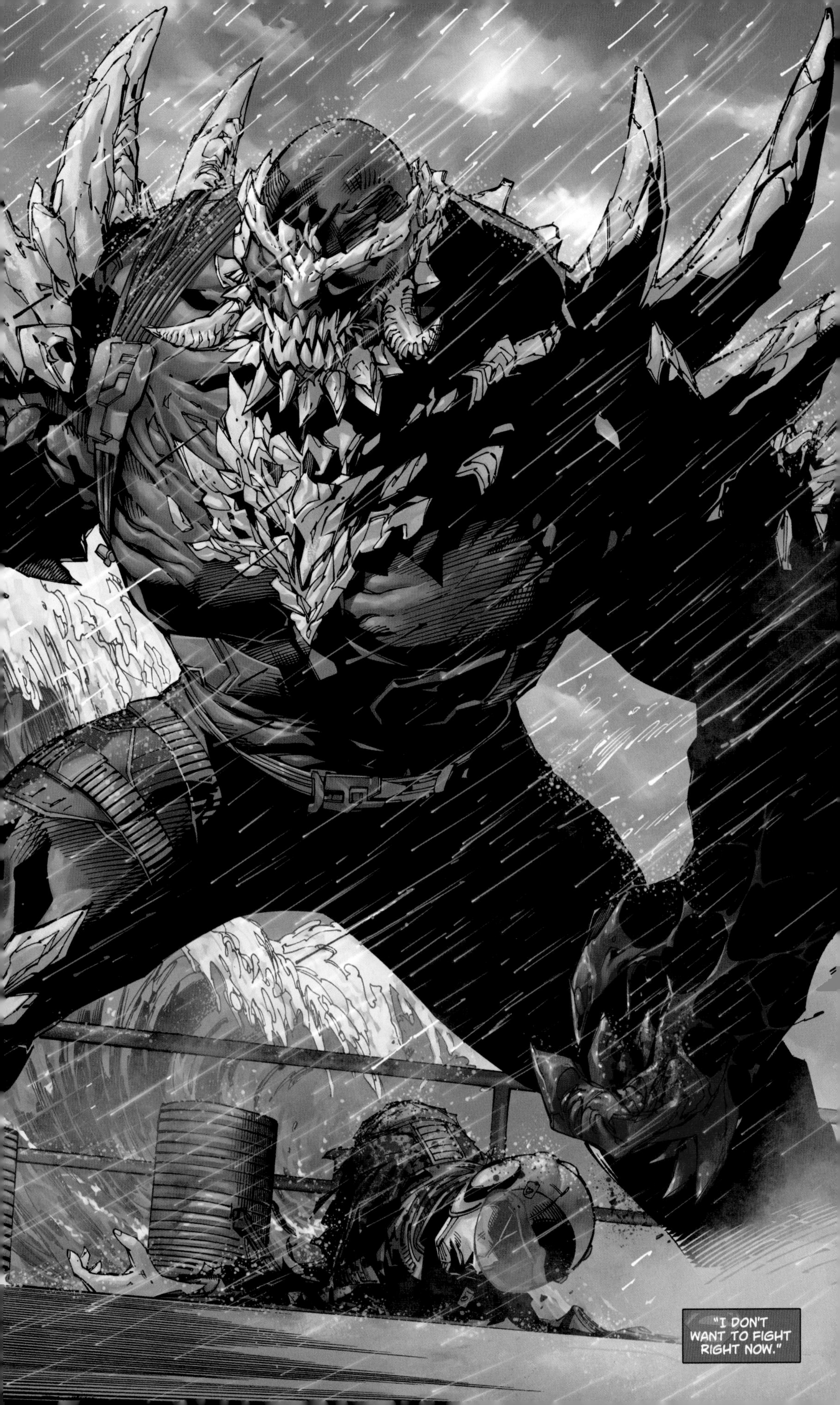
"I DON'T
WANT TO FIGHT
RIGHT NOW."

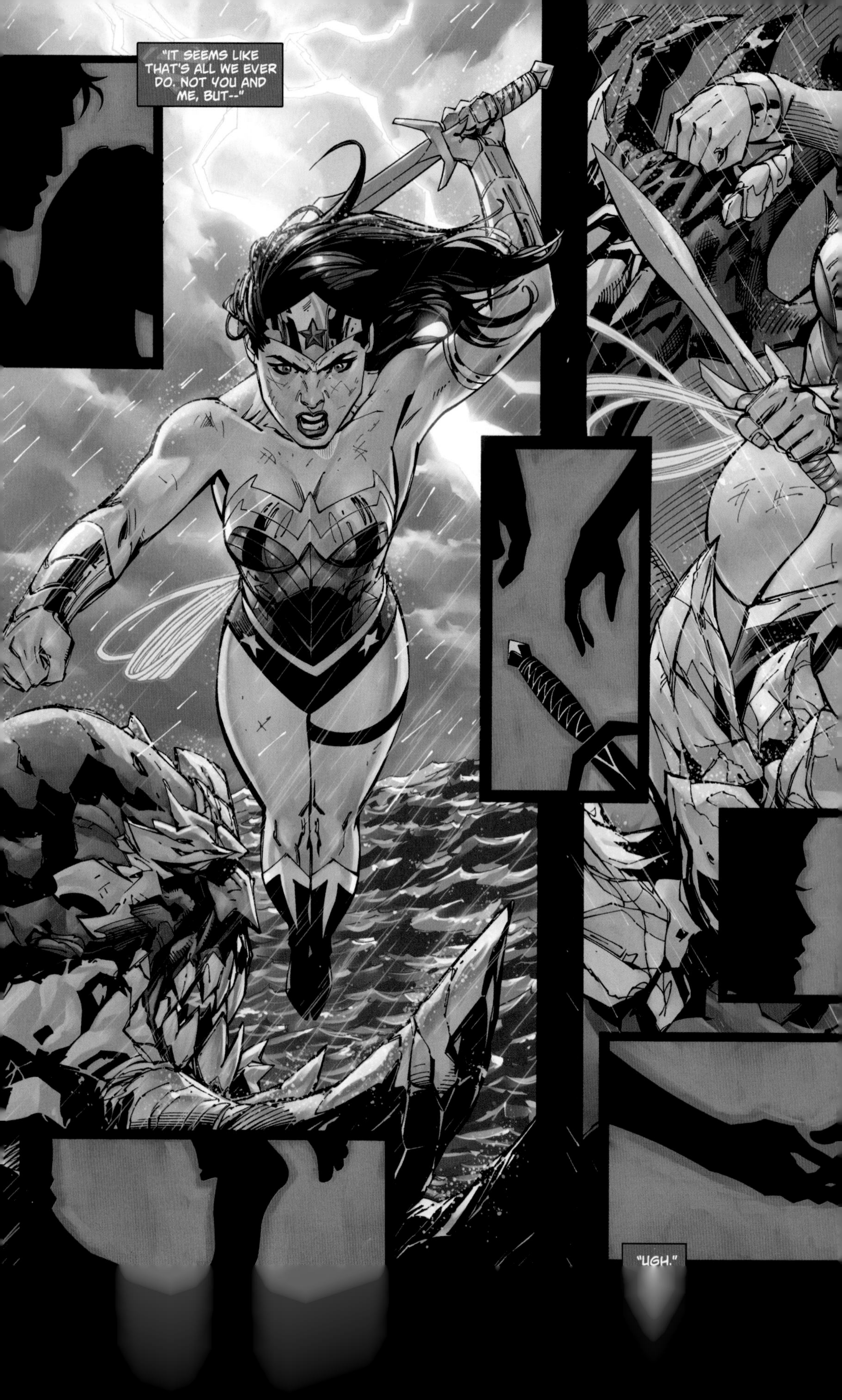
"IT SEEMS LIKE THAT'S ALL WE EVER DO. NOT YOU AND ME, BUT--"
"UGH."

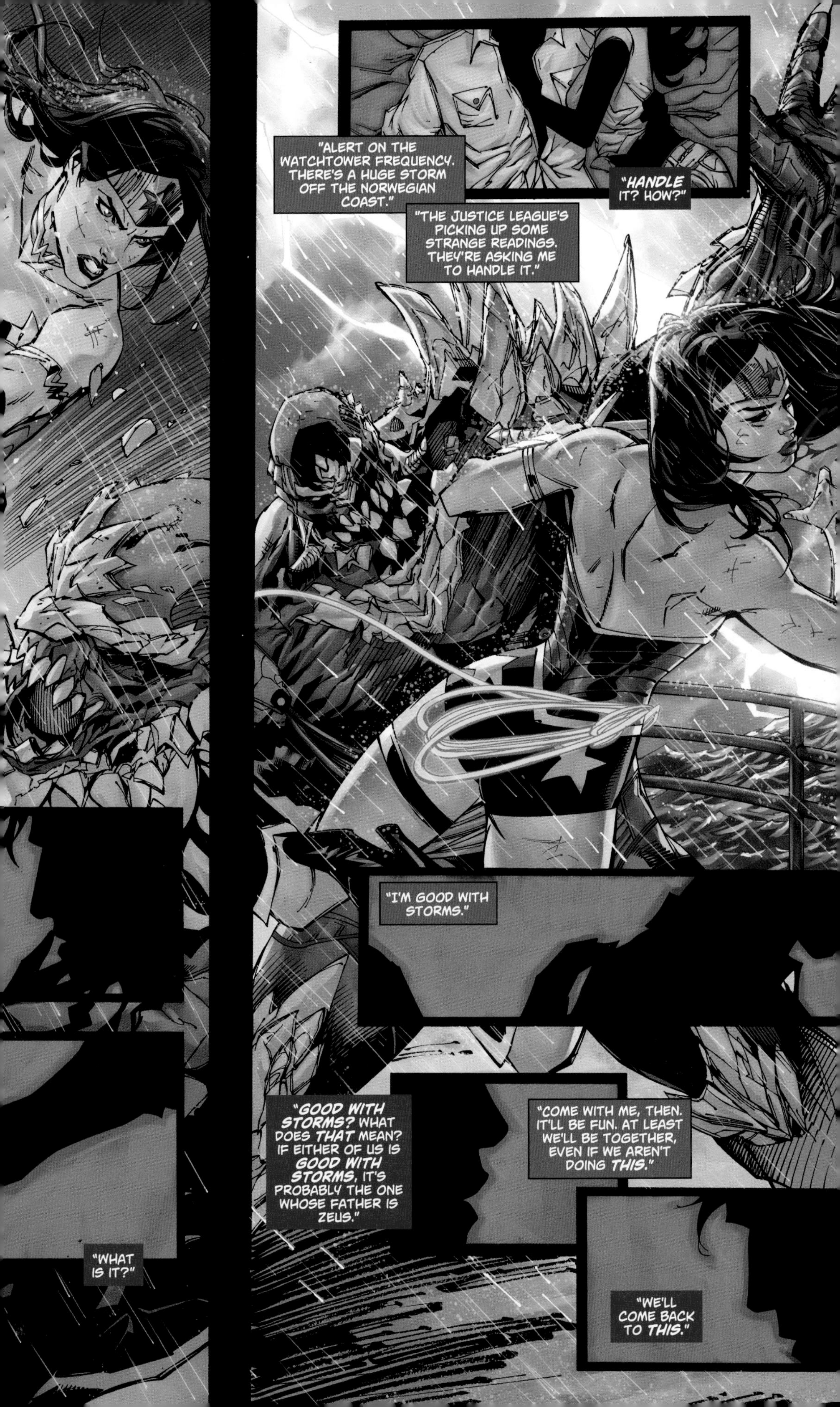
"ALERT ON THE WATCHTOWER FREQUENCY. THERE'S A HUGE STORM OFF THE NORWEGIAN COAST."
"THE JUSTICE LEAGUE'S PICKING UP SOME STRANGE READINGS. THEY'RE ASKING ME TO HANDLE IT."
"HANDLE IT? HOW?"
"I'M GOOD WITH STORMS."
"WHAT IS IT?"
"GOOD WITH STORMS? WHAT DOES THAT MEAN? IF EITHER OF US IS GOOD WITH STORMS, IT'S PROBABLY THE ONE WHOSE FATHER IS ZEUS."
"COME WITH ME, THEN. IT'LL BE FUN. AT LEAST WE'LL BE TOGETHER, EVEN IF WE AREN'T DOING THIS."
"WE'LL COME BACK TO THIS."

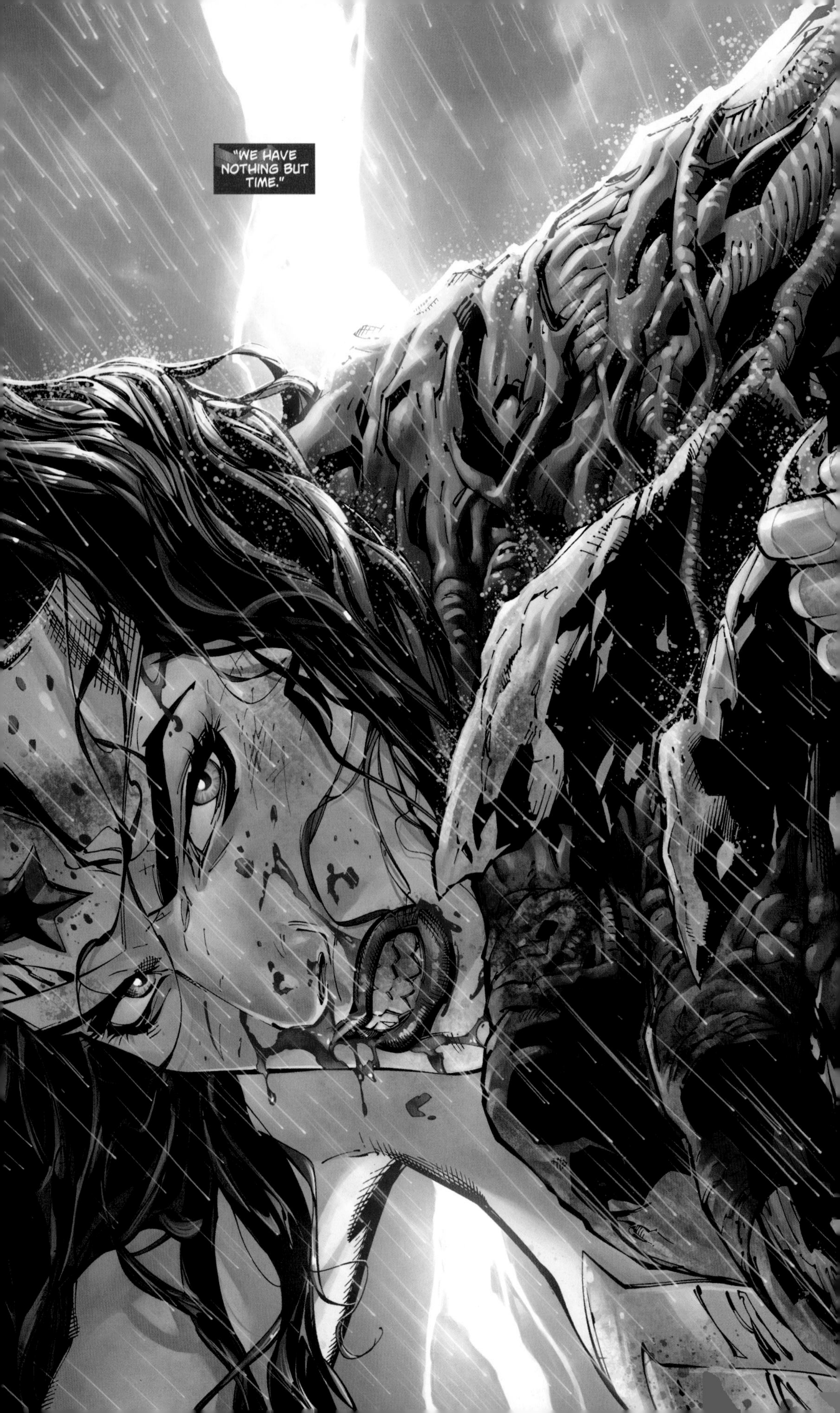
"WE HAVE NOTHING BUT TIME."

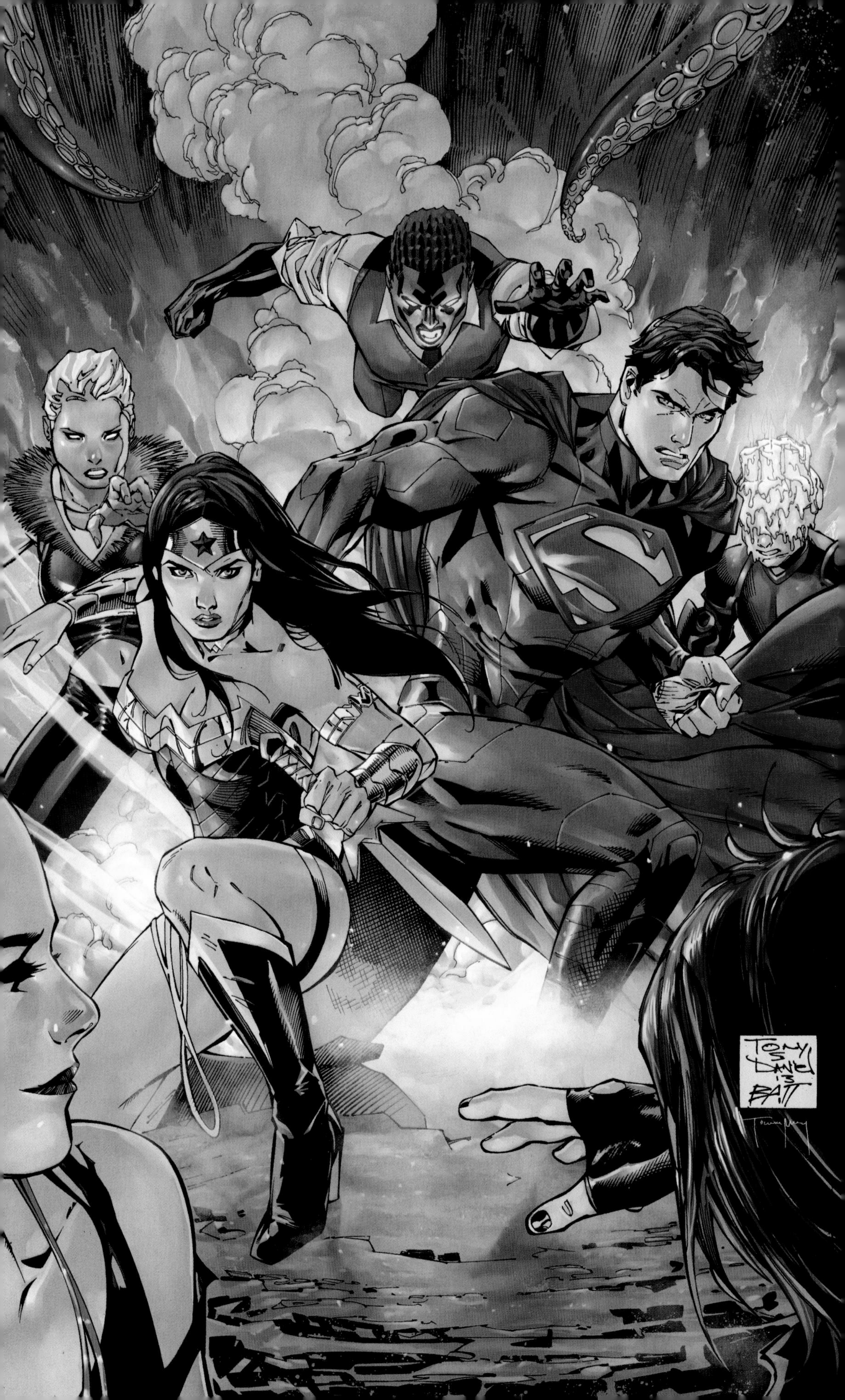
TONY S DANIEL '13 BATT

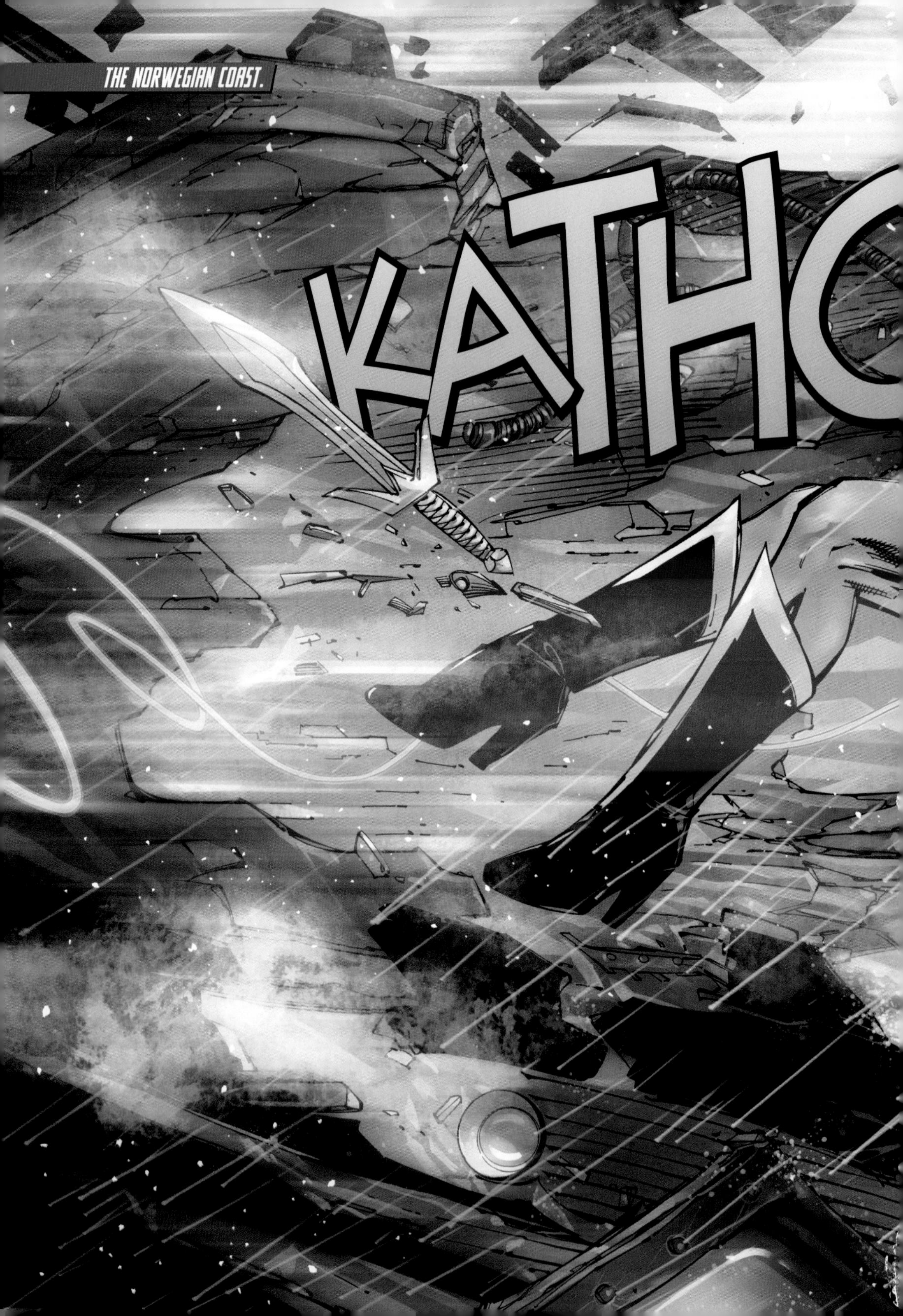
THE NORWEGIAN COAST.
KATHO

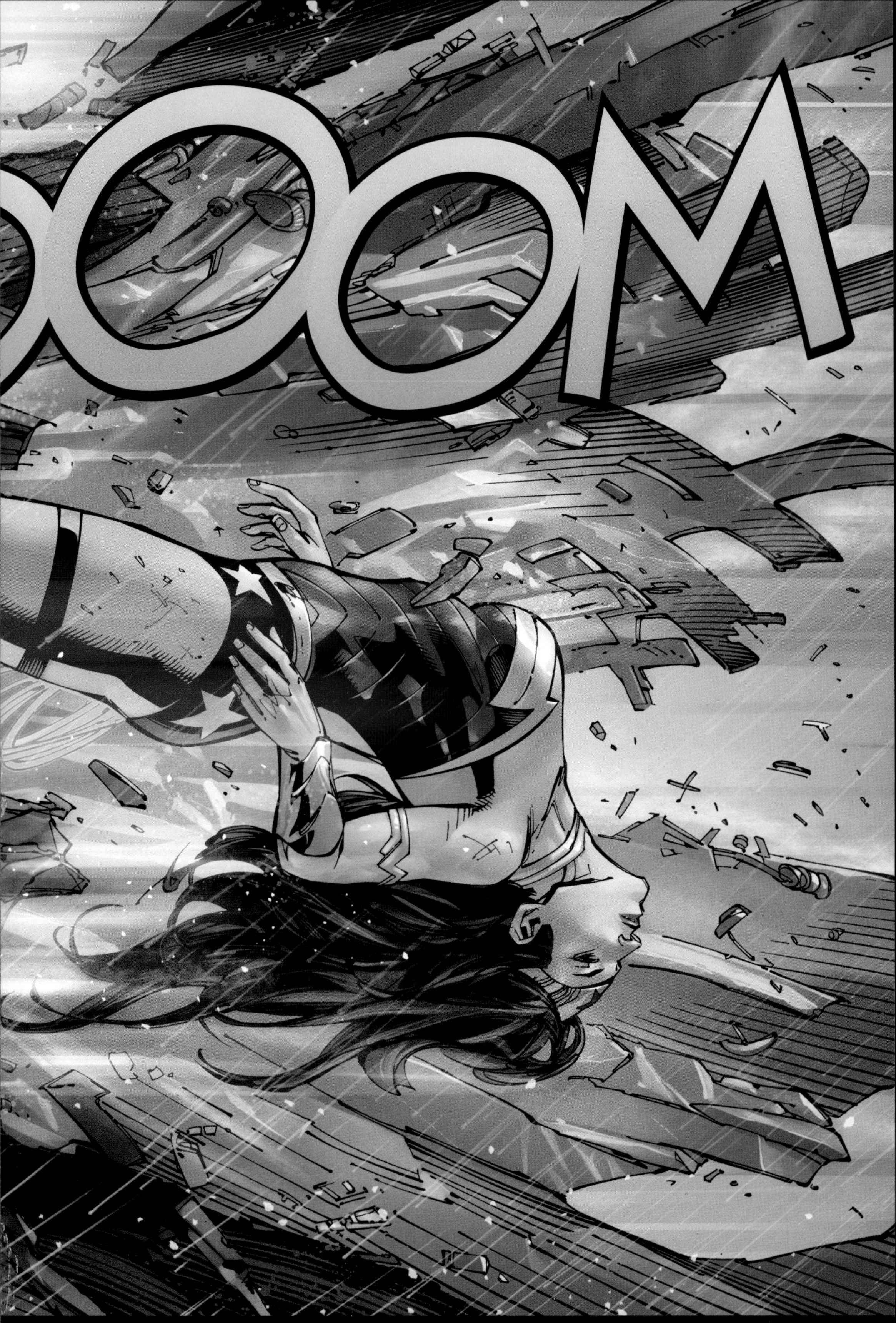
OOM

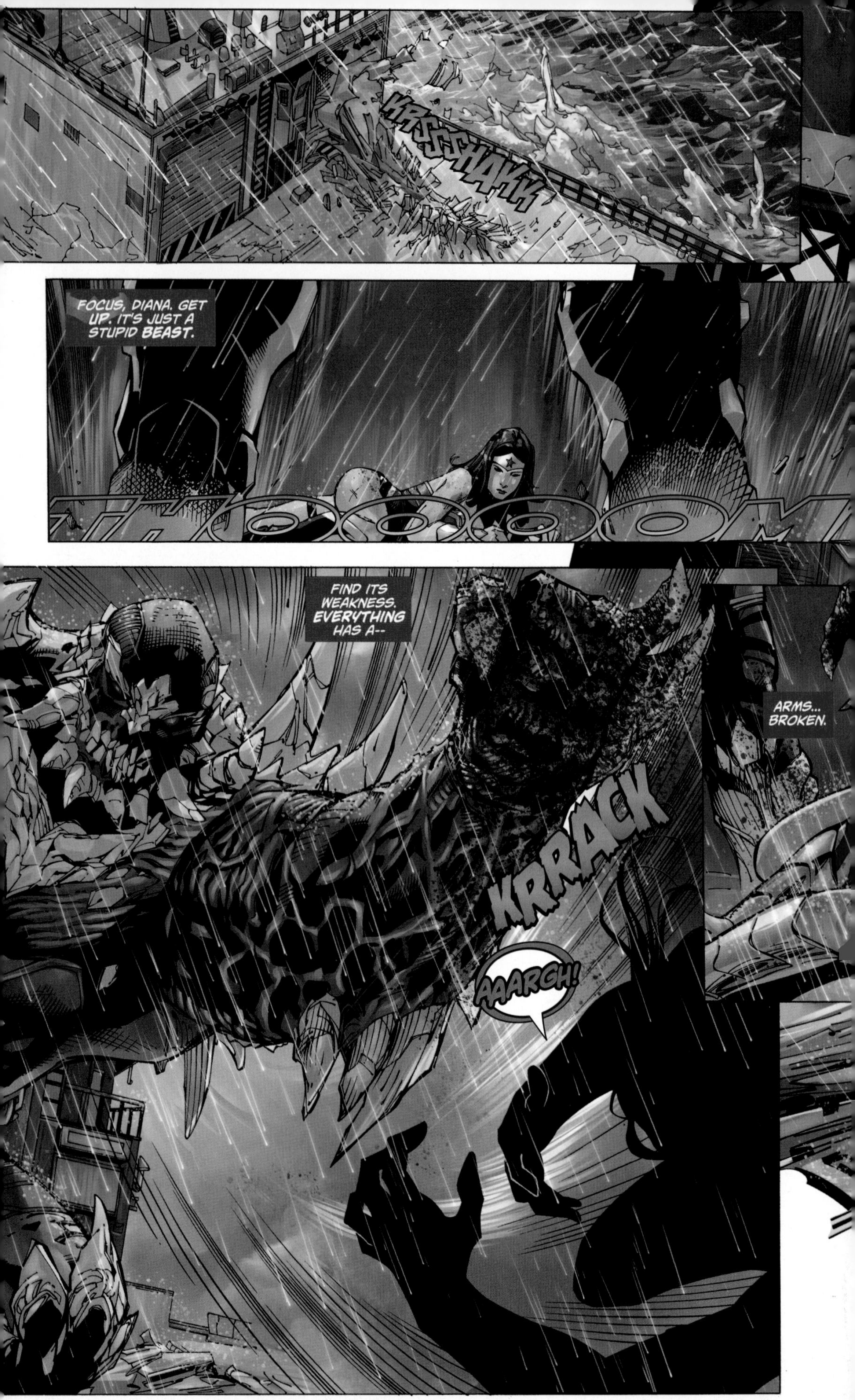
KRSSCHAKK
FOCUS, DIANA. GET UP. IT'S JUST A STUPID BEAST.
THOOOOOM
FIND ITS WEAKNESS. EVERYTHING HAS A--
ARMS... BROKEN.
KRRACK
AAARGH!

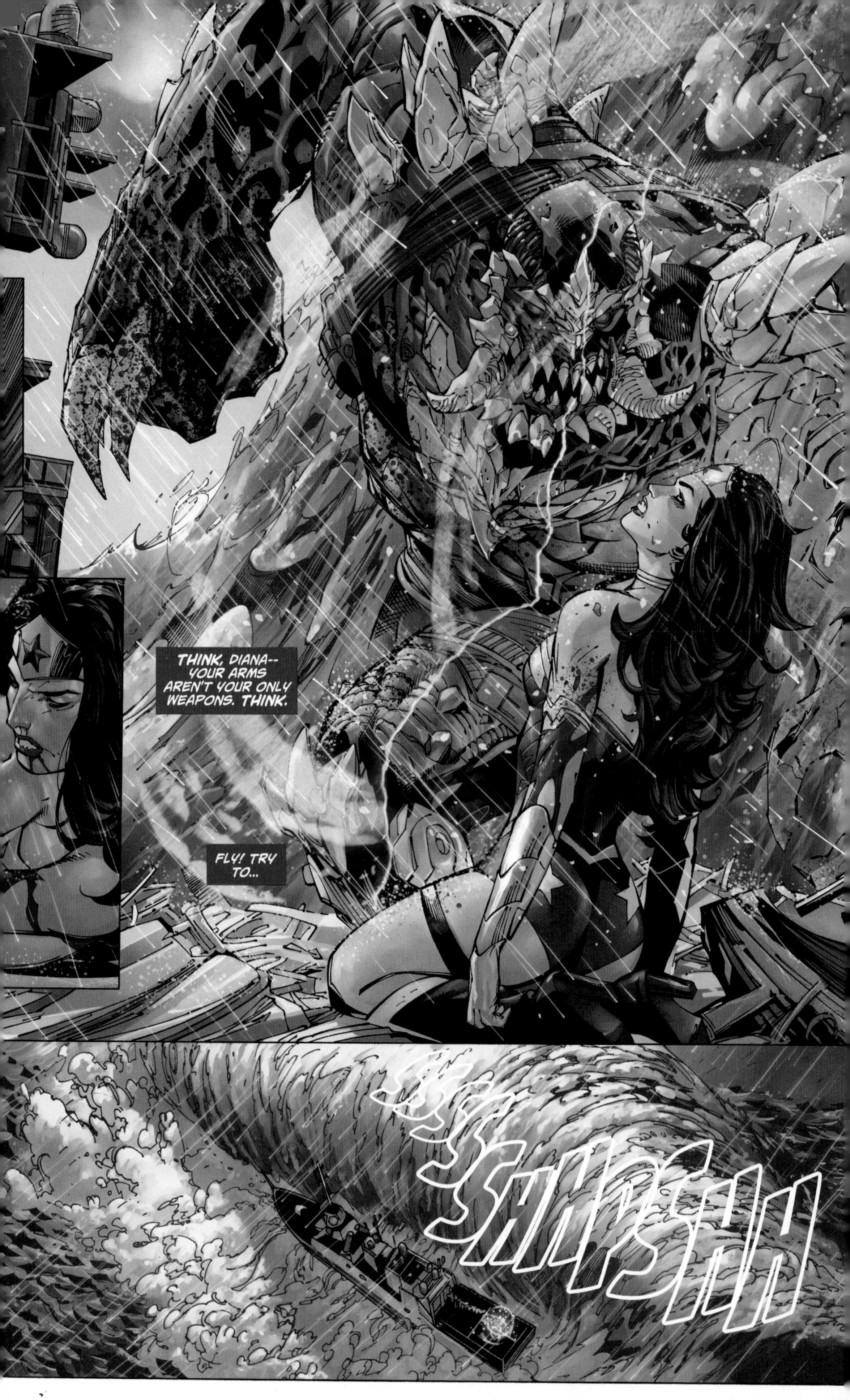
THINK, DIANA--
YOUR ARMS
AREN'T YOUR ONLY
WEAPONS. THINK.
FLY! TRY
TO...
SHHPSHH

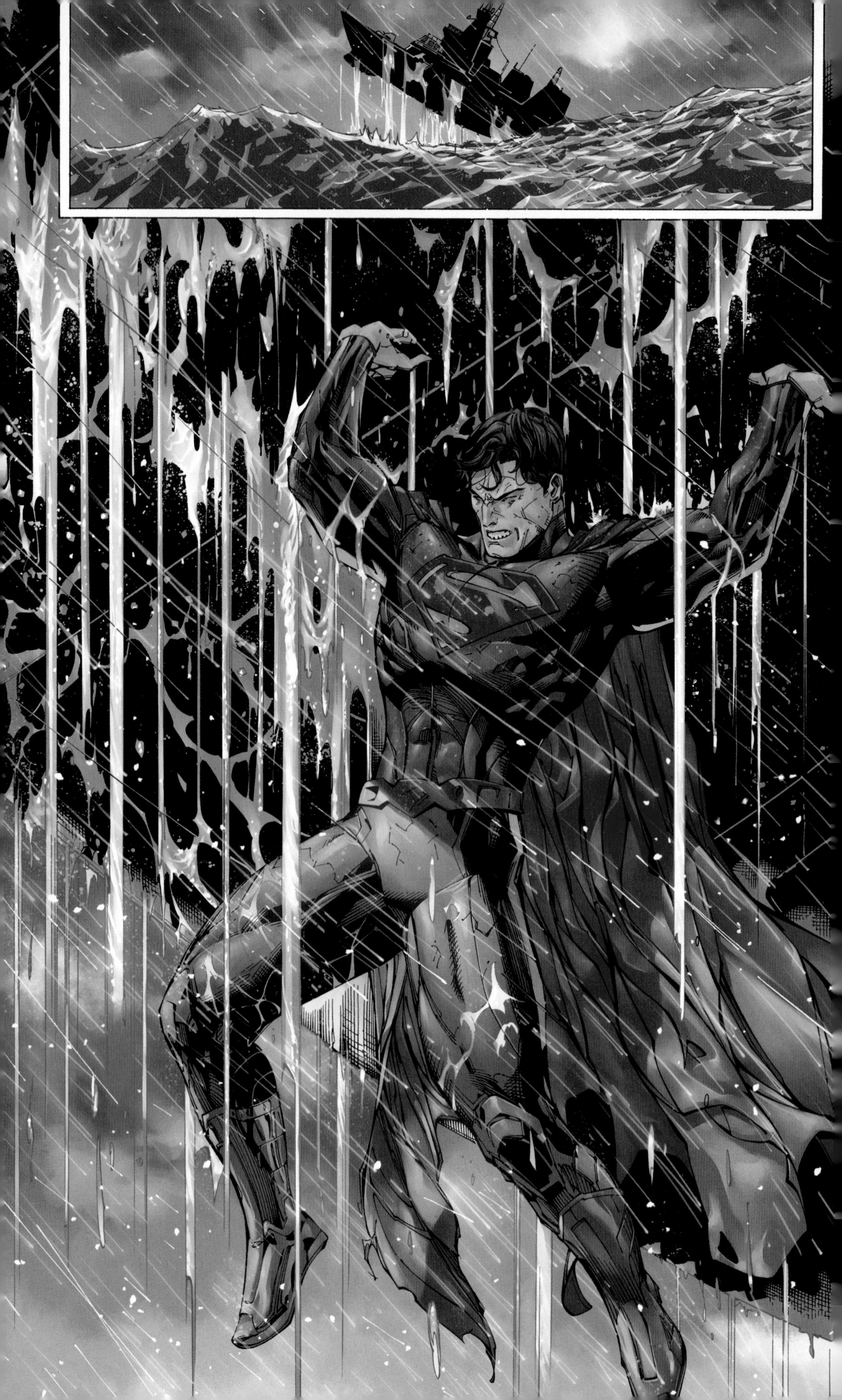

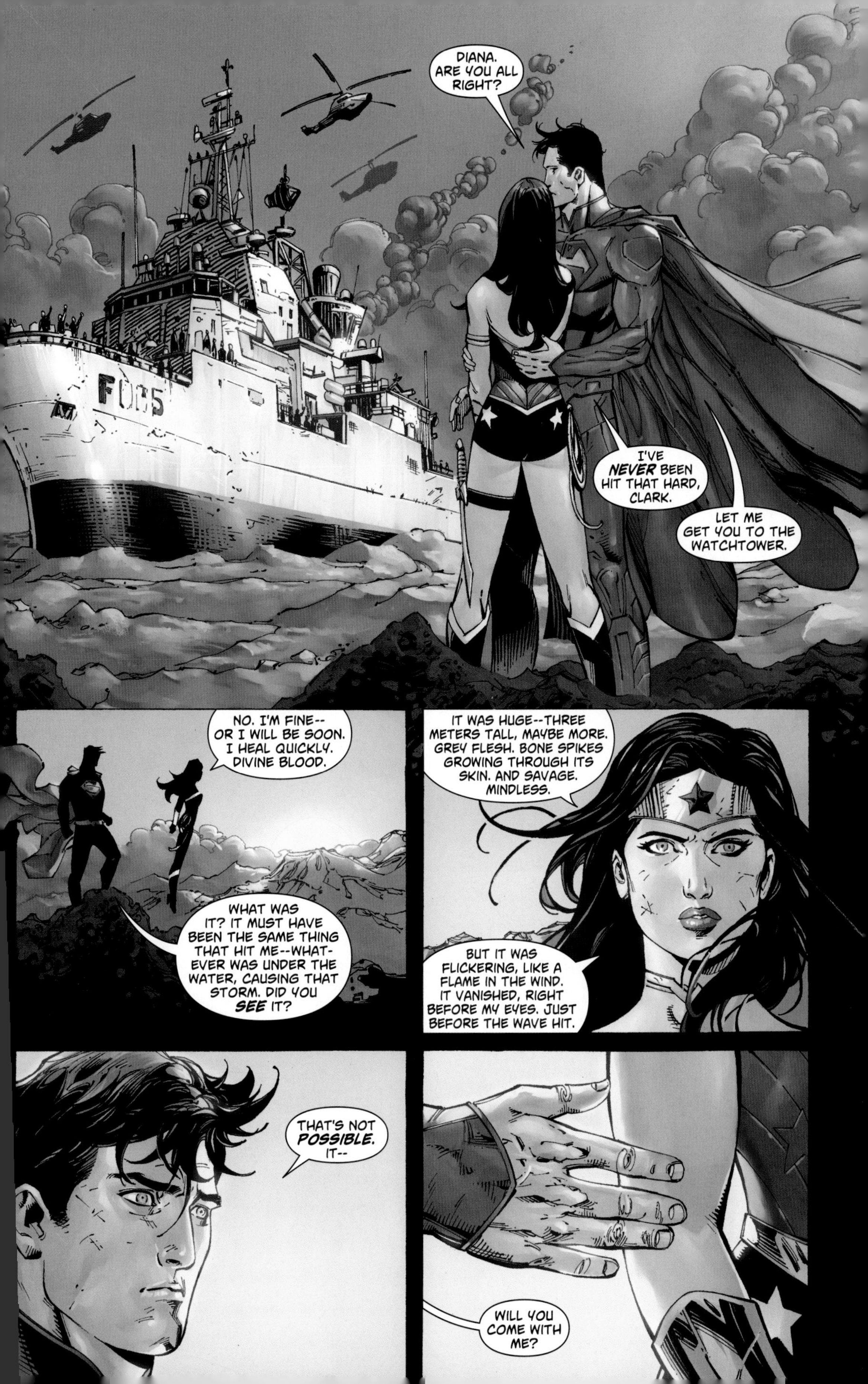
DIANA. ARE YOU ALL RIGHT?
I'VE NEVER BEEN HIT THAT HARD, CLARK.
LET ME GET YOU TO THE WATCHTOWER.
NO. I'M FINE-- OR I WILL BE SOON. I HEAL QUICKLY. DIVINE BLOOD.
WHAT WAS IT? IT MUST HAVE BEEN THE SAME THING THAT HIT ME--WHATEVER WAS UNDER THE WATER, CAUSING THAT STORM. DID YOU SEE IT?
IT WAS HUGE--THREE METERS TALL, MAYBE MORE. GREY FLESH. BONE SPIKES GROWING THROUGH ITS SKIN. AND SAVAGE. MINDLESS.
BUT IT WAS FLICKERING, LIKE A FLAME IN THE WIND. IT VANISHED, RIGHT BEFORE MY EYES. JUST BEFORE THE WAVE HIT.
THAT'S NOT POSSIBLE. IT--
WILL YOU COME WITH ME?

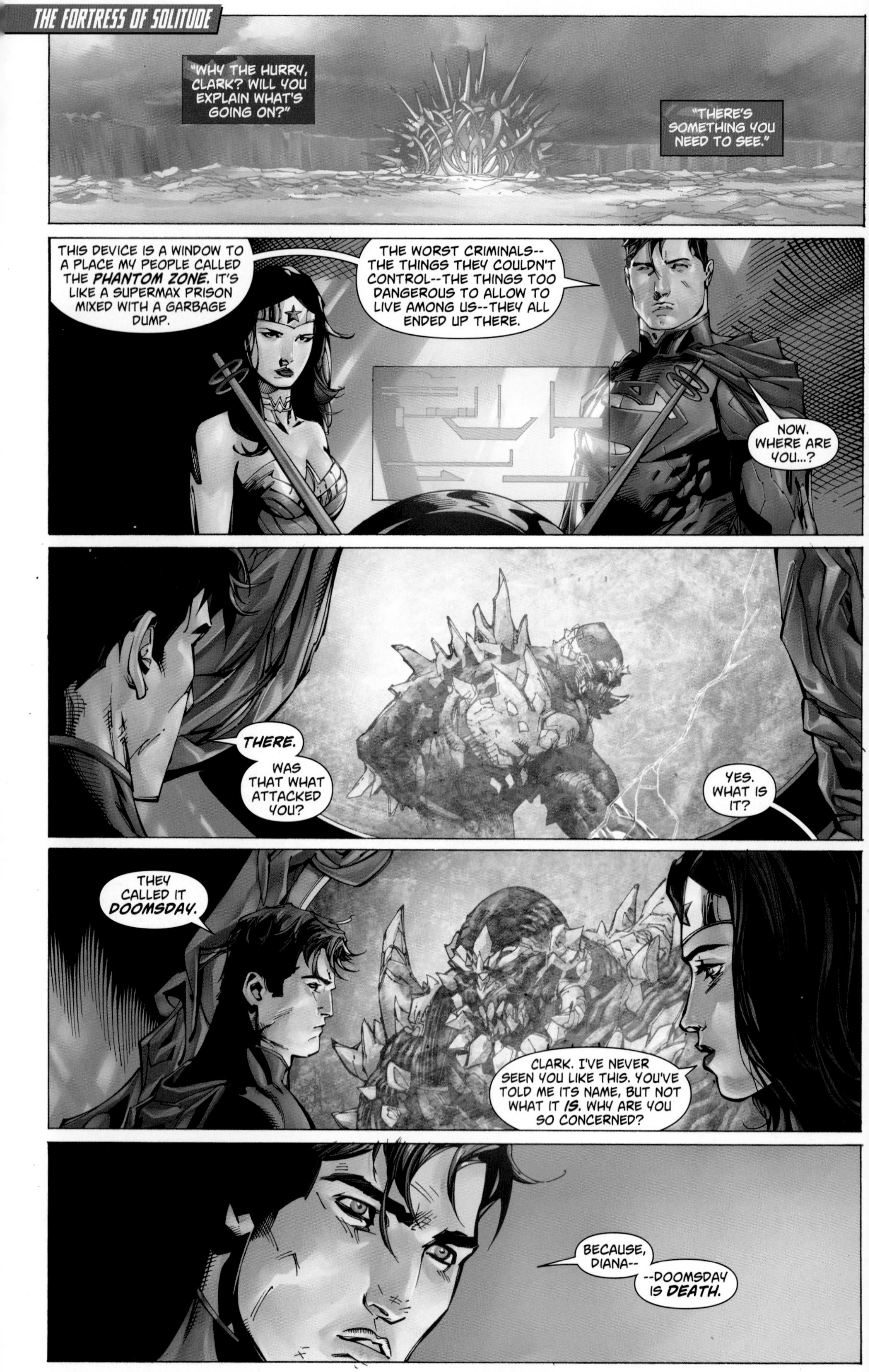

THE FORTRESS OF SOLITUDE
"WHY THE HURRY, CLARK? WILL YOU EXPLAIN WHAT'S GOING ON?"
"THERE'S SOMETHING YOU NEED TO SEE."
THIS DEVICE IS A WINDOW TO A PLACE MY PEOPLE CALLED THE PHANTOM ZONE. IT'S LIKE A SUPERMAX PRISON MIXED WITH A GARBAGE DUMP.
THE WORST CRIMINALS-- THE THINGS THEY COULDN'T CONTROL--THE THINGS TOO DANGEROUS TO ALLOW TO LIVE AMONG US--THEY ALL ENDED UP THERE.
NOW. WHERE ARE YOU...?
THERE.
WAS THAT WHAT ATTACKED YOU?
YES. WHAT IS IT?
THEY CALLED IT DOOMSDAY.
CLARK. I'VE NEVER SEEN YOU LIKE THIS. YOU'VE TOLD ME ITS NAME, BUT NOT WHAT IT IS. WHY ARE YOU SO CONCERNED?
BECAUSE, DIANA--
--DOOMSDAY IS DEATH.

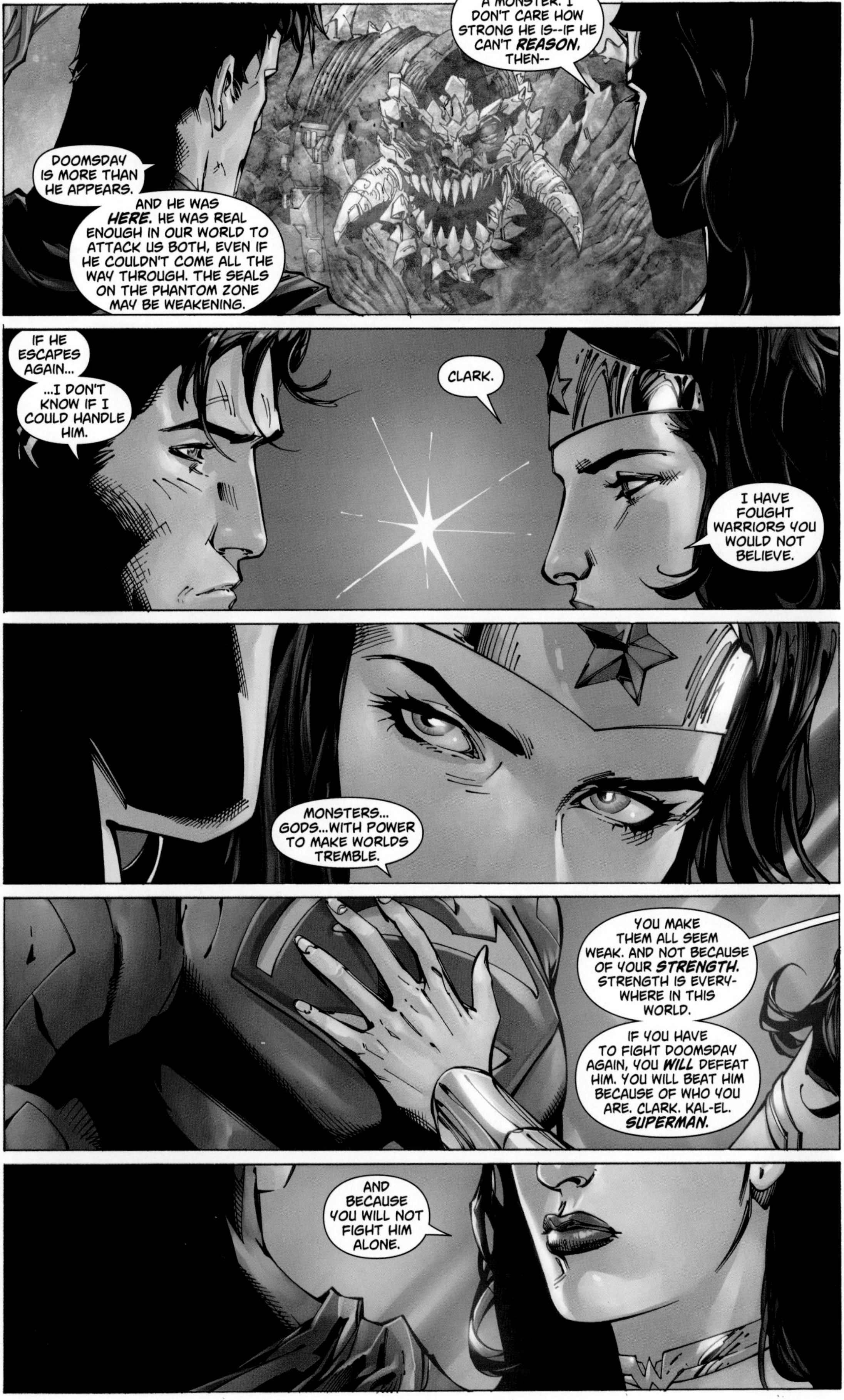
HE'S JUST A MONSTER. I DON'T CARE HOW STRONG HE IS--IF HE CAN'T REASON, THEN--
DOOMSDAY IS MORE THAN HE APPEARS.
AND HE WAS HERE. HE WAS REAL ENOUGH IN OUR WORLD TO ATTACK US BOTH, EVEN IF HE COULDN'T COME ALL THE WAY THROUGH. THE SEALS ON THE PHANTOM ZONE MAY BE WEAKENING.
IF HE ESCAPES AGAIN...
...I DON'T KNOW IF I COULD HANDLE HIM.
CLARK.
I HAVE FOUGHT WARRIORS YOU WOULD NOT BELIEVE.
MONSTERS... GODS...WITH POWER TO MAKE WORLDS TREMBLE.
YOU MAKE THEM ALL SEEM WEAK. AND NOT BECAUSE OF YOUR STRENGTH. STRENGTH IS EVERY-WHERE IN THIS WORLD.
IF YOU HAVE TO FIGHT DOOMSDAY AGAIN, YOU WILL DEFEAT HIM. YOU WILL BEAT HIM BECAUSE OF WHO YOU ARE. CLARK. KAL-EL. SUPERMAN.
AND BECAUSE YOU WILL NOT FIGHT HIM ALONE.

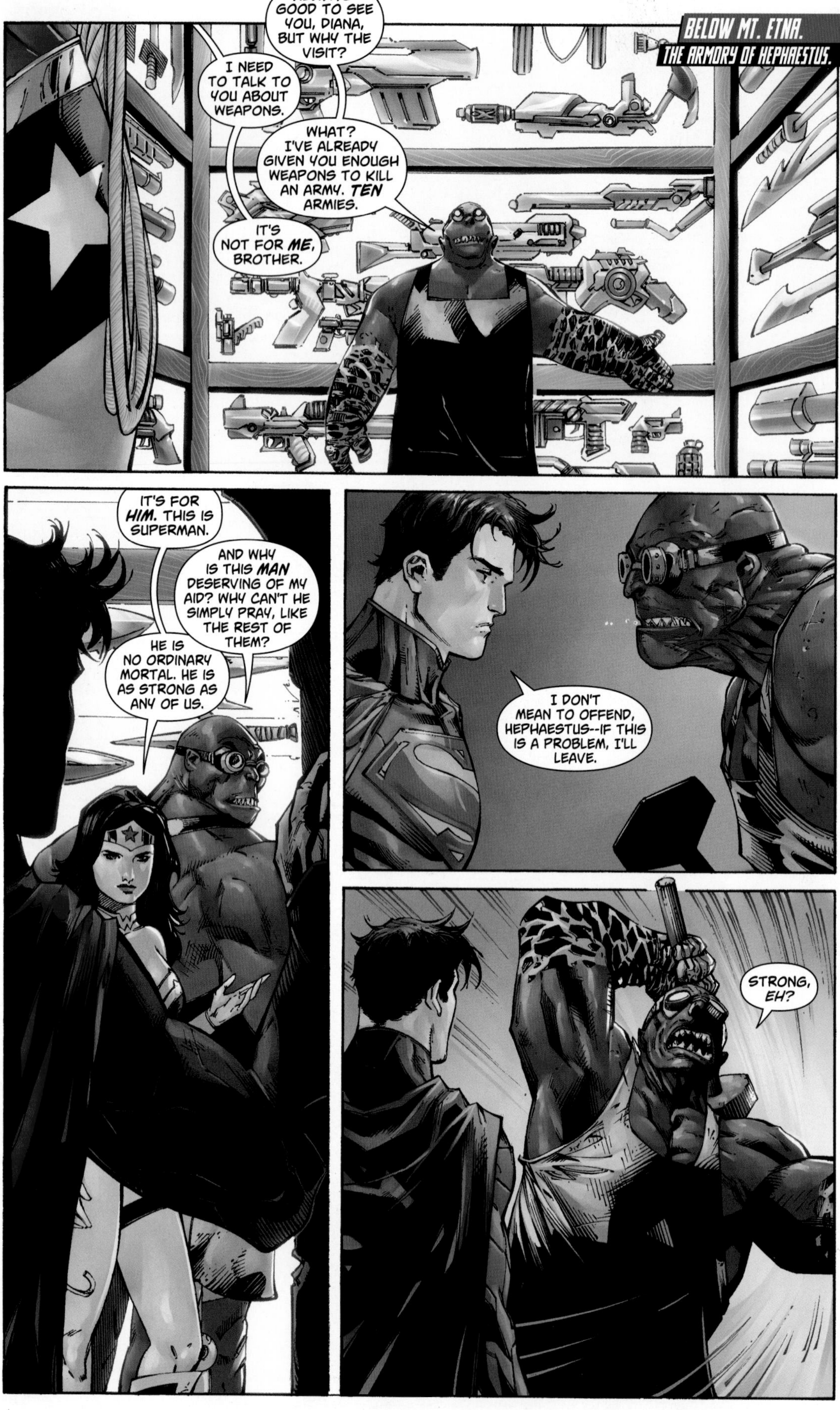
BELOW MT. ETNA.
THE ARMORY OF HEPHAESTUS.
ALWAYS GOOD TO SEE YOU, DIANA, BUT WHY THE VISIT?
I NEED TO TALK TO YOU ABOUT WEAPONS.
WHAT? I'VE ALREADY GIVEN YOU ENOUGH WEAPONS TO KILL AN ARMY. TEN ARMIES.
IT'S NOT FOR ME, BROTHER.
IT'S FOR HIM. THIS IS SUPERMAN.
AND WHY IS THIS MAN DESERVING OF MY AID? WHY CAN'T HE SIMPLY PRAY, LIKE THE REST OF THEM?
HE IS NO ORDINARY MORTAL. HE IS AS STRONG AS ANY OF US.
I DON'T MEAN TO OFFEND, HEPHAESTUS--IF THIS IS A PROBLEM, I'LL LEAVE.
STRONG, EH?

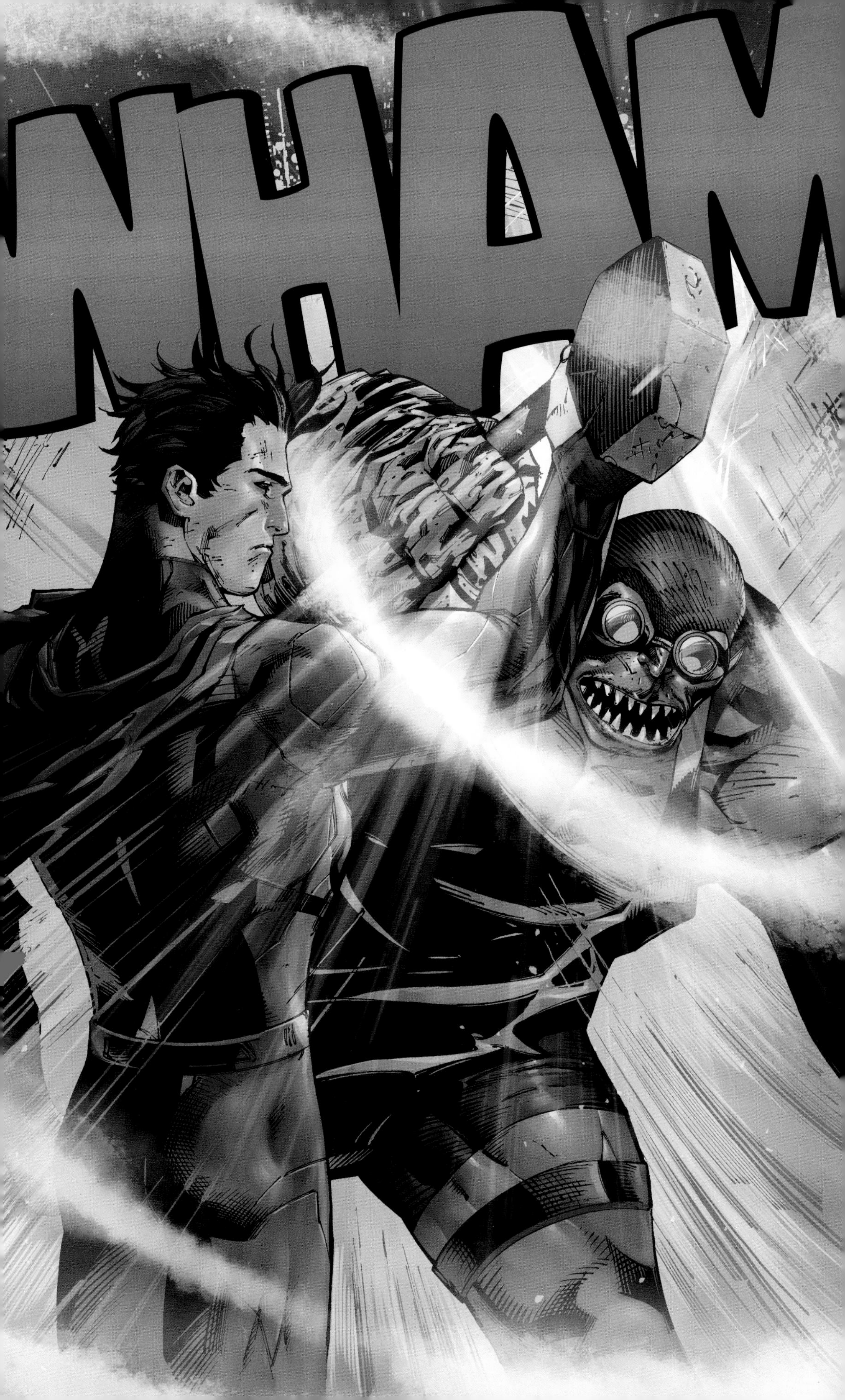
WHAM

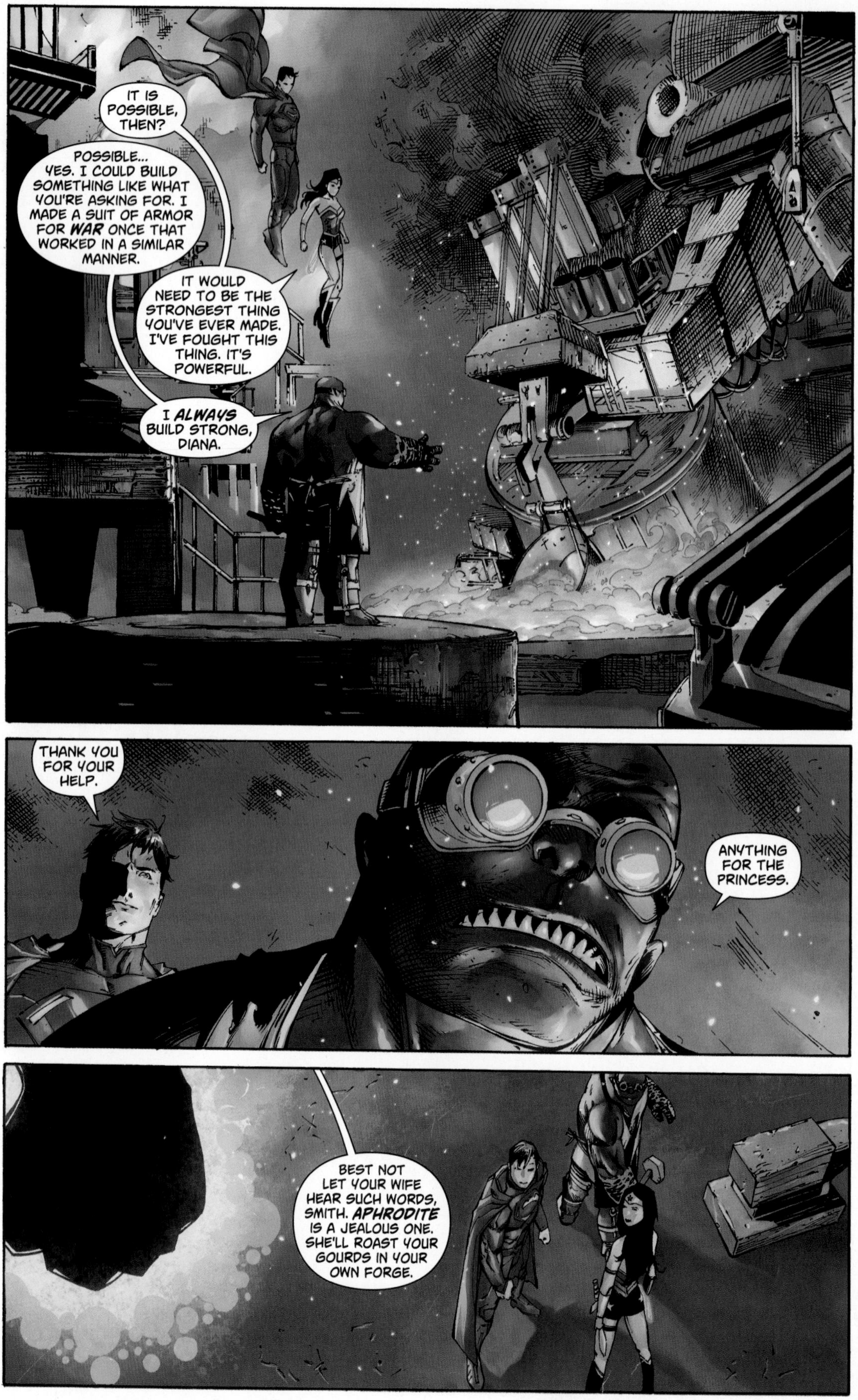
IT IS POSSIBLE, THEN?
POSSIBLE... YES. I COULD BUILD SOMETHING LIKE WHAT YOU'RE ASKING FOR. I MADE A SUIT OF ARMOR FOR *WAR* ONCE THAT WORKED IN A SIMILAR MANNER.
IT WOULD NEED TO BE THE STRONGEST THING YOU'VE EVER MADE. I'VE FOUGHT THIS THING. IT'S POWERFUL.
I *ALWAYS* BUILD STRONG, DIANA.
THANK YOU FOR YOUR HELP.
ANYTHING FOR THE PRINCESS.
BEST NOT LET YOUR WIFE HEAR SUCH WORDS, SMITH. *APHRODITE* IS A JEALOUS ONE. SHE'LL ROAST YOUR GOURDS IN YOUR OWN FORGE.

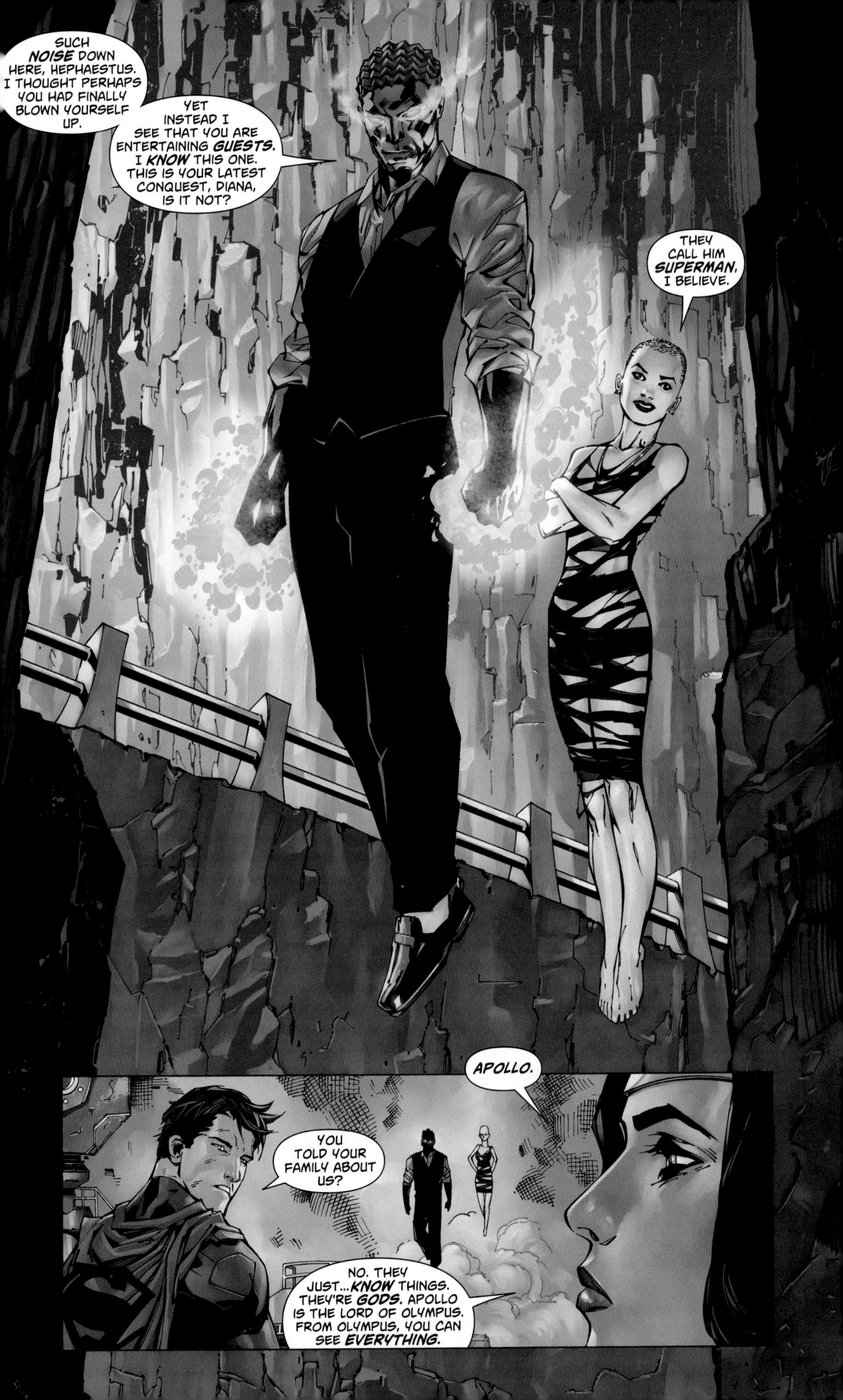
SUCH NOISE DOWN HERE, HEPHAESTUS. I THOUGHT PERHAPS YOU HAD FINALLY BLOWN YOURSELF UP.
YET INSTEAD I SEE THAT YOU ARE ENTERTAINING GUESTS. I KNOW THIS ONE. THIS IS YOUR LATEST CONQUEST, DIANA, IS IT NOT?
THEY CALL HIM SUPERMAN, I BELIEVE.
APOLLO.
YOU TOLD YOUR FAMILY ABOUT US?
NO. THEY JUST...KNOW THINGS. THEY'RE GODS. APOLLO IS THE LORD OF OLYMPUS. FROM OLYMPUS, YOU CAN SEE EVERYTHING.

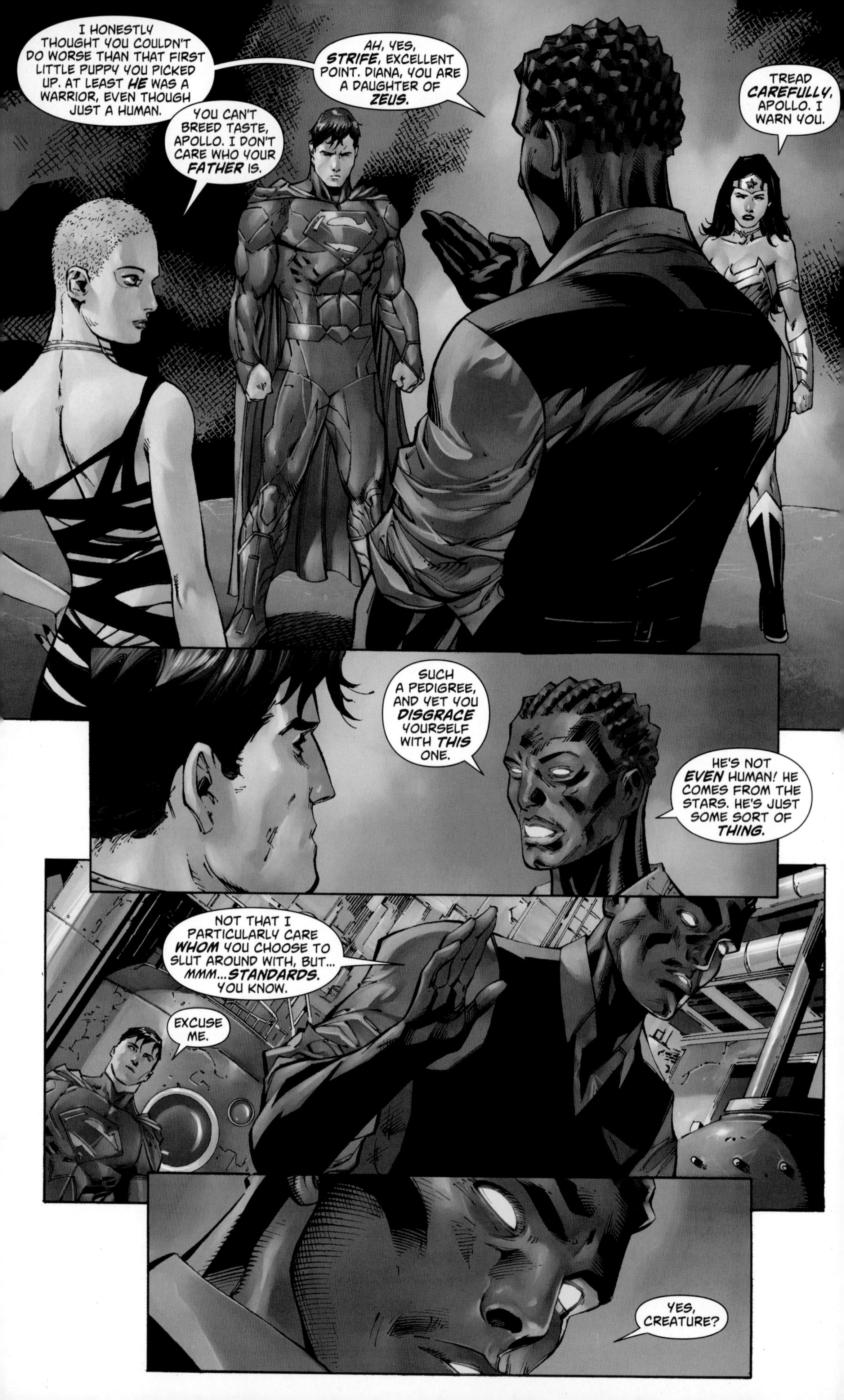
I HONESTLY THOUGHT YOU COULDN'T DO WORSE THAN THAT FIRST LITTLE PUPPY YOU PICKED UP. AT LEAST **HE** WAS A WARRIOR, EVEN THOUGH JUST A HUMAN.
AH, YES, **STRIFE**, EXCELLENT POINT. DIANA, YOU ARE A DAUGHTER OF **ZEUS**.
YOU CAN'T BREED TASTE, APOLLO. I DON'T CARE WHO YOUR **FATHER** IS.
TREAD **CAREFULLY**, APOLLO. I WARN YOU.
SUCH A PEDIGREE, AND YET YOU **DISGRACE** YOURSELF WITH **THIS** ONE.
HE'S NOT **EVEN** HUMAN! HE COMES FROM THE STARS. HE'S JUST SOME SORT OF **THING**.
NOT THAT I PARTICULARLY CARE **WHOM** YOU CHOOSE TO SLUT AROUND WITH, BUT... MMM...**STANDARDS**. YOU KNOW.
EXCUSE ME.
YES, CREATURE?

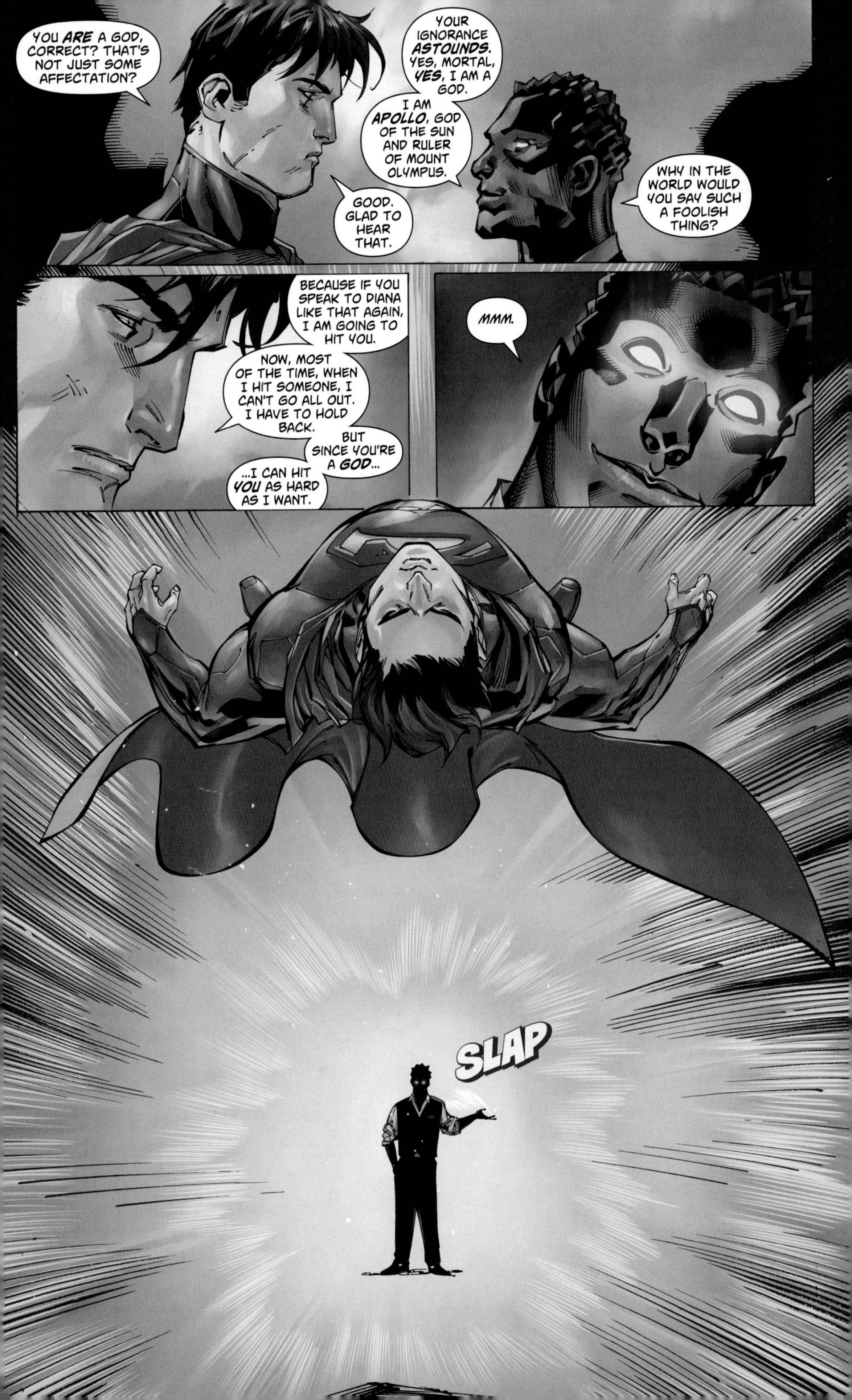
YOU ARE A GOD, CORRECT? THAT'S NOT JUST SOME AFFECTATION?
YOUR IGNORANCE ASTOUNDS. YES, MORTAL, YES, I AM A GOD.
I AM APOLLO, GOD OF THE SUN AND RULER OF MOUNT OLYMPUS.
GOOD. GLAD TO HEAR THAT.
WHY IN THE WORLD WOULD YOU SAY SUCH A FOOLISH THING?
BECAUSE IF YOU SPEAK TO DIANA LIKE THAT AGAIN, I AM GOING TO HIT YOU.
NOW, MOST OF THE TIME, WHEN I HIT SOMEONE, I CAN'T GO ALL OUT. I HAVE TO HOLD BACK.
BUT SINCE YOU'RE A GOD...
...I CAN HIT YOU AS HARD AS I WANT.
MMM.
SLAP

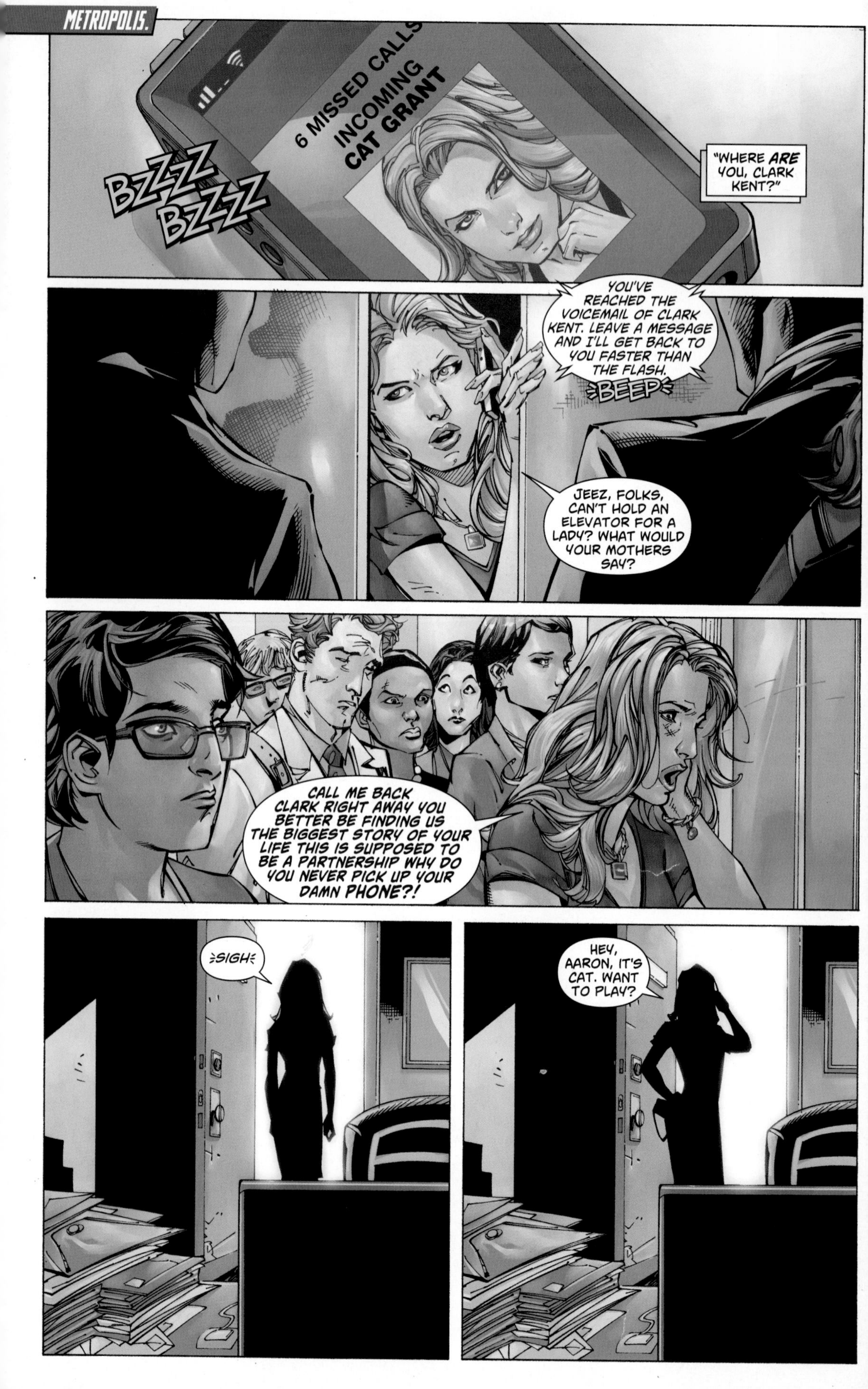
METROPOLIS.
6 MISSED CALLS
INCOMING
CAT GRANT
BZZZZ BZZZZ
"WHERE ARE YOU, CLARK KENT?"
YOU'VE REACHED THE VOICEMAIL OF CLARK KENT. LEAVE A MESSAGE AND I'LL GET BACK TO YOU FASTER THAN THE FLASH.
BEEP
JEEZ, FOLKS, CAN'T HOLD AN ELEVATOR FOR A LADY? WHAT WOULD YOUR MOTHERS SAY?
CALL ME BACK CLARK RIGHT AWAY YOU BETTER BE FINDING US THE BIGGEST STORY OF YOUR LIFE THIS IS SUPPOSED TO BE A PARTNERSHIP WHY DO YOU NEVER PICK UP YOUR DAMN PHONE?!
SIGH
HEY, AARON, IT'S CAT. WANT TO PLAY?

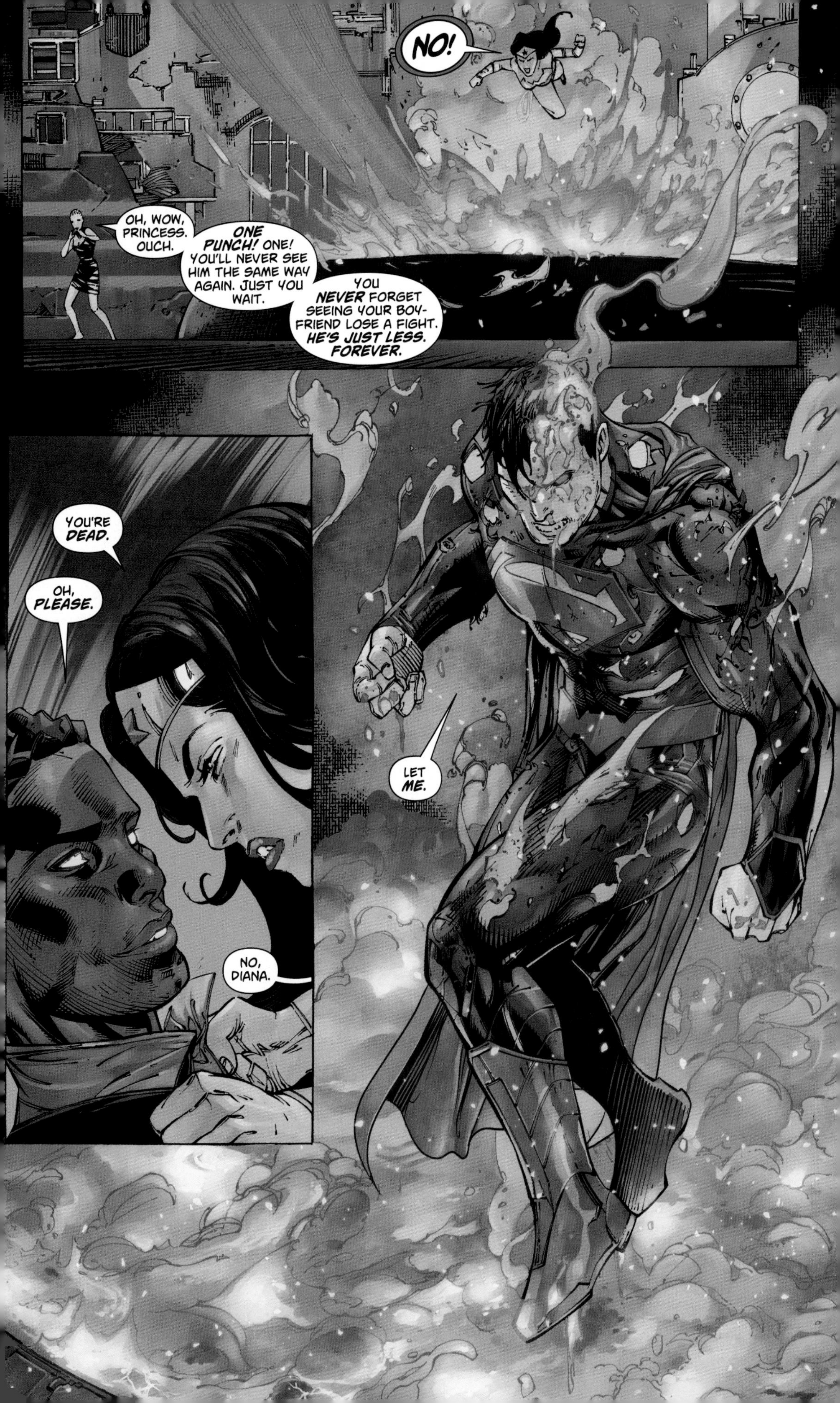
NO!
OH, WOW, PRINCESS. OUCH.
ONE PUNCH! ONE! YOU'LL NEVER SEE HIM THE SAME WAY AGAIN. JUST YOU WAIT.
YOU NEVER FORGET SEEING YOUR BOY-FRIEND LOSE A FIGHT. HE'S JUST LESS. FOREVER.
YOU'RE DEAD.
OH, PLEASE.
NO, DIANA.
LET ME.

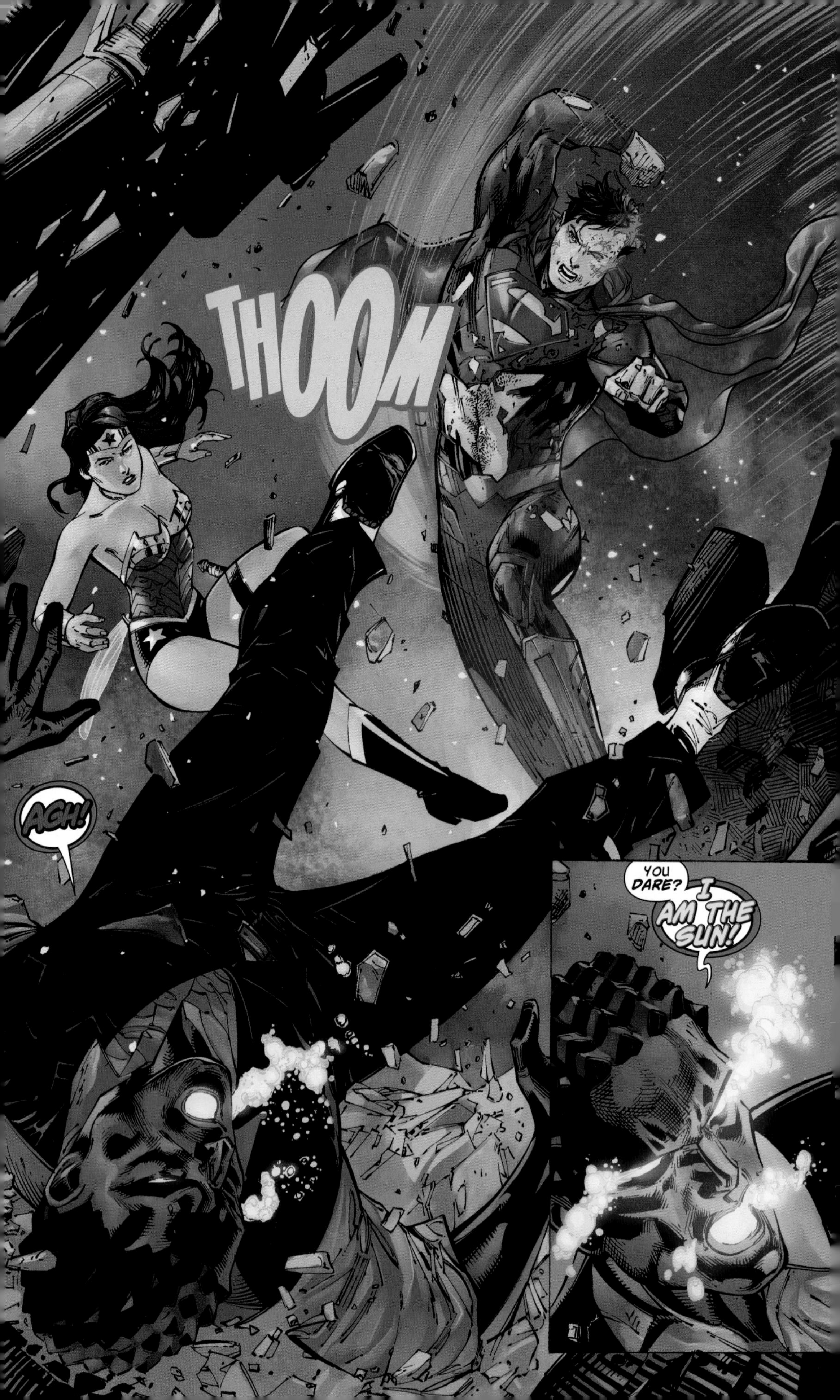
THOOM
AGH!
YOU DARE?
I AM THE SUN!

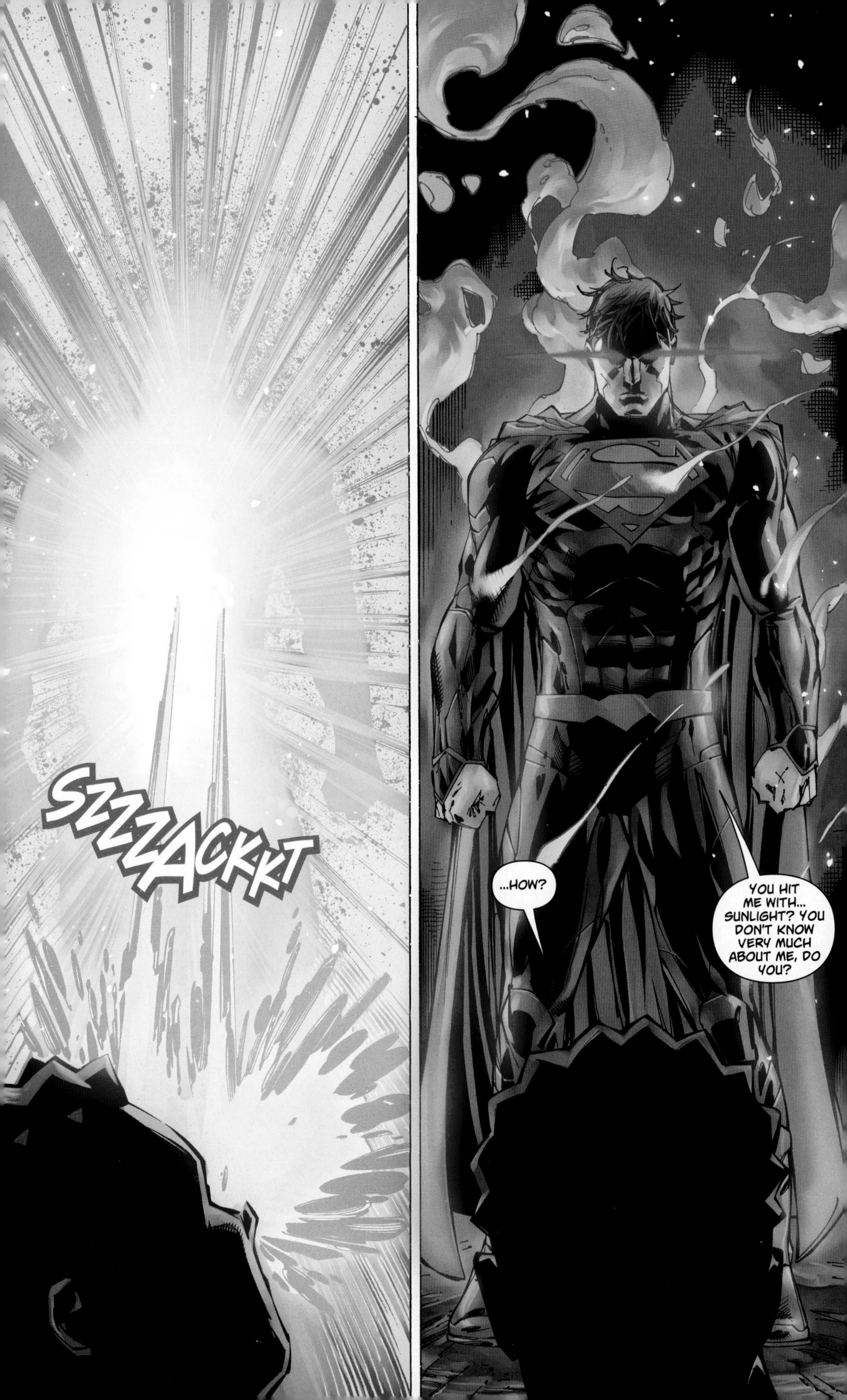
SZZZACKKT
...HOW?
YOU HIT ME WITH... SUNLIGHT? YOU DON'T KNOW VERY MUCH ABOUT ME, DO YOU?

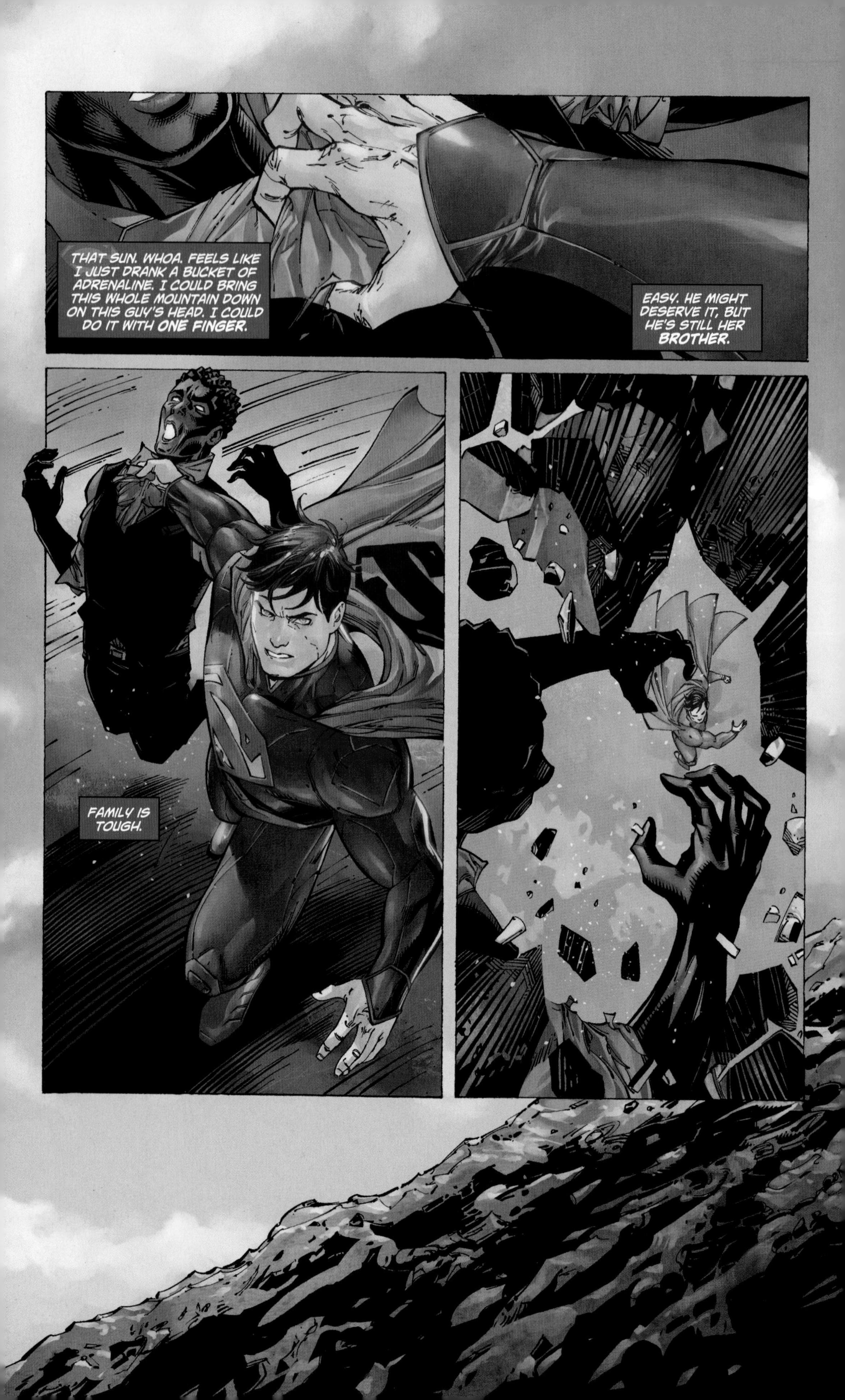
THAT SUN. WHOA. FEELS LIKE I JUST DRANK A BUCKET OF ADRENALINE. I COULD BRING THIS WHOLE MOUNTAIN DOWN ON THIS GUY'S HEAD. I COULD DO IT WITH ONE FINGER.
EASY. HE MIGHT DESERVE IT, BUT HE'S STILL HER BROTHER.
FAMILY IS TOUGH.

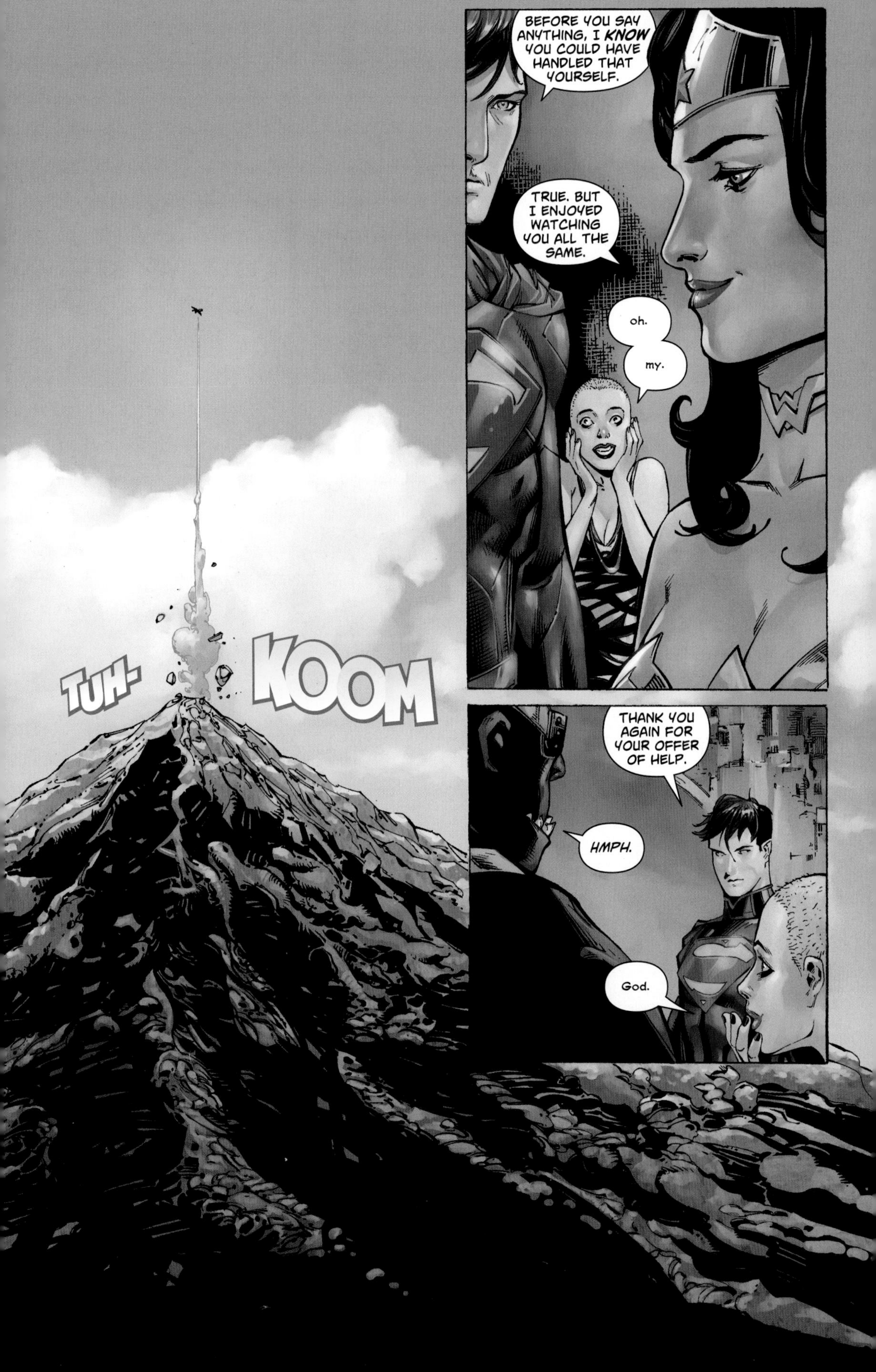
TUH-
KOOM
BEFORE YOU SAY ANYTHING, I KNOW YOU COULD HAVE HANDLED THAT YOURSELF.
TRUE. BUT I ENJOYED WATCHING YOU ALL THE SAME.
oh.
my.
THANK YOU AGAIN FOR YOUR OFFER OF HELP.
HMPH.
God.

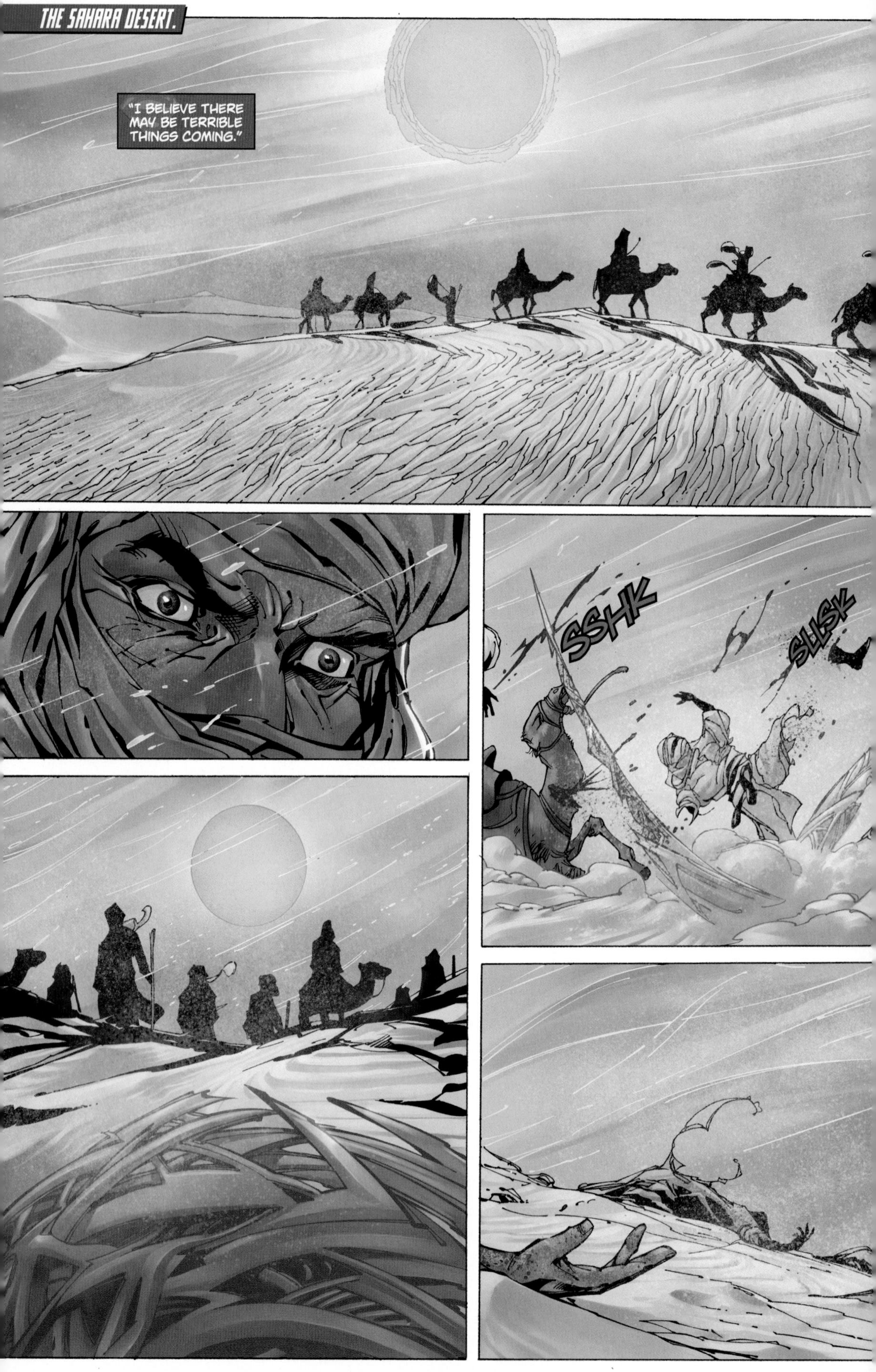
THE SAHARA DESERT.
"I BELIEVE THERE MAY BE TERRIBLE THINGS COMING."
SSHK
SLISK

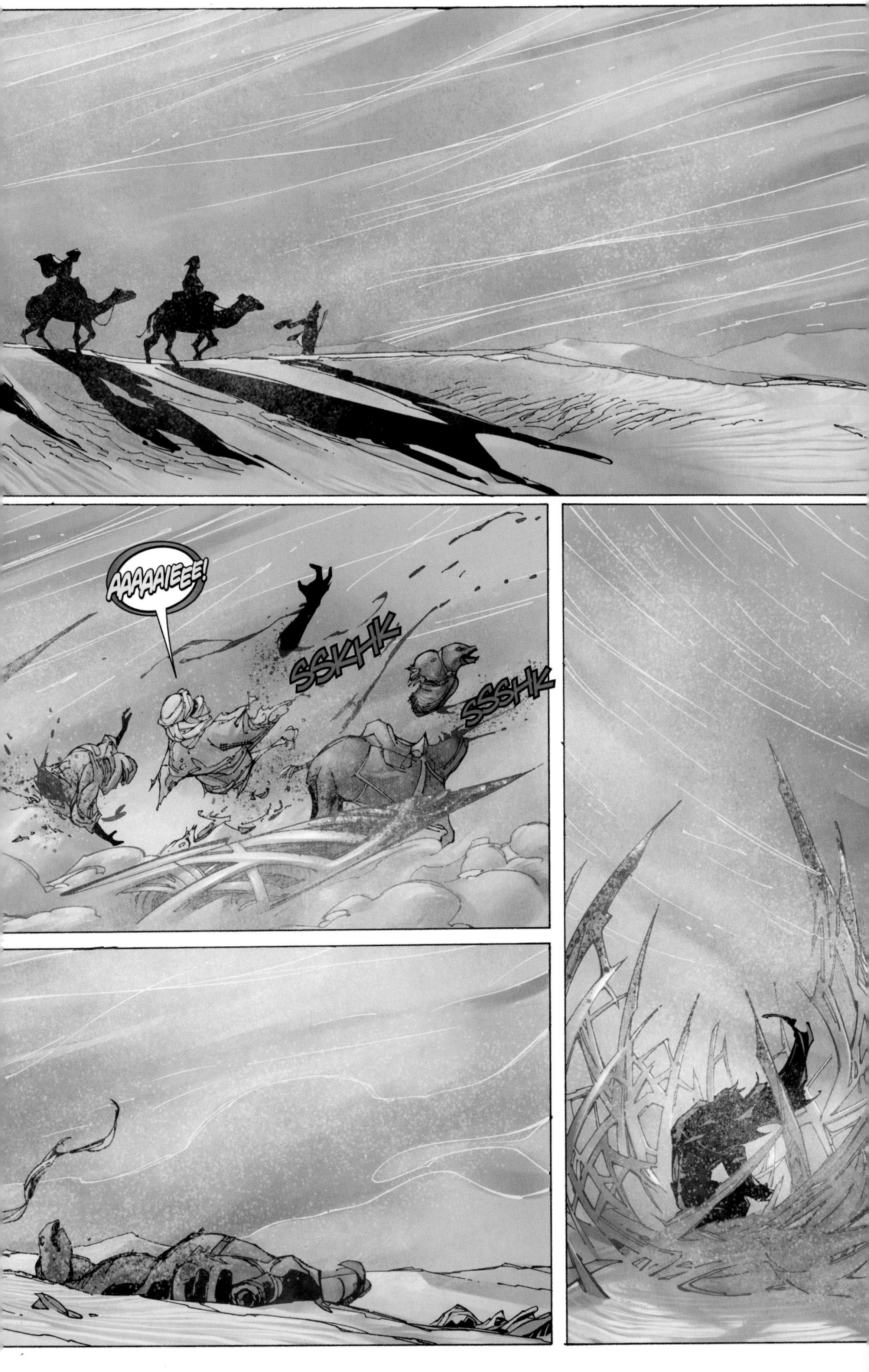
AAAAAIEEE!
SSKHK
SSSHK

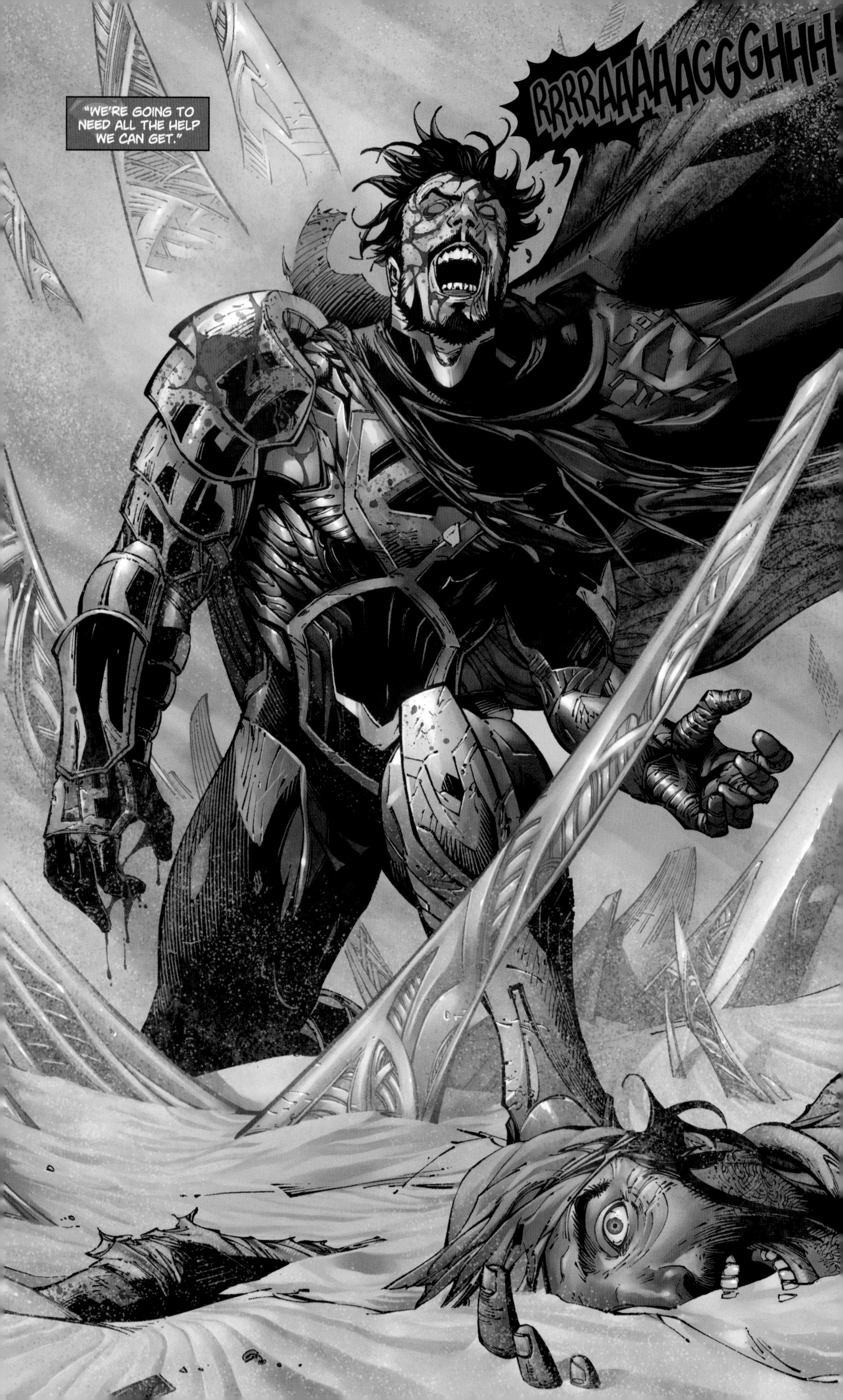
"WE'RE GOING TO NEED ALL THE HELP WE CAN GET."
RRRRAAAAAAGGGHHH

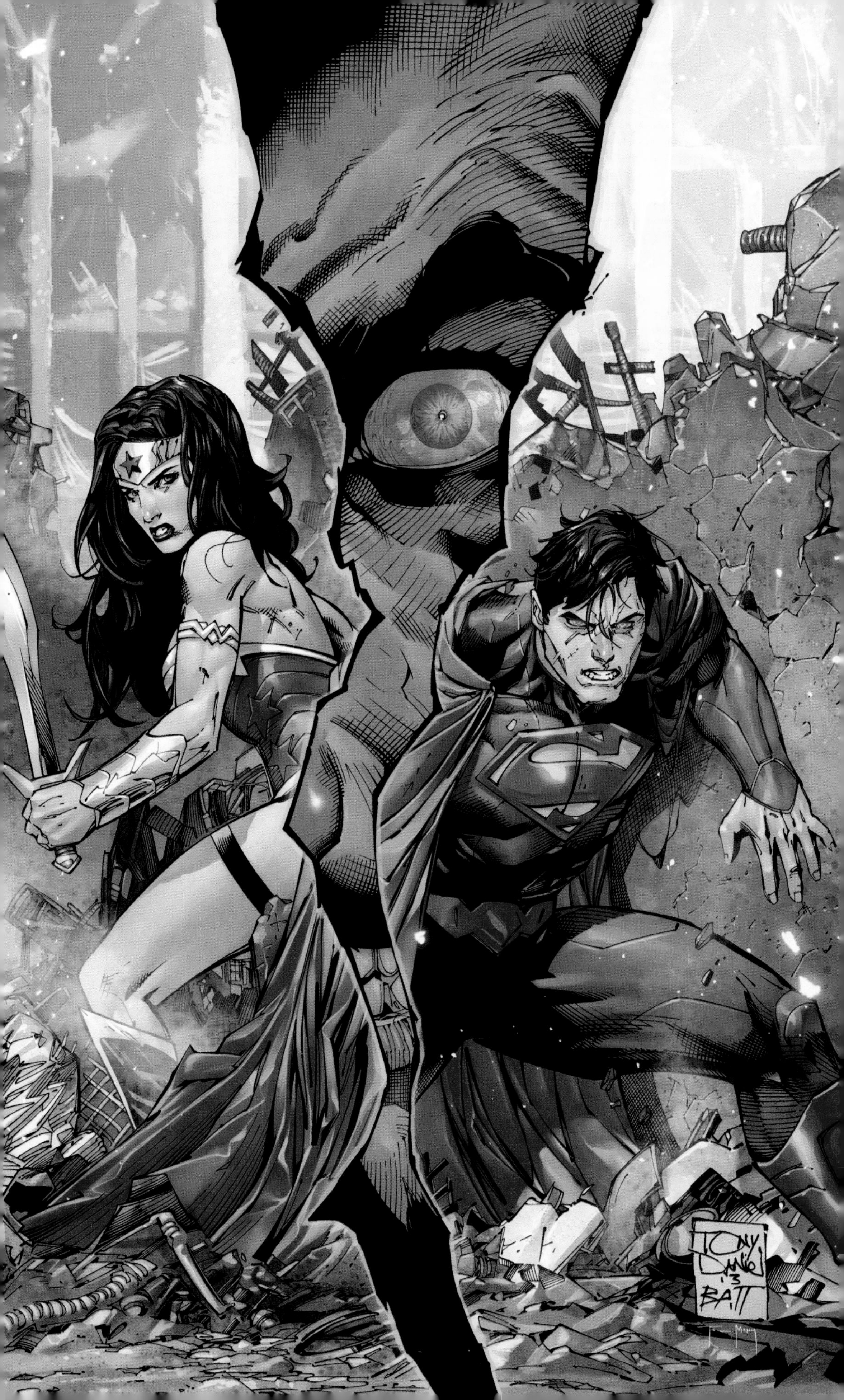

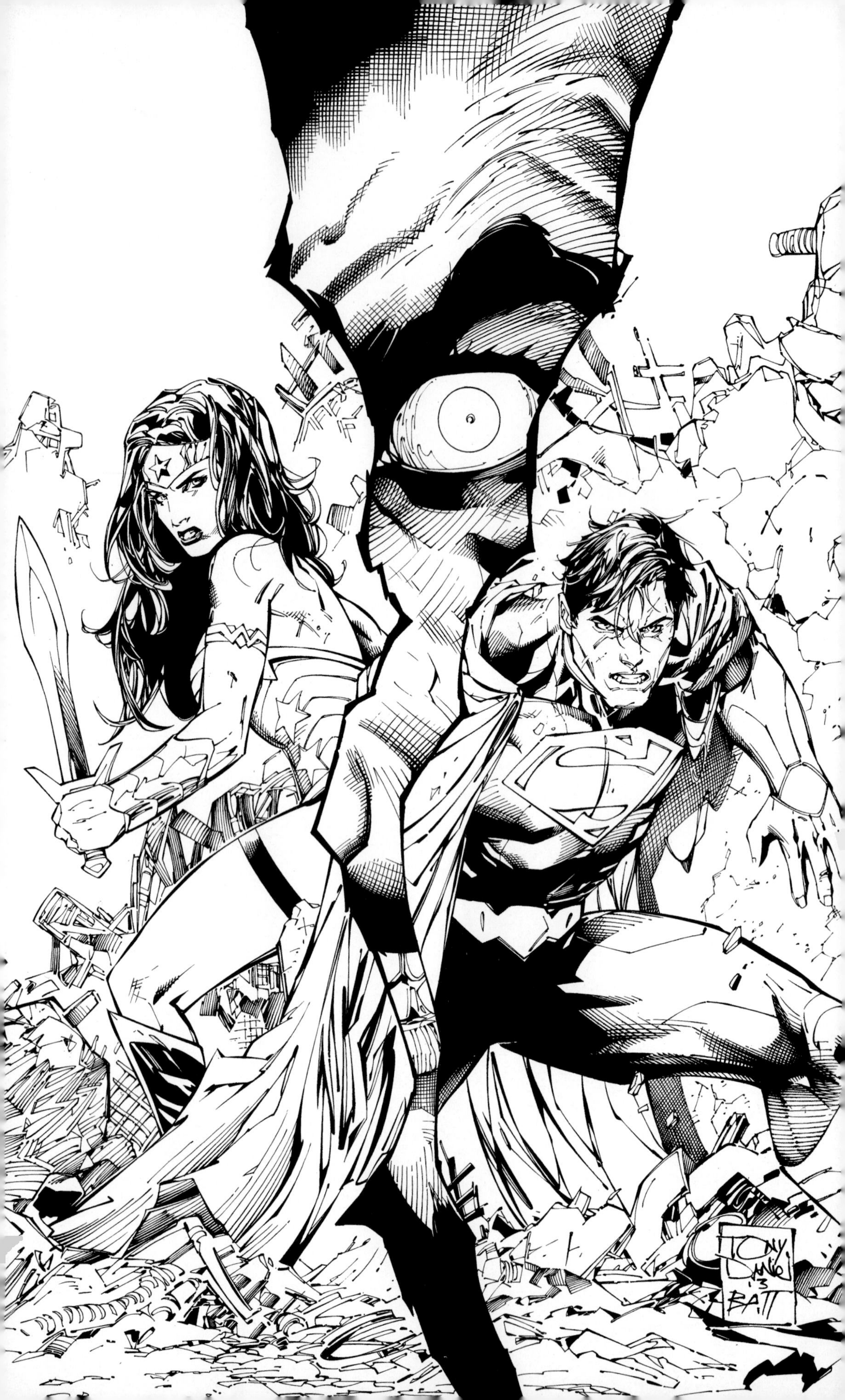

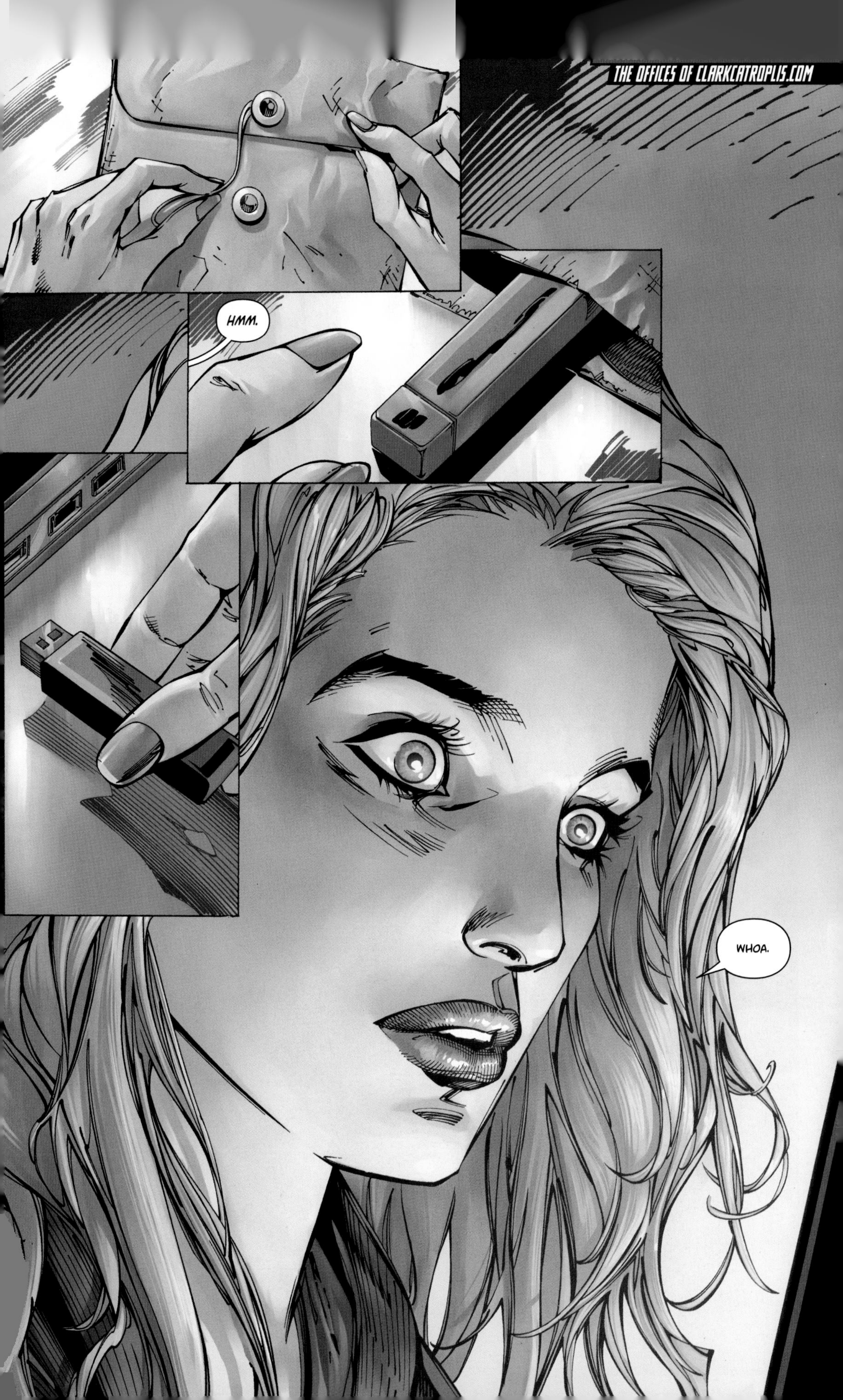
THE OFFICES OF CLARKCATROPLIS.COM
HMM.
WHOA.

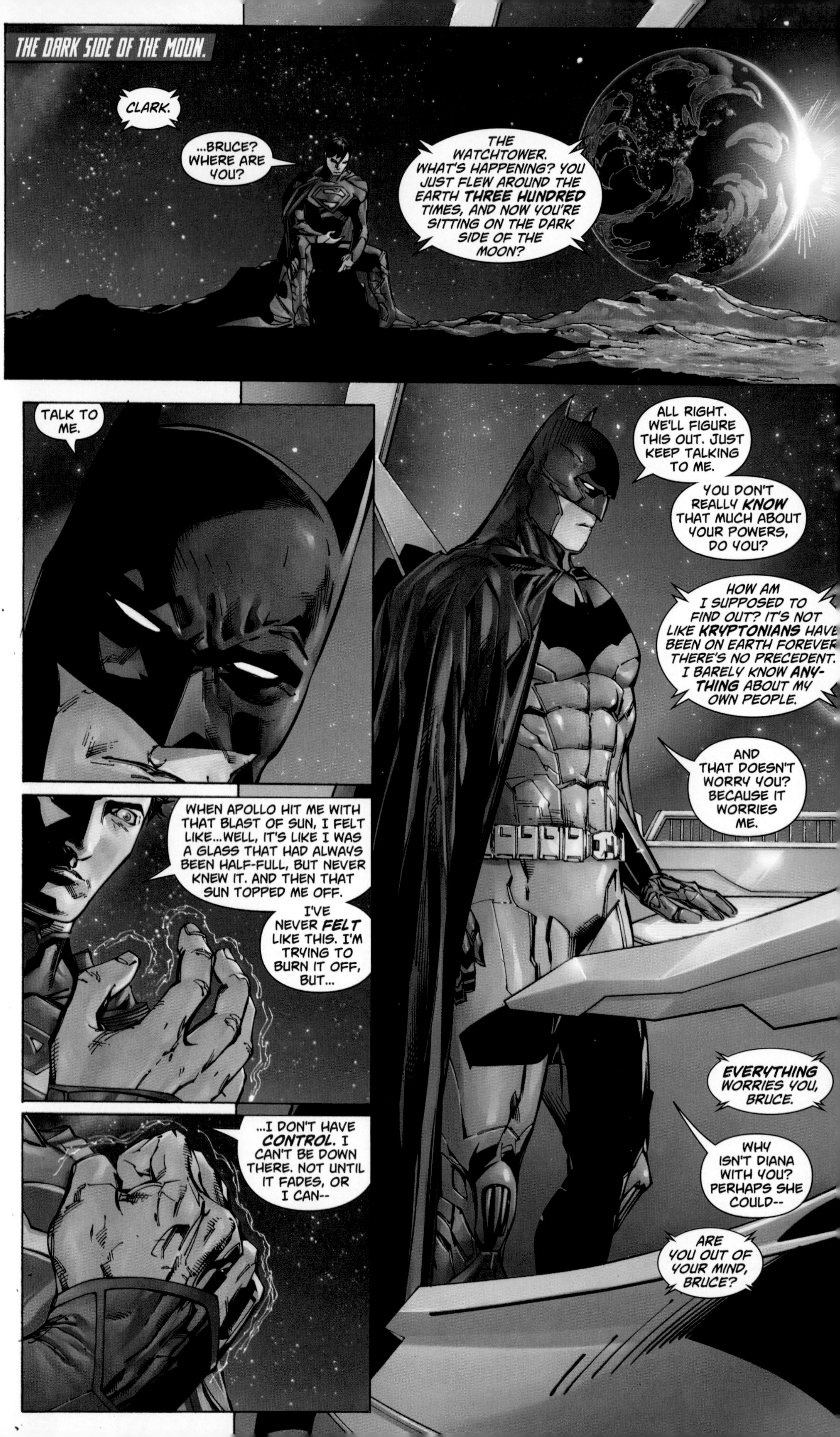
THE DARK SIDE OF THE MOON.
CLARK.
...BRUCE? WHERE ARE YOU?
THE WATCHTOWER. WHAT'S HAPPENING? YOU JUST FLEW AROUND THE EARTH THREE HUNDRED TIMES, AND NOW YOU'RE SITTING ON THE DARK SIDE OF THE MOON?
TALK TO ME.
ALL RIGHT. WE'LL FIGURE THIS OUT. JUST KEEP TALKING TO ME.
YOU DON'T REALLY KNOW THAT MUCH ABOUT YOUR POWERS, DO YOU?
HOW AM I SUPPOSED TO FIND OUT? IT'S NOT LIKE KRYPTONIANS HAVE BEEN ON EARTH FOREVER. THERE'S NO PRECEDENT. I BARELY KNOW ANYTHING ABOUT MY OWN PEOPLE.
AND THAT DOESN'T WORRY YOU? BECAUSE IT WORRIES ME.
WHEN APOLLO HIT ME WITH THAT BLAST OF SUN, I FELT LIKE...WELL, IT'S LIKE I WAS A GLASS THAT HAD ALWAYS BEEN HALF-FULL, BUT NEVER KNEW IT. AND THEN THAT SUN TOPPED ME OFF.
I'VE NEVER FELT LIKE THIS. I'M TRYING TO BURN IT OFF, BUT...
...I DON'T HAVE CONTROL. I CAN'T BE DOWN THERE. NOT UNTIL IT FADES, OR I CAN--
EVERYTHING WORRIES YOU, BRUCE.
WHY ISN'T DIANA WITH YOU? PERHAPS SHE COULD--
ARE YOU OUT OF YOUR MIND, BRUCE?

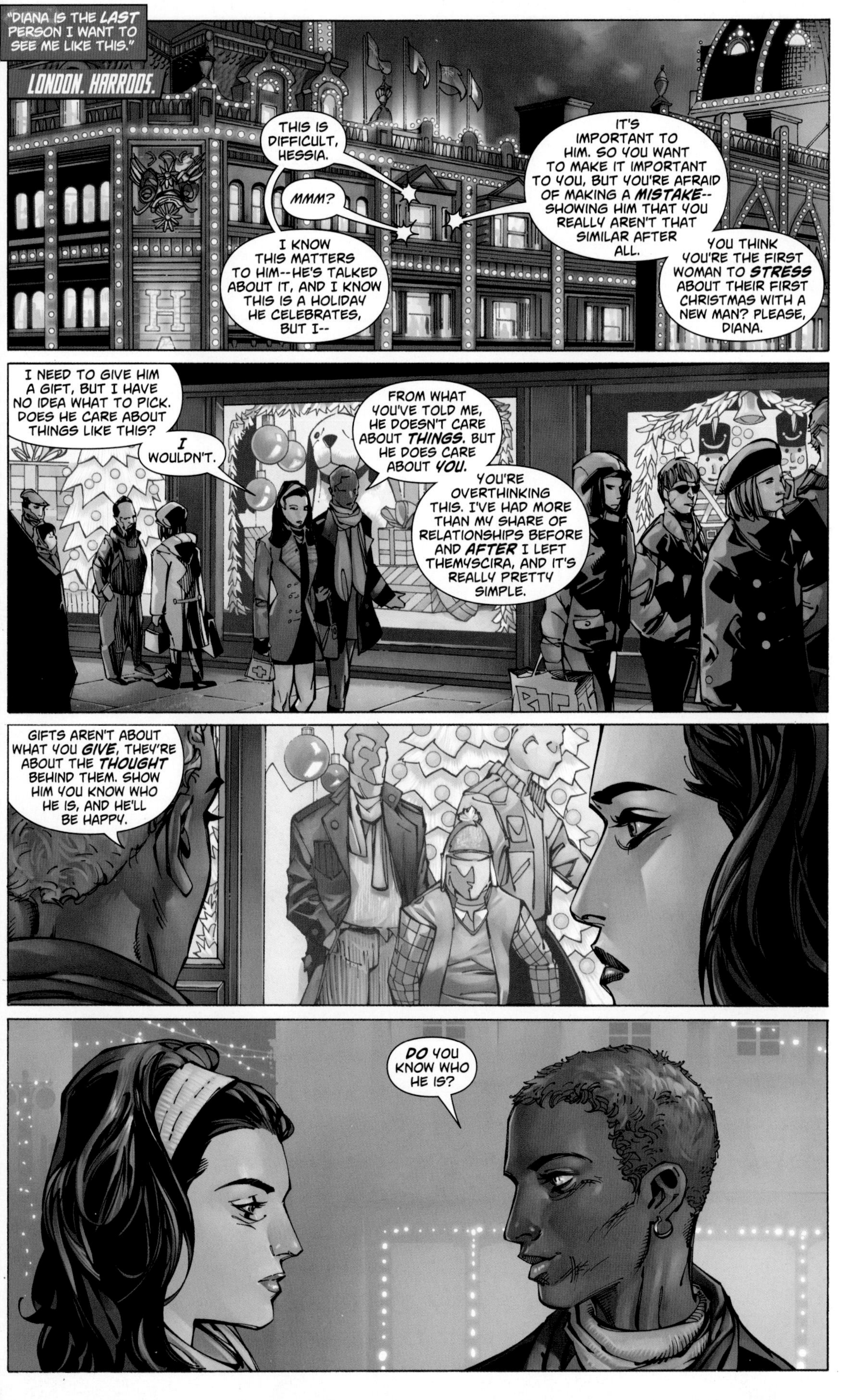
"DIANA IS THE LAST PERSON I WANT TO SEE ME LIKE THIS."
LONDON. HARRODS.
THIS IS DIFFICULT, HESSIA.
MMM?
I KNOW THIS MATTERS TO HIM--HE'S TALKED ABOUT IT, AND I KNOW THIS IS A HOLIDAY HE CELEBRATES, BUT I--
IT'S IMPORTANT TO HIM. SO YOU WANT TO MAKE IT IMPORTANT TO YOU, BUT YOU'RE AFRAID OF MAKING A MISTAKE-- SHOWING HIM THAT YOU REALLY AREN'T THAT SIMILAR AFTER ALL.
YOU THINK YOU'RE THE FIRST WOMAN TO STRESS ABOUT THEIR FIRST CHRISTMAS WITH A NEW MAN? PLEASE, DIANA.
I NEED TO GIVE HIM A GIFT, BUT I HAVE NO IDEA WHAT TO PICK. DOES HE CARE ABOUT THINGS LIKE THIS?
I WOULDN'T.
FROM WHAT YOU'VE TOLD ME, HE DOESN'T CARE ABOUT THINGS. BUT HE DOES CARE ABOUT YOU.
YOU'RE OVERTHINKING THIS. I'VE HAD MORE THAN MY SHARE OF RELATIONSHIPS BEFORE AND AFTER I LEFT THEMYSCIRA, AND IT'S REALLY PRETTY SIMPLE.
GIFTS AREN'T ABOUT WHAT YOU GIVE, THEY'RE ABOUT THE THOUGHT BEHIND THEM. SHOW HIM YOU KNOW WHO HE IS, AND HE'LL BE HAPPY.
DO YOU KNOW WHO HE IS?

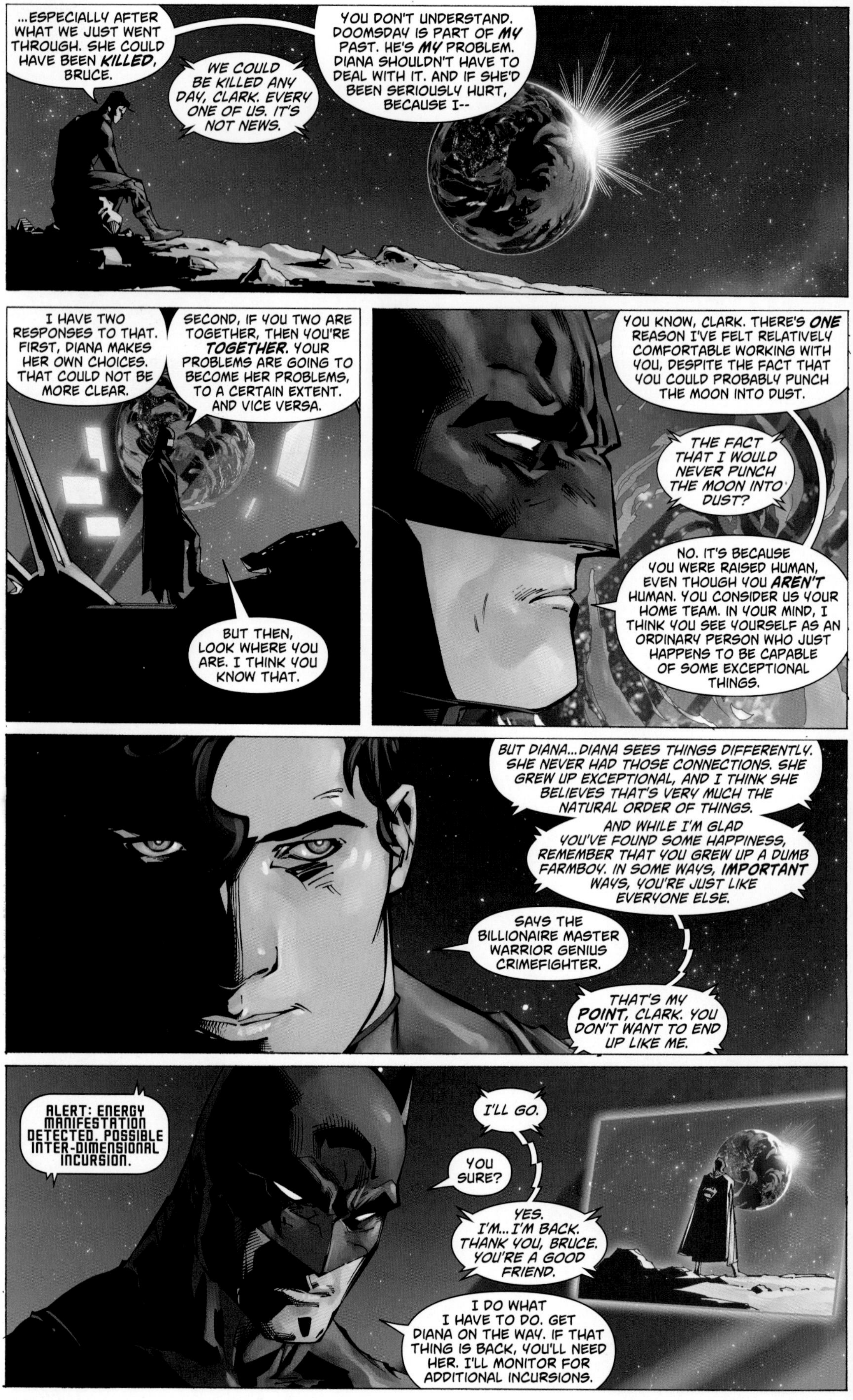
...ESPECIALLY AFTER WHAT WE JUST WENT THROUGH. SHE COULD HAVE BEEN KILLED, BRUCE.
WE COULD BE KILLED ANY DAY, CLARK. EVERY ONE OF US. IT'S NOT NEWS.
YOU DON'T UNDERSTAND. DOOMSDAY IS PART OF MY PAST. HE'S MY PROBLEM. DIANA SHOULDN'T HAVE TO DEAL WITH IT. AND IF SHE'D BEEN SERIOUSLY HURT, BECAUSE I--
I HAVE TWO RESPONSES TO THAT. FIRST, DIANA MAKES HER OWN CHOICES. THAT COULD NOT BE MORE CLEAR.
SECOND, IF YOU TWO ARE TOGETHER, THEN YOU'RE TOGETHER. YOUR PROBLEMS ARE GOING TO BECOME HER PROBLEMS, TO A CERTAIN EXTENT. AND VICE VERSA.
BUT THEN, LOOK WHERE YOU ARE. I THINK YOU KNOW THAT.
YOU KNOW, CLARK. THERE'S ONE REASON I'VE FELT RELATIVELY COMFORTABLE WORKING WITH YOU, DESPITE THE FACT THAT YOU COULD PROBABLY PUNCH THE MOON INTO DUST.
THE FACT THAT I WOULD NEVER PUNCH THE MOON INTO DUST?
NO. IT'S BECAUSE YOU WERE RAISED HUMAN, EVEN THOUGH YOU AREN'T HUMAN. YOU CONSIDER US YOUR HOME TEAM. IN YOUR MIND, I THINK YOU SEE YOURSELF AS AN ORDINARY PERSON WHO JUST HAPPENS TO BE CAPABLE OF SOME EXCEPTIONAL THINGS.
BUT DIANA...DIANA SEES THINGS DIFFERENTLY. SHE NEVER HAD THOSE CONNECTIONS. SHE GREW UP EXCEPTIONAL, AND I THINK SHE BELIEVES THAT'S VERY MUCH THE NATURAL ORDER OF THINGS.
AND WHILE I'M GLAD YOU'VE FOUND SOME HAPPINESS, REMEMBER THAT YOU GREW UP A DUMB FARMBOY. IN SOME WAYS, IMPORTANT WAYS, YOU'RE JUST LIKE EVERYONE ELSE.
SAYS THE BILLIONAIRE MASTER WARRIOR GENIUS CRIMEFIGHTER.
THAT'S MY POINT, CLARK. YOU DON'T WANT TO END UP LIKE ME.
ALERT: ENERGY MANIFESTATION DETECTED. POSSIBLE INTER-DIMENSIONAL INCURSION.
I'LL GO.
YOU SURE?
YES. I'M...I'M BACK. THANK YOU, BRUCE. YOU'RE A GOOD FRIEND.
I DO WHAT I HAVE TO DO. GET DIANA ON THE WAY. IF THAT THING IS BACK, YOU'LL NEED HER. I'LL MONITOR FOR ADDITIONAL INCURSIONS.

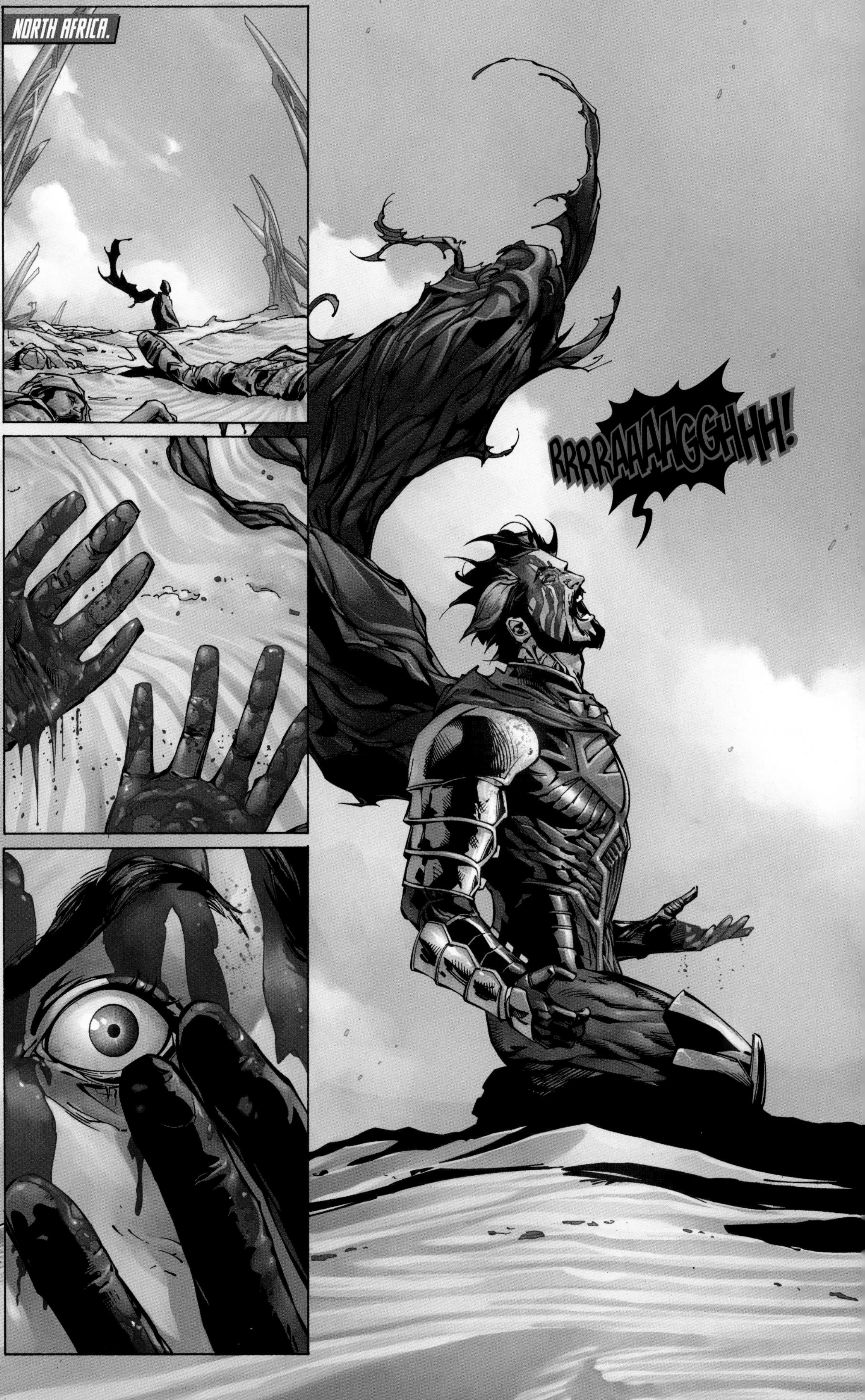
NORTH AFRICA.
RRRRAAAAGGHHH!

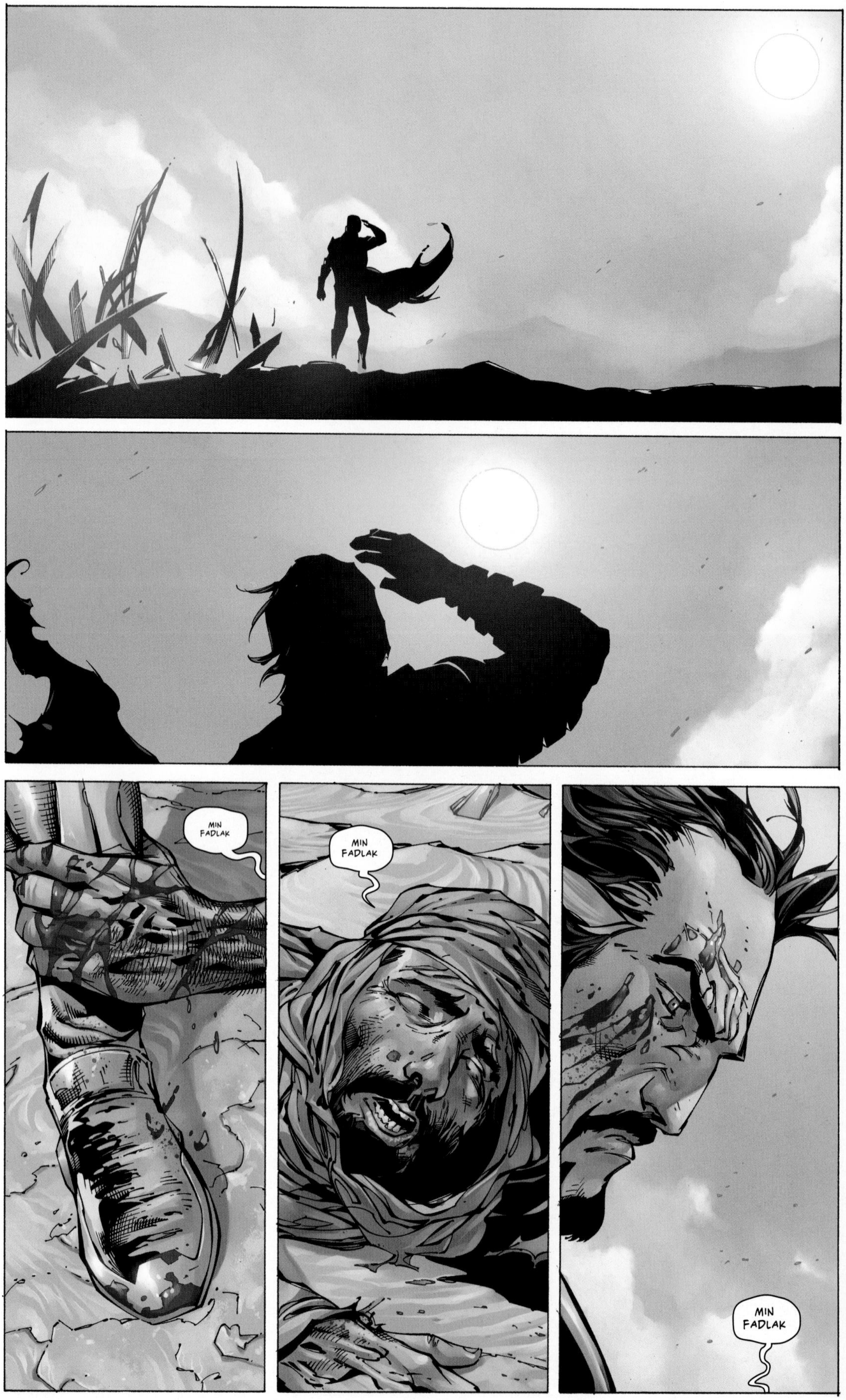
MIN FADLAK
MIN FADLAK
MIN FADLAK

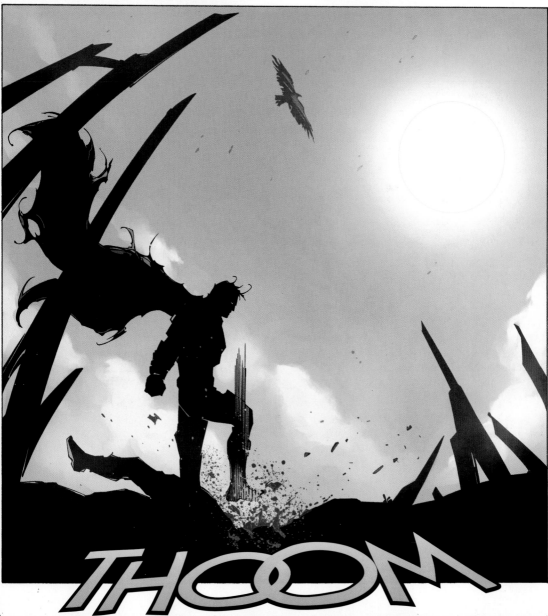

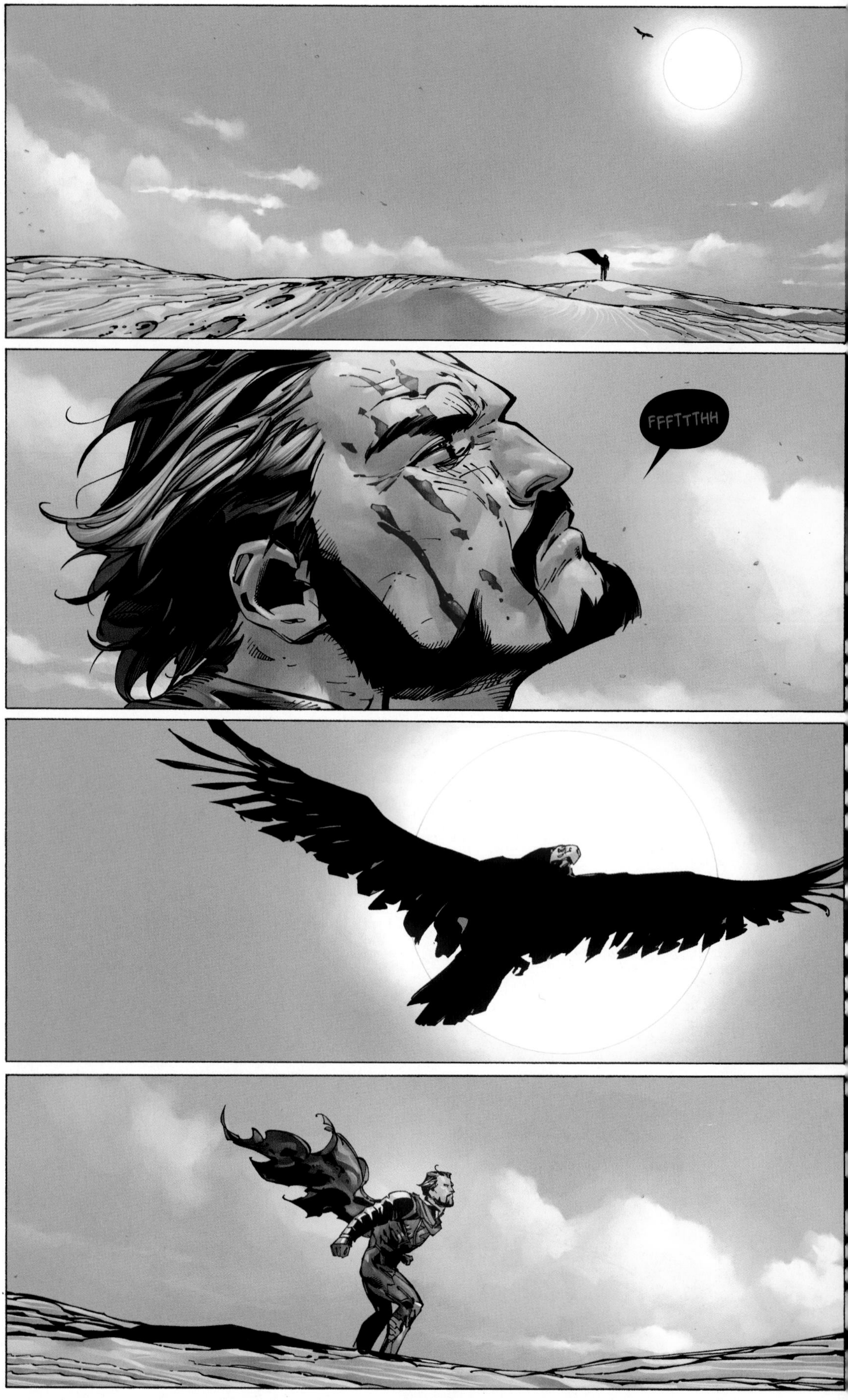
FFFTTTHH

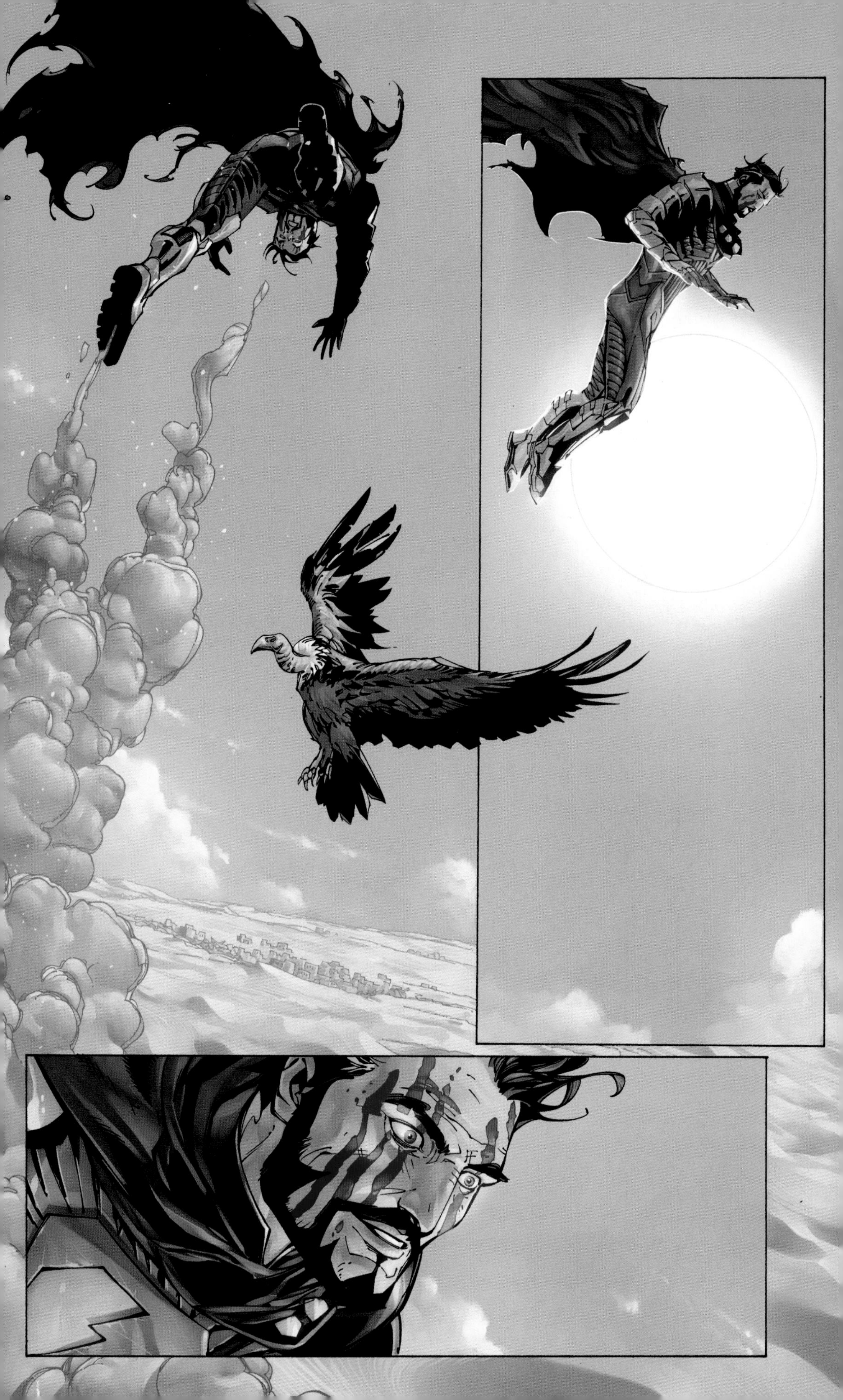

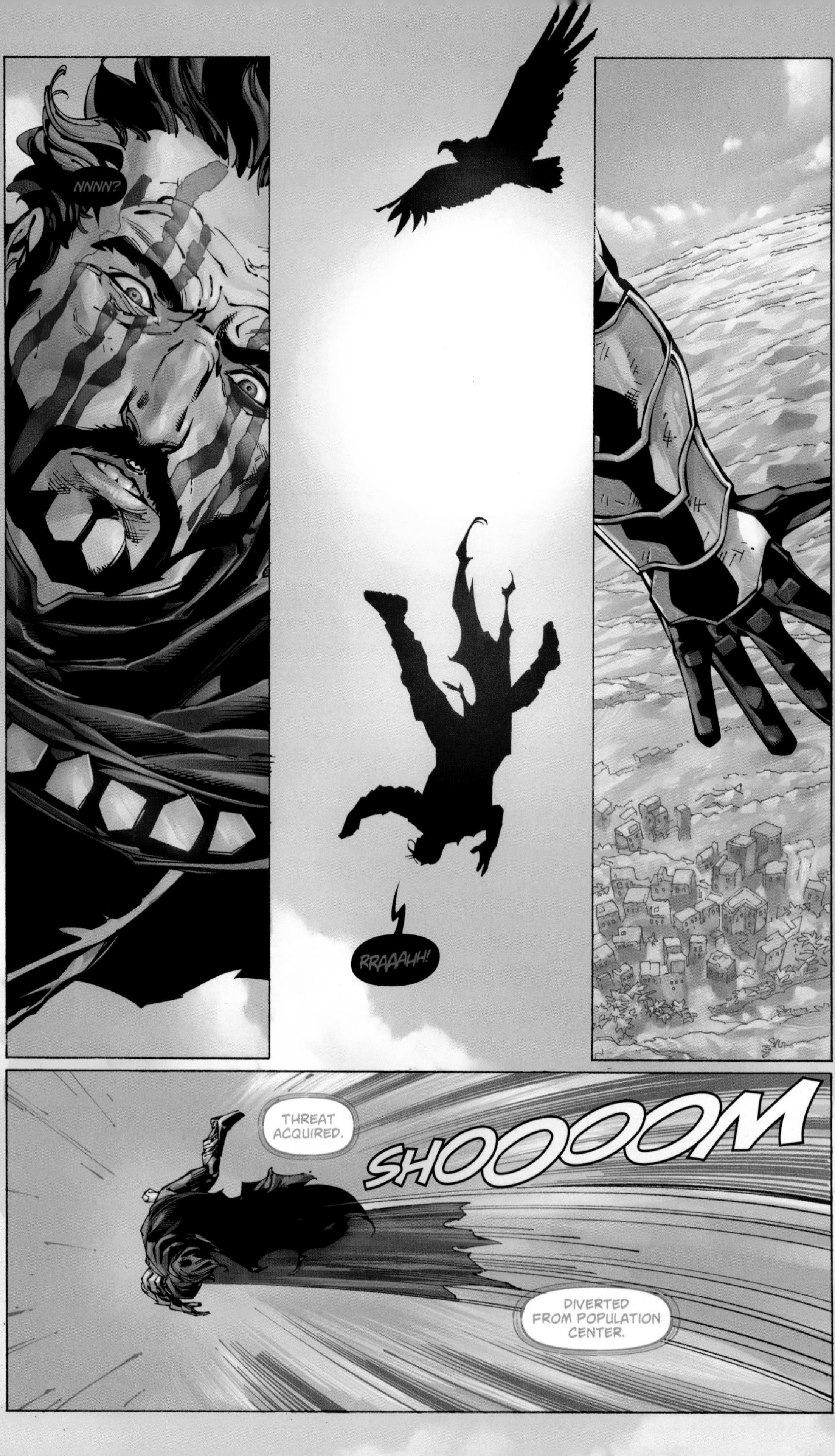
NNNN?
RRAAAHH!
THREAT ACQUIRED.
SHOOOOOM
DIVERTED FROM POPULATION CENTER.

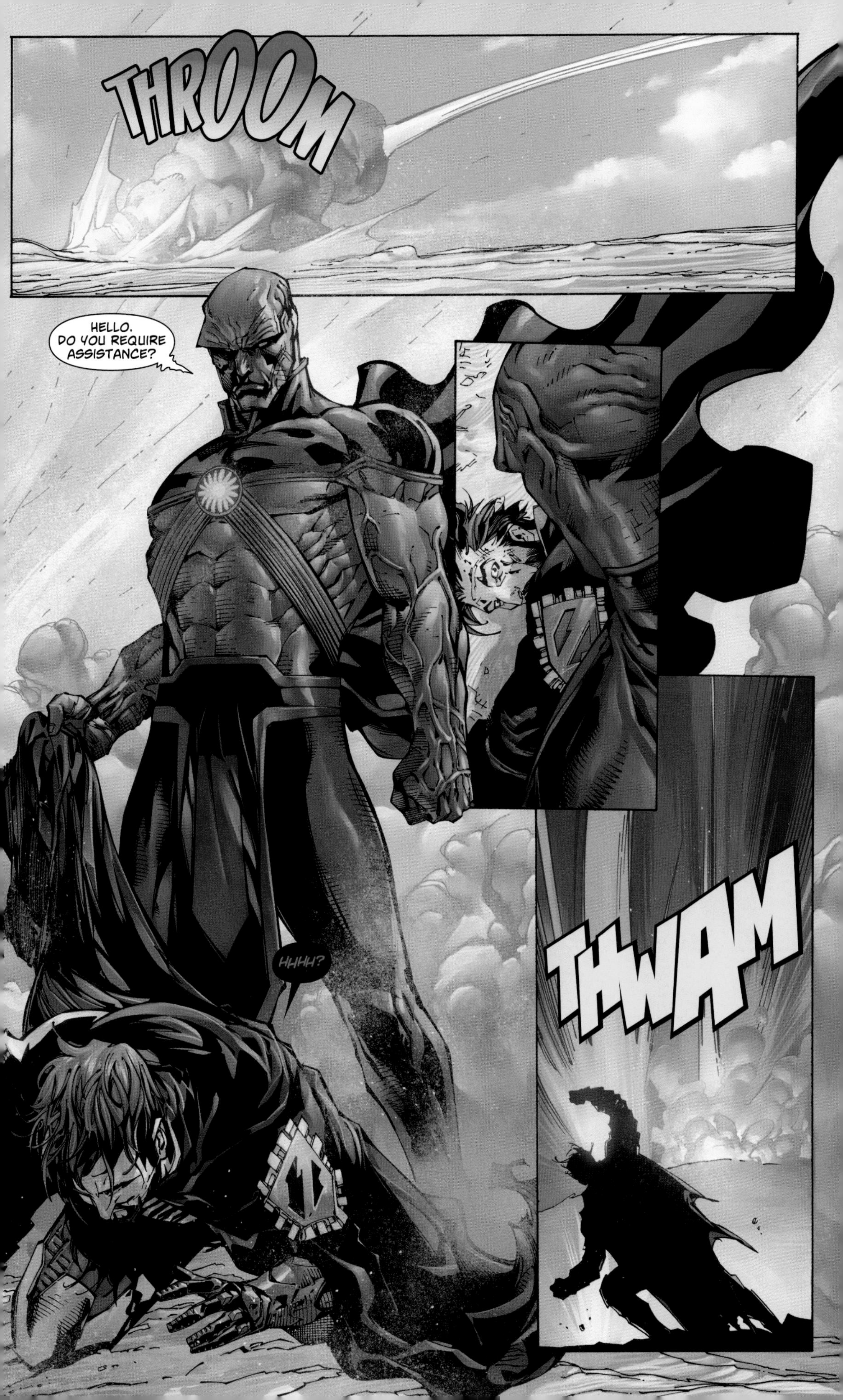
THROOM
HELLO. DO YOU REQUIRE ASSISTANCE?
HHHH?
THWAM

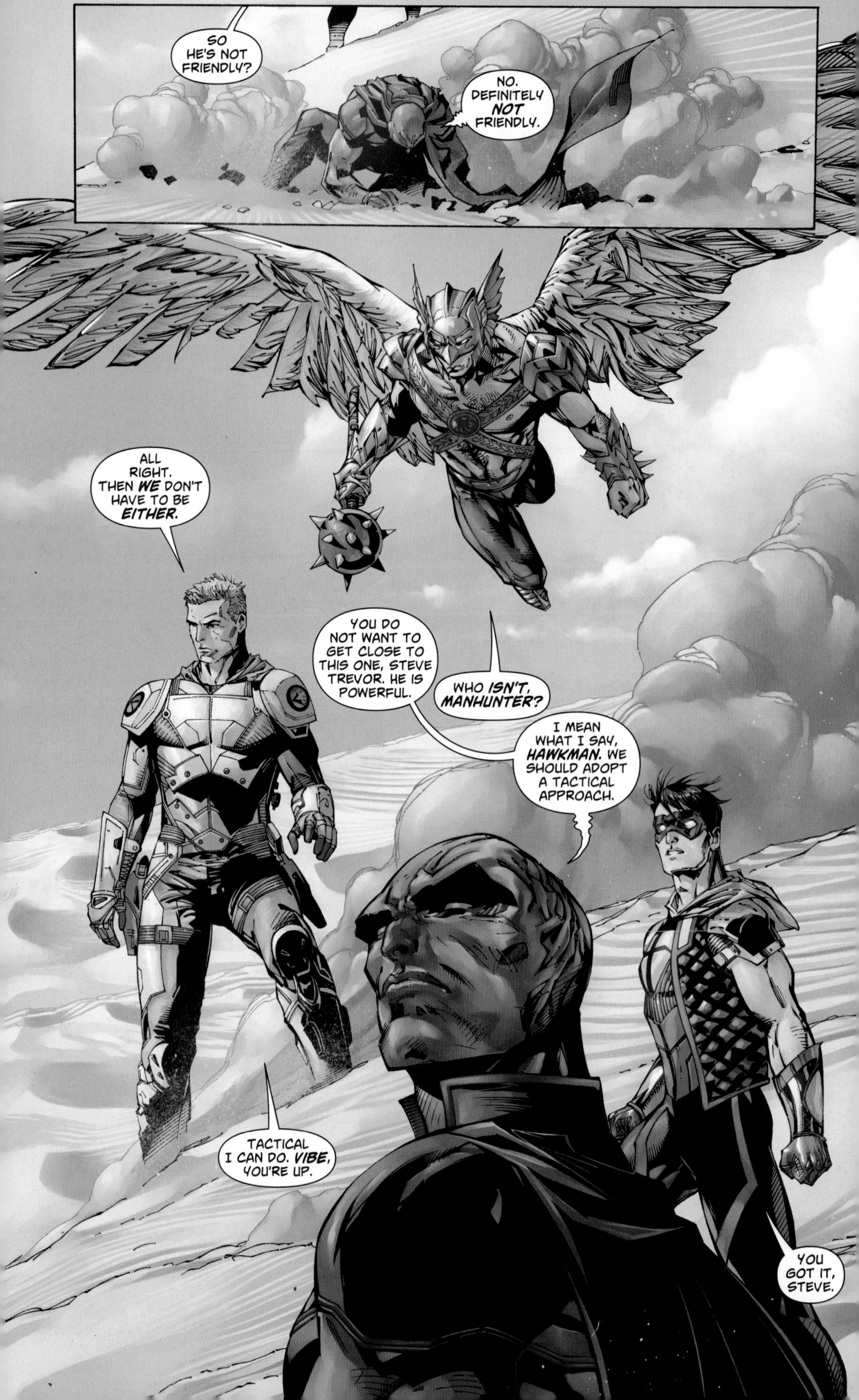

SO HE'S NOT FRIENDLY?
NO. DEFINITELY **NOT** FRIENDLY.
ALL RIGHT. THEN **WE** DON'T HAVE TO BE **EITHER.**
YOU DO NOT WANT TO GET CLOSE TO THIS ONE, STEVE TREVOR. HE IS POWERFUL.
WHO **ISN'T, MANHUNTER?**
I MEAN WHAT I SAY, **HAWKMAN.** WE SHOULD ADOPT A TACTICAL APPROACH.
TACTICAL I CAN DO. **VIBE,** YOU'RE UP.
YOU GOT IT, STEVE.

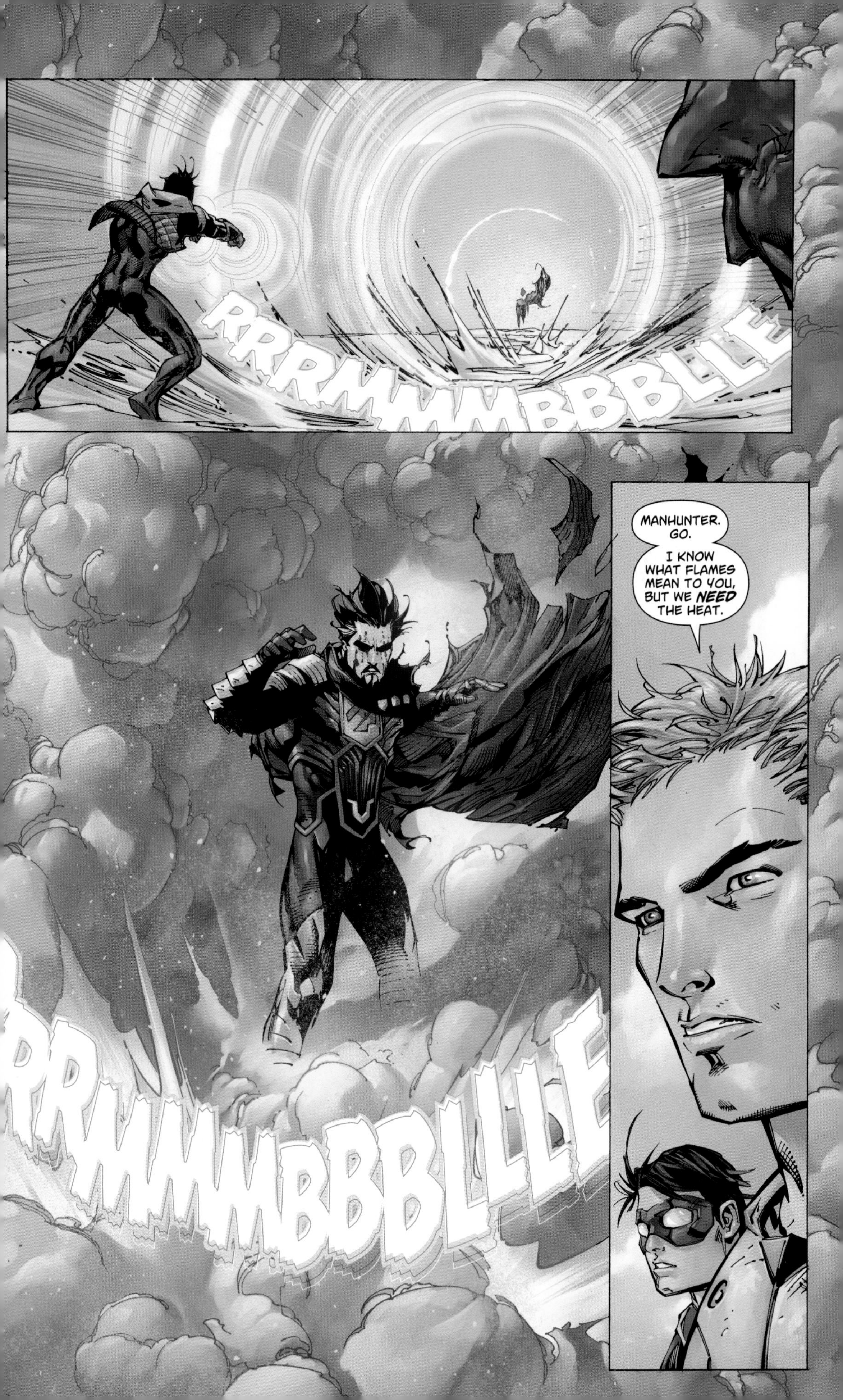
RRRMMMMBBBLLE
MANHUNTER. GO.
I KNOW WHAT FLAMES MEAN TO YOU, BUT WE NEED THE HEAT.
RRMMMBBBLLE

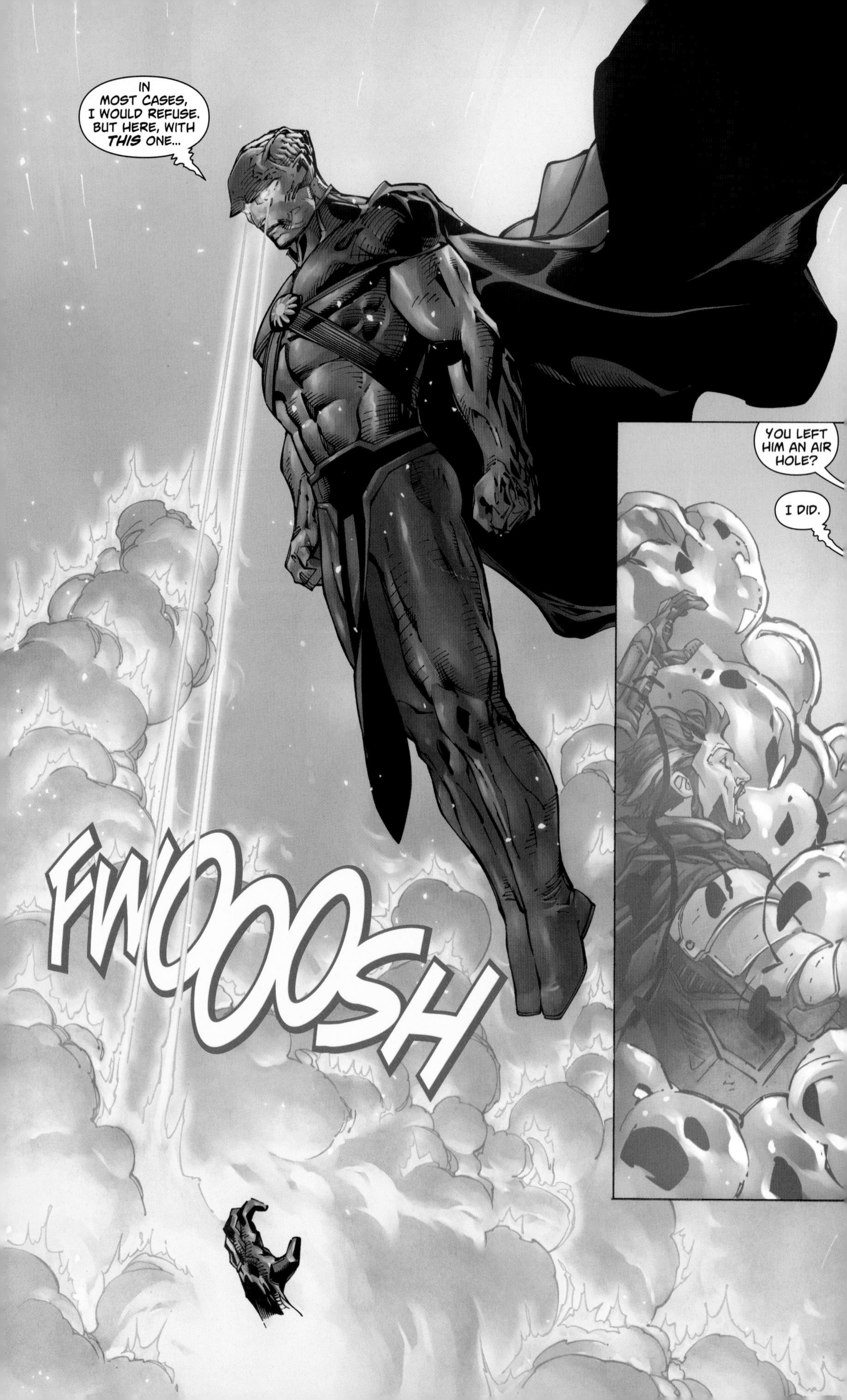
IN MOST CASES, I WOULD REFUSE. BUT HERE, WITH THIS ONE...
FWOOOSH
YOU LEFT HIM AN AIR HOLE?
I DID.

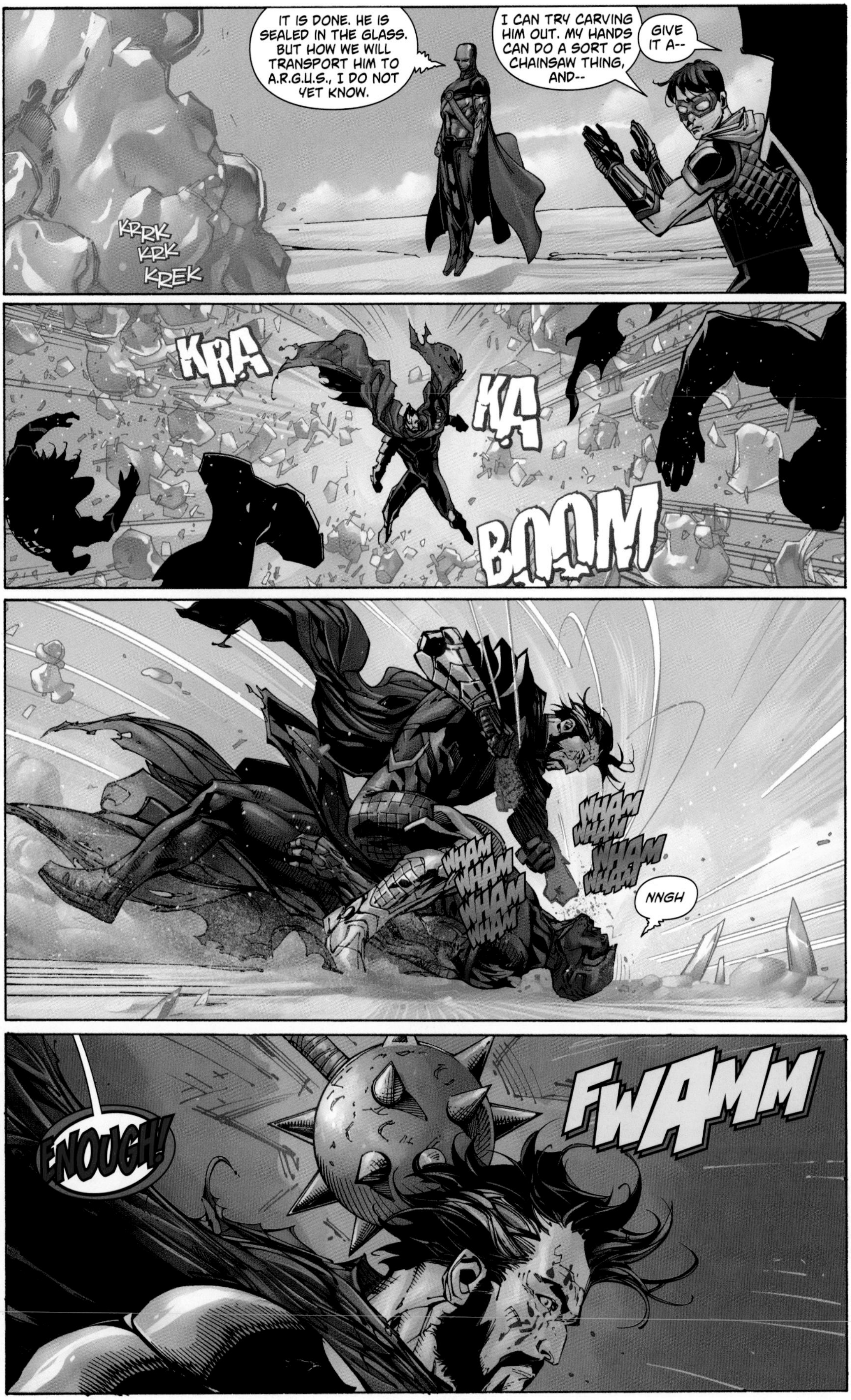
IT IS DONE. HE IS SEALED IN THE GLASS. BUT HOW WE WILL TRANSPORT HIM TO A.R.G.U.S., I DO NOT YET KNOW.
I CAN TRY CARVING HIM OUT. MY HANDS CAN DO A SORT OF CHAINSAW THING, AND--
GIVE IT A--
KRRK KRK KREK
KRA KA BOOM
WHAM WHAM WHAM WHAM WHAM
WHAM WHAM WHAM WHAM
NNGH
ENOUGH!
FWAMM

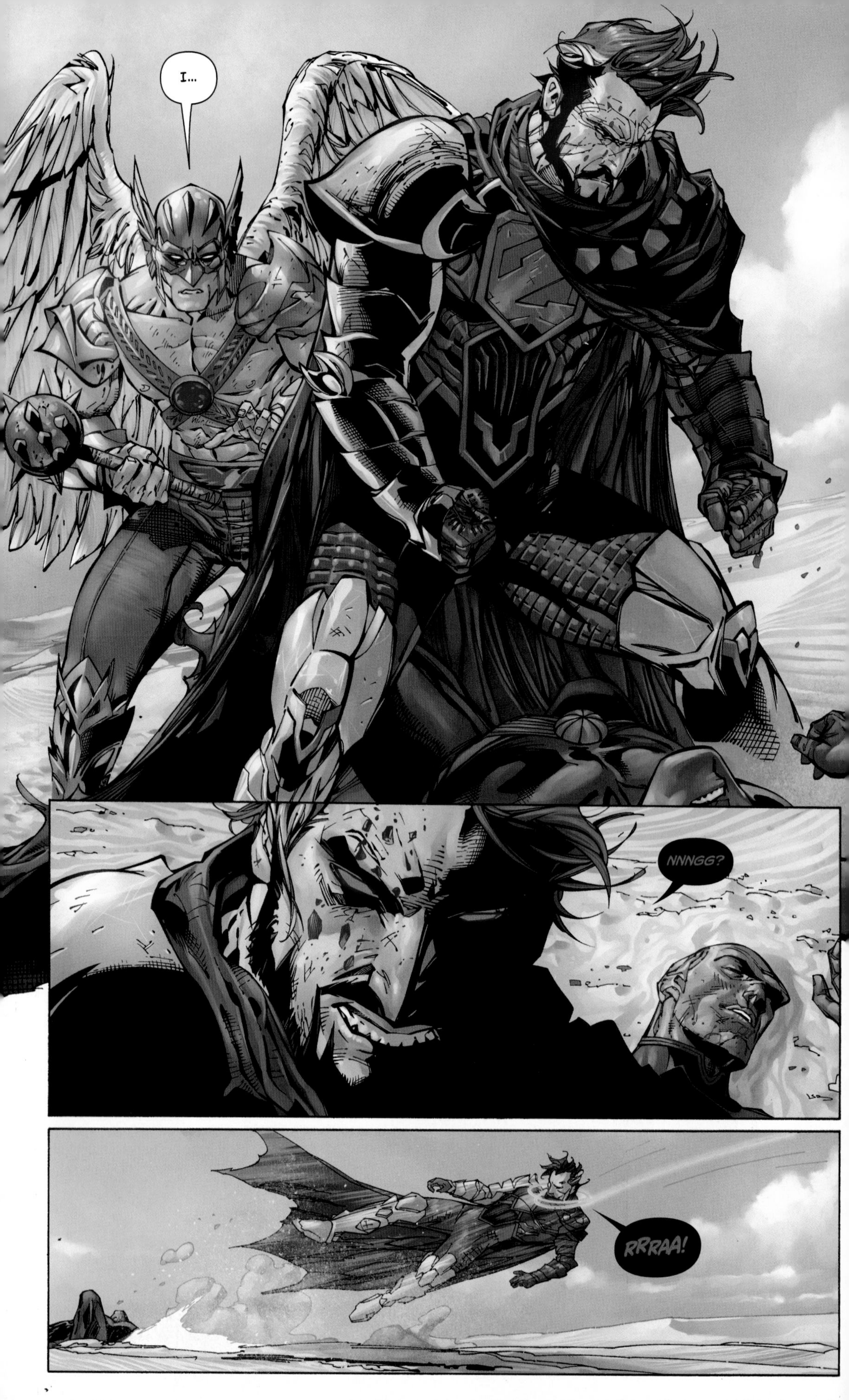
I...
NNNGG?
RRRAA!

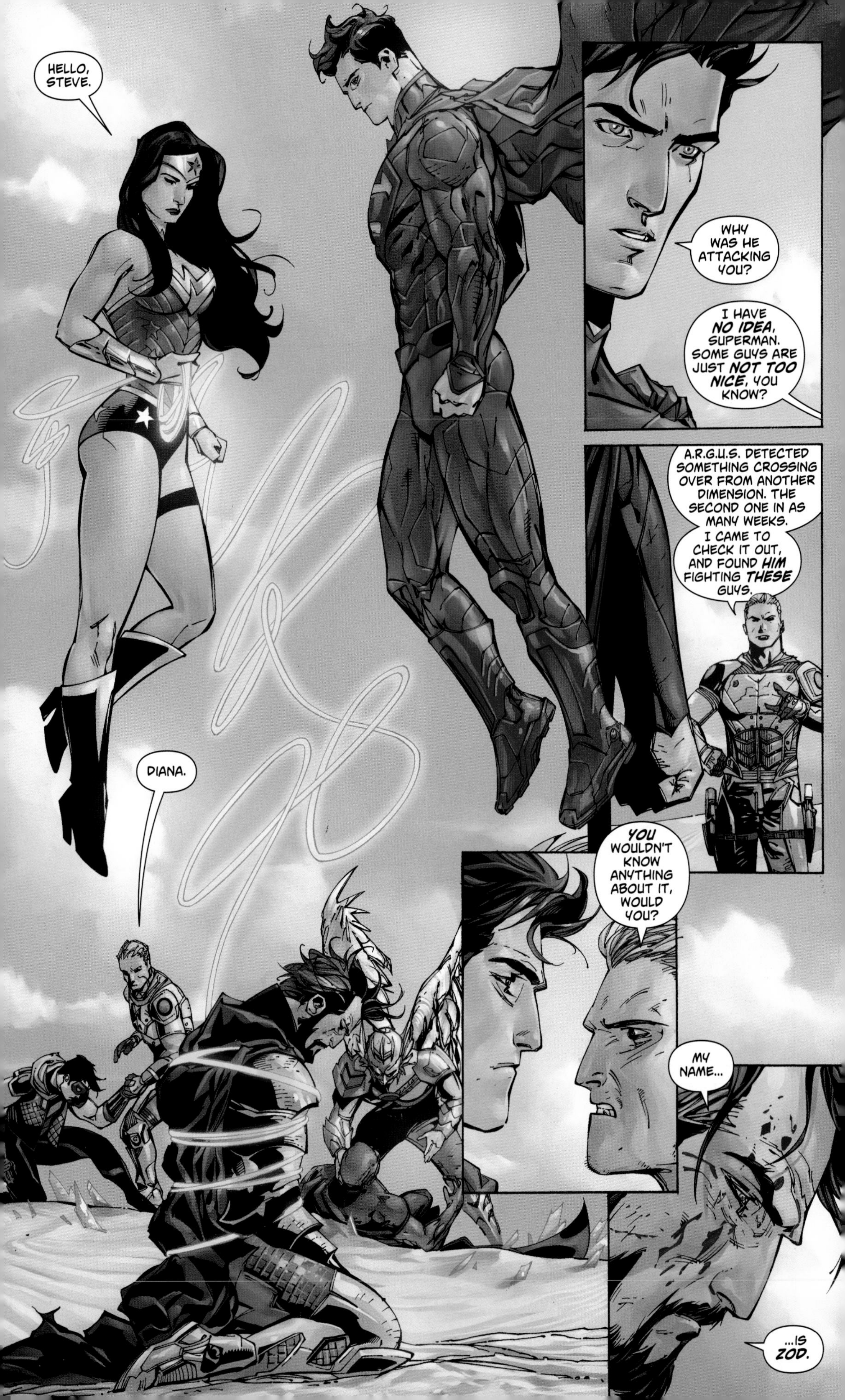
HELLO, STEVE.
DIANA.
WHY WAS HE ATTACKING YOU?
I HAVE NO IDEA, SUPERMAN. SOME GUYS ARE JUST NOT TOO NICE, YOU KNOW?
A.R.G.U.S. DETECTED SOMETHING CROSSING OVER FROM ANOTHER DIMENSION. THE SECOND ONE IN AS MANY WEEKS.
I CAME TO CHECK IT OUT, AND FOUND HIM FIGHTING THESE GUYS.
YOU WOULDN'T KNOW ANYTHING ABOUT IT, WOULD YOU?
MY NAME...
...IS ZOD.

A ZOO?

I APOLOGIZE, ZOD. IT'S WHAT I HAD AVAILABLE, AND I TRIED TO MAKE IT COMFORTABLE. THE SCREEN CAN CALL UP ENTERTAINMENT FROM EARTH, AND I'VE LEFT A FEW KRYPTONIAN TEXTS, AS WELL

I'LL MOVE YOU AS SOON AS I CAN.

I UNDERSTAND, KAL-EL. I CAME OUT OF THE *PHANTOM ZONE.* I WOULD BE *CAUTIOUS* IN YOUR POSITION AS WELL. THIS IS MORE THAN SUITABLE.

I LOOK FORWARD TO SPEAKING WITH YOU MORE IN THE DAYS TO COME. I WOULD TELL YOU OF YOUR FATHER.

I...WOULD LIKE THAT VERY MUCH.

BUT PLEASE. IF SOMEONE ELSE COMES THROUGH... FAORA...

I KNOW, ZOD. I WILL.

WILL IT HOLD HIM?

IT WOULD HOLD *ME.*

I...I HAVE A CHRISTMAS GIFT FOR YOU. I KNOW IT'S A BIT EARLY, BUT THIS SEEMS LIKE THE RIGHT MOMENT FOR IT. WOULD YOU LIKE IT?

WHAT? YOU DIDN'T HAVE TO... YOU DON'T WANT TO WAIT?

NO. THINGS NEVER GET THIS CALM. THIS IS THE TIME.

ALL RIGHT. WHAT IS IT?

IT'S *TIME,* BRUCE.

GOOD, DIANA. WE'RE ON IT. ENJOY YOUR-SELVES.

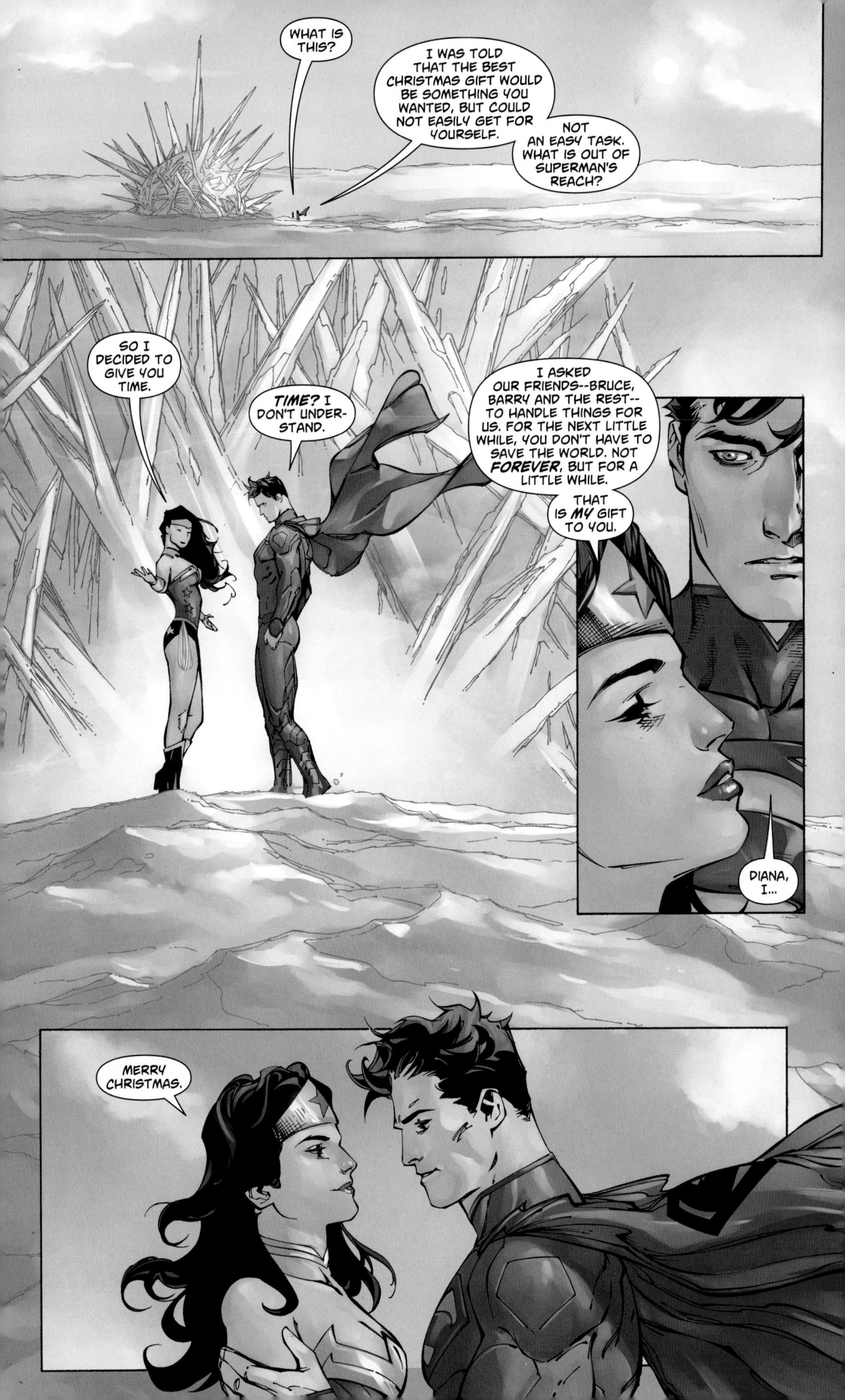
WHAT IS THIS?
I WAS TOLD THAT THE BEST CHRISTMAS GIFT WOULD BE SOMETHING YOU WANTED, BUT COULD NOT EASILY GET FOR YOURSELF.
NOT AN EASY TASK. WHAT IS OUT OF SUPERMAN'S REACH?
SO I DECIDED TO GIVE YOU TIME.
TIME? I DON'T UNDERSTAND.
I ASKED OUR FRIENDS--BRUCE, BARRY AND THE REST--TO HANDLE THINGS FOR US. FOR THE NEXT LITTLE WHILE, YOU DON'T HAVE TO SAVE THE WORLD. NOT FOREVER, BUT FOR A LITTLE WHILE.
THAT IS MY GIFT TO YOU.
DIANA, I...
MERRY CHRISTMAS.

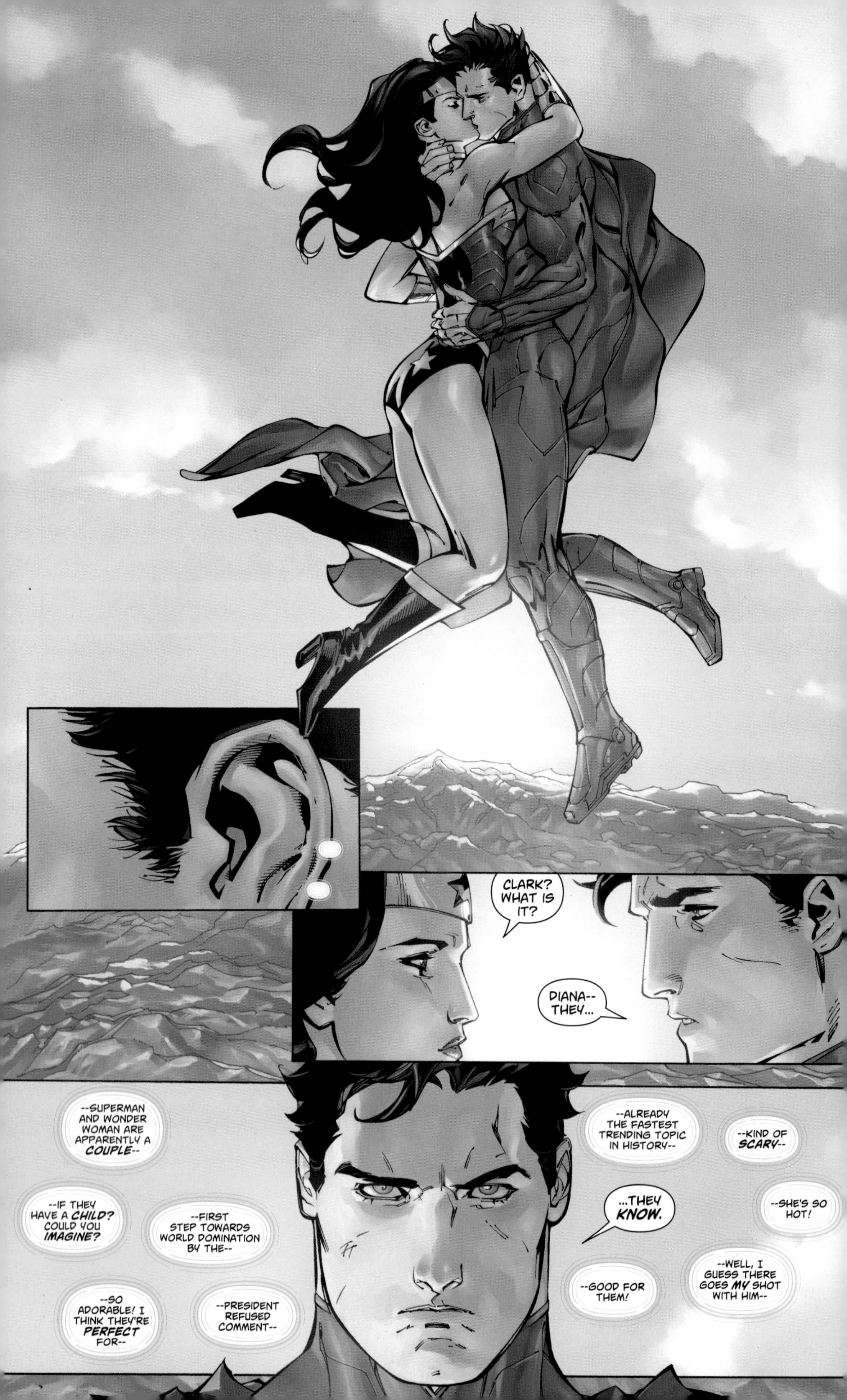
CLARK? WHAT IS IT?
DIANA-- THEY...
--SUPERMAN AND WONDER WOMAN ARE APPARENTLY A COUPLE--
--ALREADY THE FASTEST TRENDING TOPIC IN HISTORY--
--KIND OF SCARY--
--IF THEY HAVE A CHILD? COULD YOU IMAGINE?
--FIRST STEP TOWARDS WORLD DOMINATION BY THE--
...THEY KNOW.
--SHE'S SO HOT!
--GOOD FOR THEM!
--WELL, I GUESS THERE GOES MY SHOT WITH HIM--
--SO ADORABLE! I THINK THEY'RE PERFECT FOR--
--PRESIDENT REFUSED COMMENT--

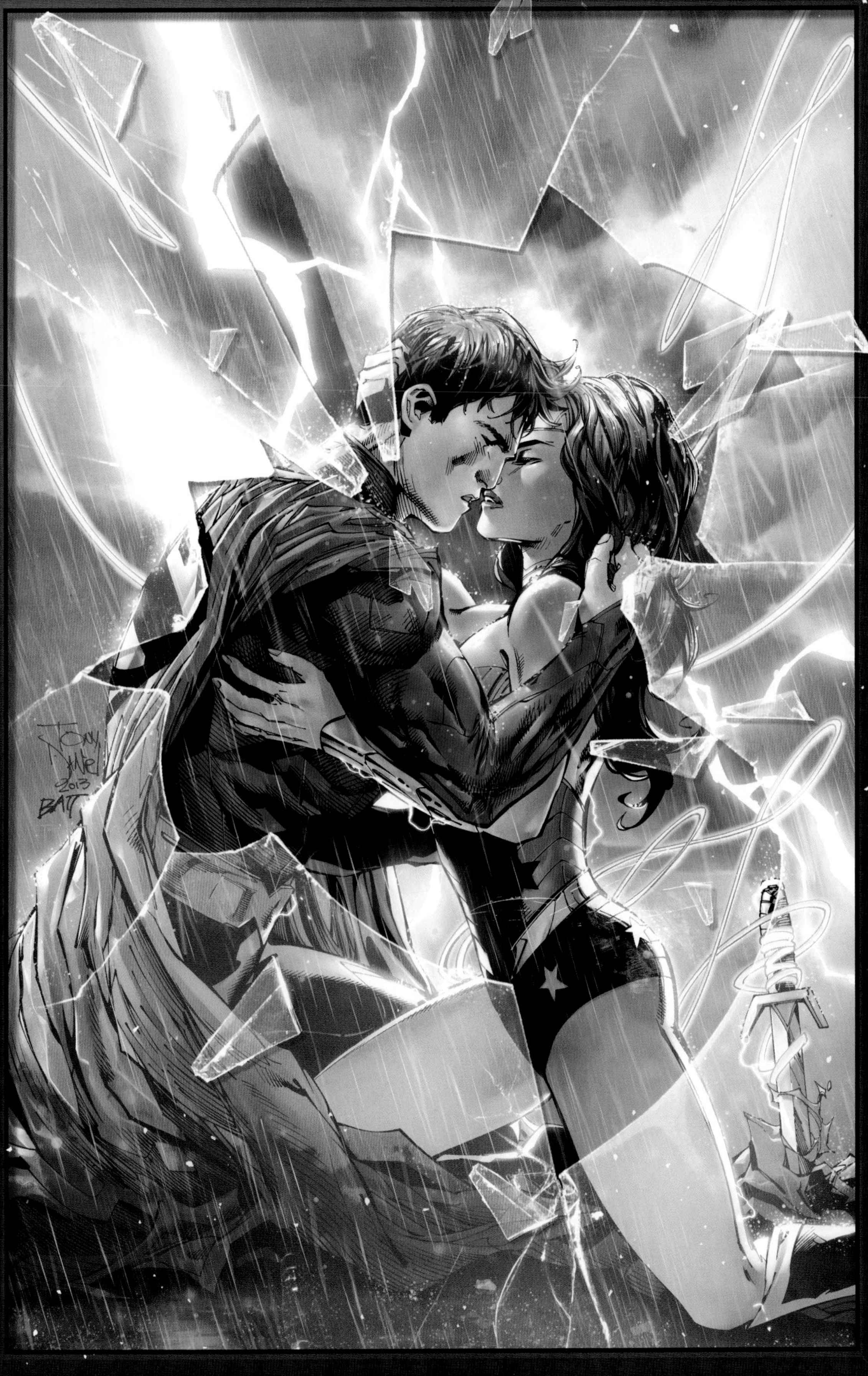

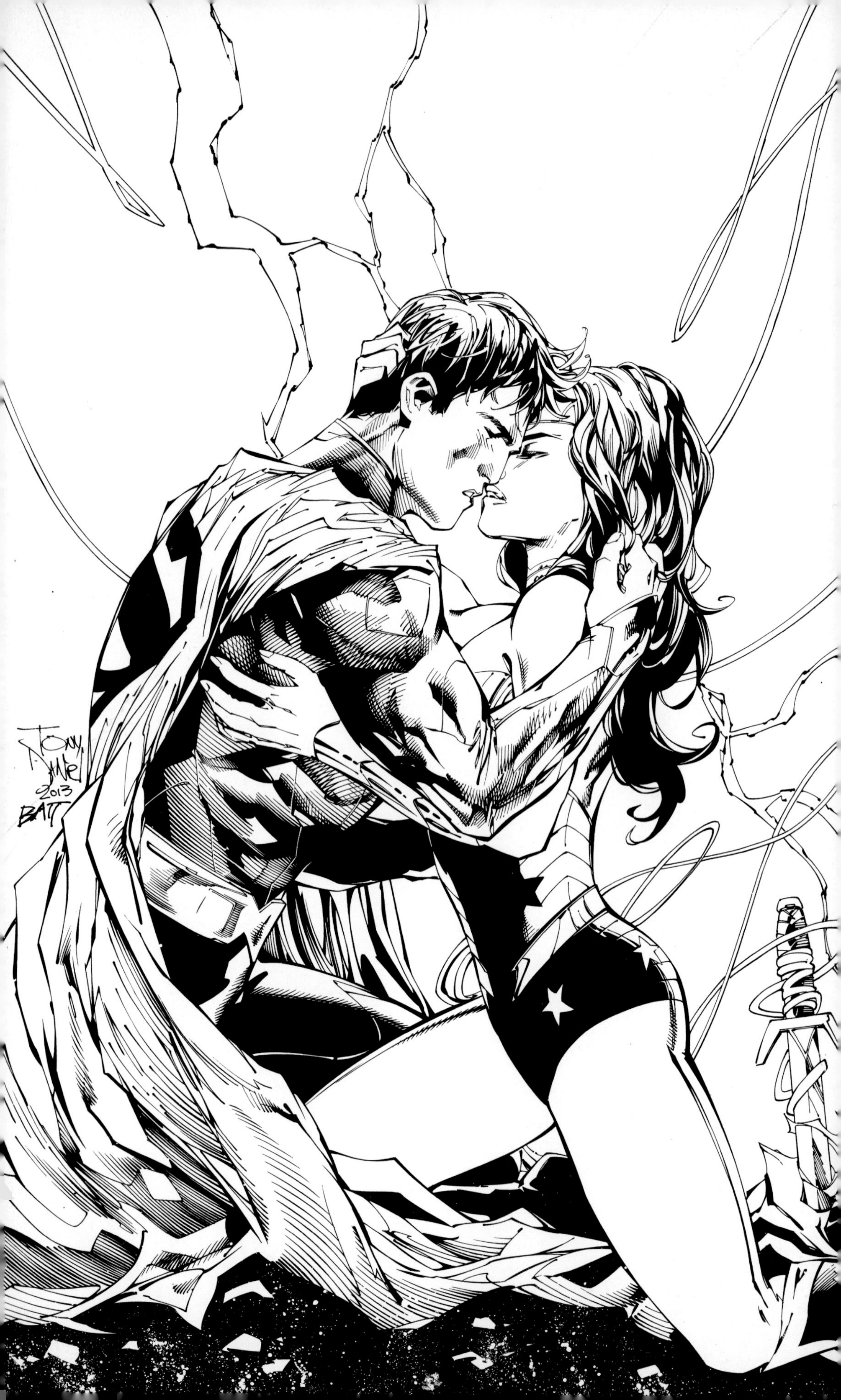

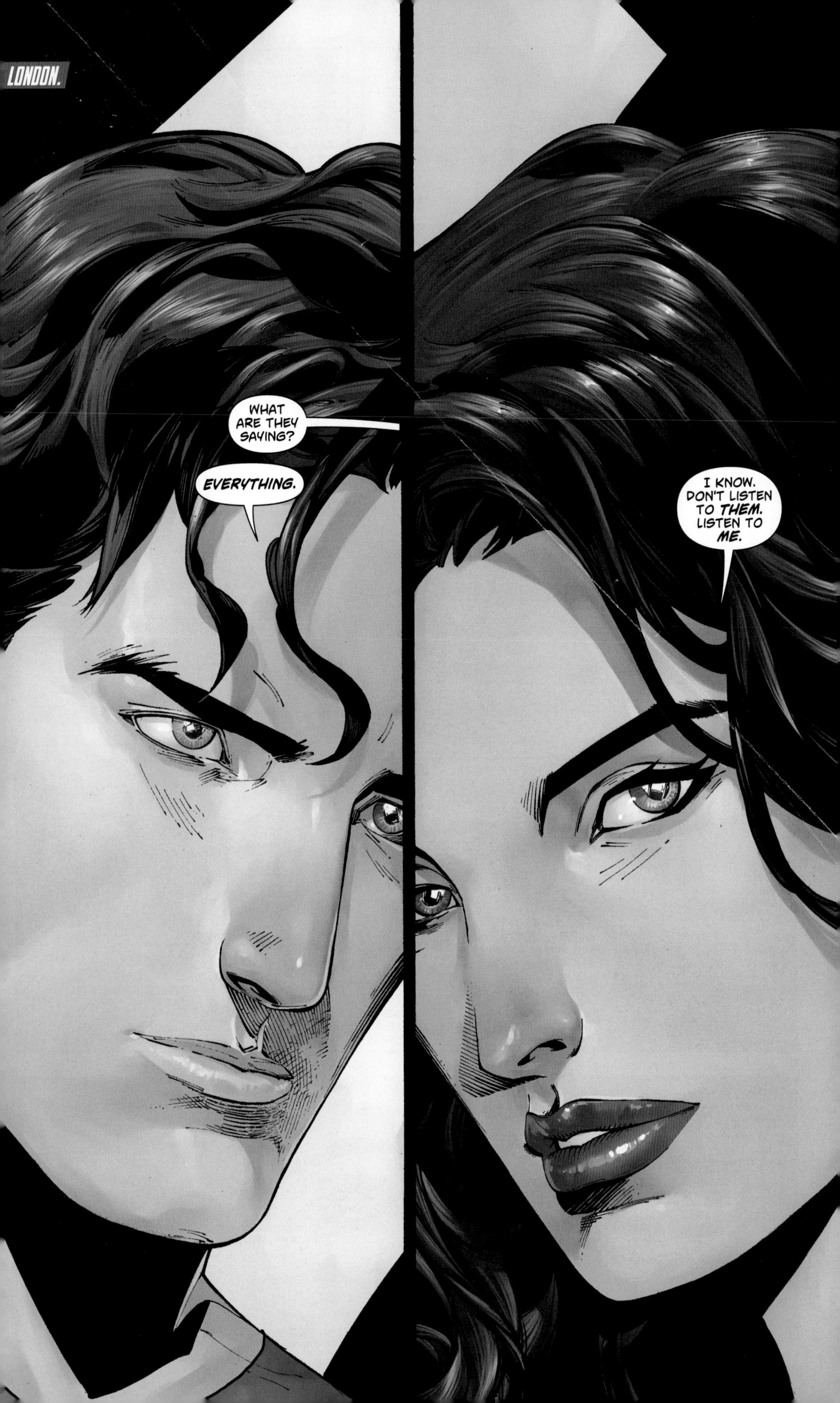
LONDON.
WHAT ARE THEY SAYING?
EVERYTHING.
I KNOW. DON'T LISTEN TO THEM. LISTEN TO ME.

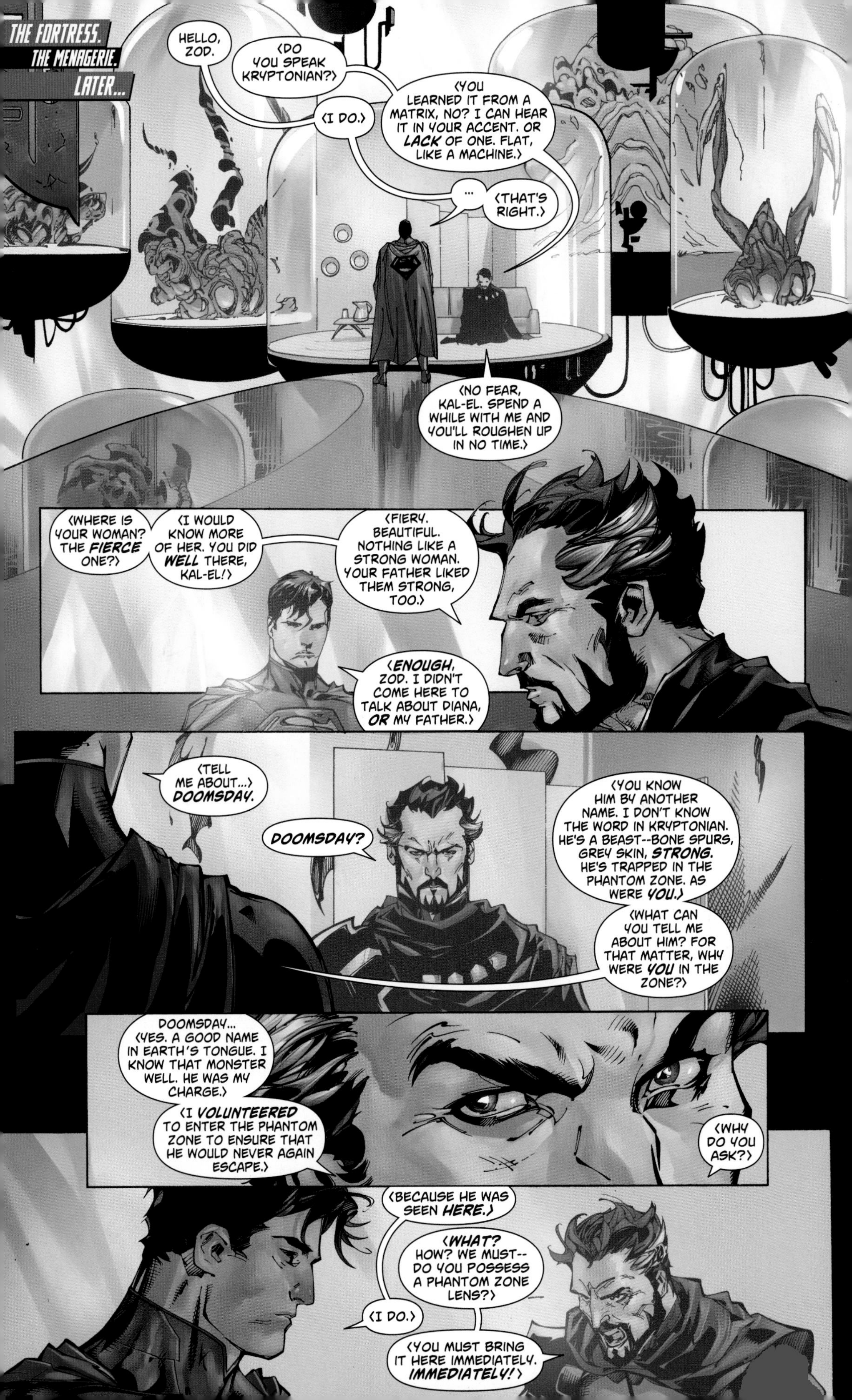

THE FORTRESS.
THE MENAGERIE.
LATER...
HELLO, ZOD.
‹DO YOU SPEAK KRYPTONIAN?›
‹I DO.›
‹YOU LEARNED IT FROM A MATRIX, NO? I CAN HEAR IT IN YOUR ACCENT. OR LACK OF ONE. FLAT, LIKE A MACHINE.›
...
‹THAT'S RIGHT.›
‹NO FEAR, KAL-EL. SPEND A WHILE WITH ME AND YOU'LL ROUGHEN UP IN NO TIME.›
‹WHERE IS YOUR WOMAN? THE FIERCE ONE?›
‹I WOULD KNOW MORE OF HER. YOU DID WELL THERE, KAL-EL!›
‹FIERY. BEAUTIFUL. NOTHING LIKE A STRONG WOMAN. YOUR FATHER LIKED THEM STRONG, TOO.›
‹ENOUGH, ZOD. I DIDN'T COME HERE TO TALK ABOUT DIANA, OR MY FATHER.›
‹TELL ME ABOUT...› DOOMSDAY.
DOOMSDAY?
‹YOU KNOW HIM BY ANOTHER NAME. I DON'T KNOW THE WORD IN KRYPTONIAN. HE'S A BEAST--BONE SPURS, GREY SKIN, STRONG. HE'S TRAPPED IN THE PHANTOM ZONE. AS WERE YOU.›
‹WHAT CAN YOU TELL ME ABOUT HIM? FOR THAT MATTER, WHY WERE YOU IN THE ZONE?›
DOOMSDAY... ‹YES. A GOOD NAME IN EARTH'S TONGUE. I KNOW THAT MONSTER WELL. HE WAS MY CHARGE.›
‹I VOLUNTEERED TO ENTER THE PHANTOM ZONE TO ENSURE THAT HE WOULD NEVER AGAIN ESCAPE.›
‹WHY DO YOU ASK?›
‹BECAUSE HE WAS SEEN HERE.›
‹WHAT? HOW? WE MUST-- DO YOU POSSESS A PHANTOM ZONE LENS?›
‹I DO.›
‹YOU MUST BRING IT HERE IMMEDIATELY. IMMEDIATELY!›

⟨AND NOW?⟩

⟨TURN IT ON. I HOPE YOU KEEP THIS MACHINE WELL PROTECTED.⟩

⟨YES. IT IS CODED TO ME. IT'S TOO DANGEROUS TO LET ANYONE ELSE OPERATE IT.⟩

⟨CLEVER, KAL-EL. YOU ARE YOUR FATHER'S SON.⟩

⟨MENTIONING MY FATHER ISN'T GOING TO GET YOU OUT OF THAT CELL, ZOD.⟩

⟨I *LET* YOU PUT ME IN A CAGE, KAL-EL. I DID NOT RESIST, AND I AM HELPING YOU NOW. WHY DO YOU FEAR ME?⟩

⟨FEAR AND CAUTION ARE NOT THE SAME THING.⟩

⟨YOU FLATTER ME.⟩

⟨THERE. THE LENS INTO THE ZONE HAS CLEARED. WHAT NEXT?⟩

⟨EXCELLENT.⟩

⟨□◇▯◇‖ï□̇⟩.

SZZK

⟨...HOW?!⟩

⟨YOU USE THESE AS CAGES. THEY ARE NOT.⟩

⟨YOU ARE AS IGNORANT OF YOUR PEOPLE'S TECHNOLOGY AS YOU ARE THEIR LANGUAGE.⟩

⟨THEY ARE *SHIPPING CONTAINERS*, AS COMMON ON KRYPTON AS WATER. DESIGNED TO BE OPENED WITH A SINGLE PASS-PHRASE, SET BY THEIR OWNER.⟩

⟨BEFORE IT IS SET, THERE IS A DEFAULT ACCESS WORD, WHICH I ASSUME YOU WOULD NOT KNOW ENOUGH TO CHANGE.⟩

⟨AND SO YOU DID NOT.⟩

⟨NOT FOR *MY* CAGE, AND NOT FOR *ANY* OF THESE OTHERS.⟩

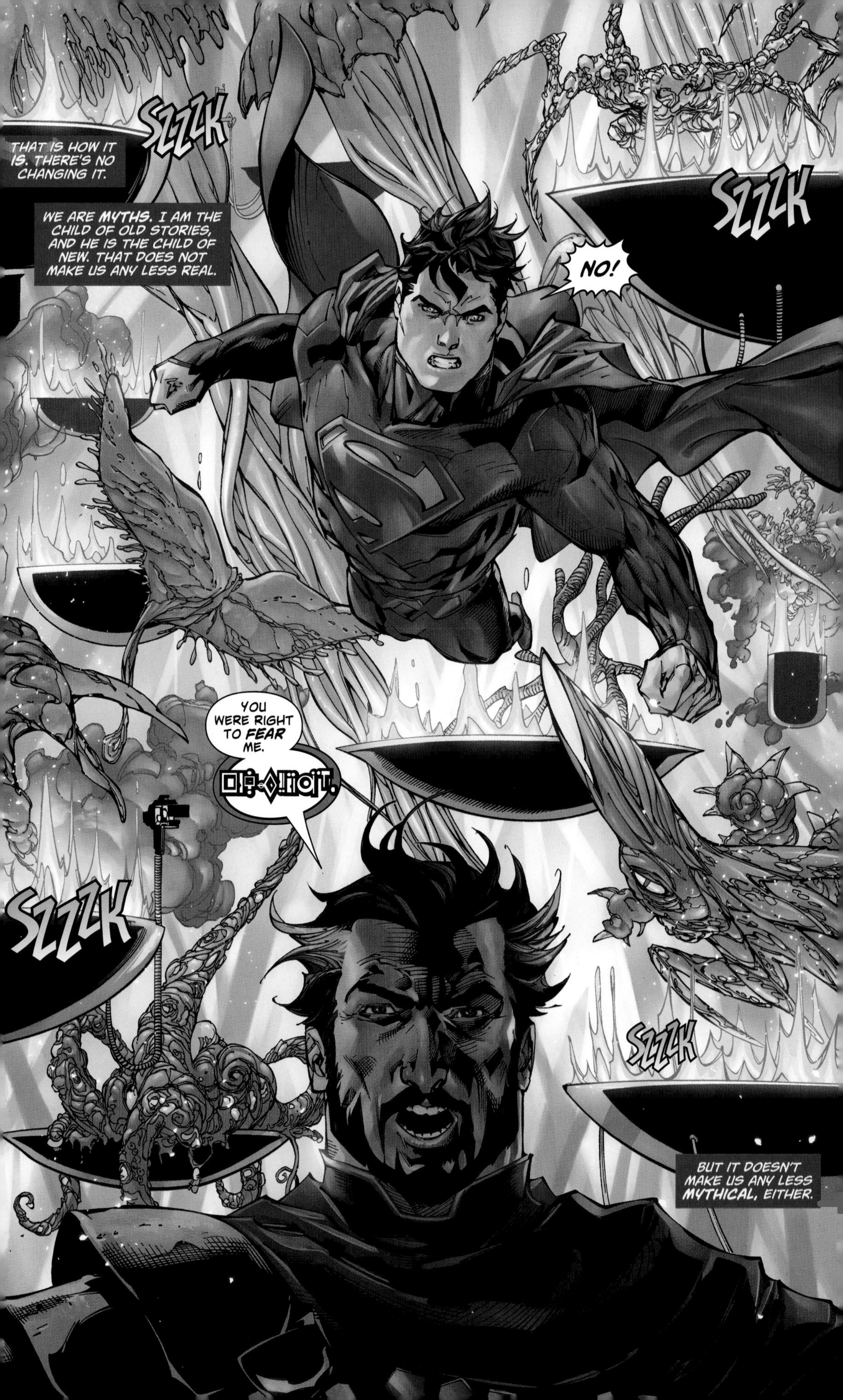
SZZZK
THAT IS HOW IT IS. THERE'S NO CHANGING IT.
SZZZK
WE ARE MYTHS. I AM THE CHILD OF OLD STORIES, AND HE IS THE CHILD OF NEW. THAT DOES NOT MAKE US ANY LESS REAL.
NO!
YOU WERE RIGHT TO FEAR ME.
SZZZK
SZZZK
BUT IT DOESN'T MAKE US ANY LESS MYTHICAL, EITHER.

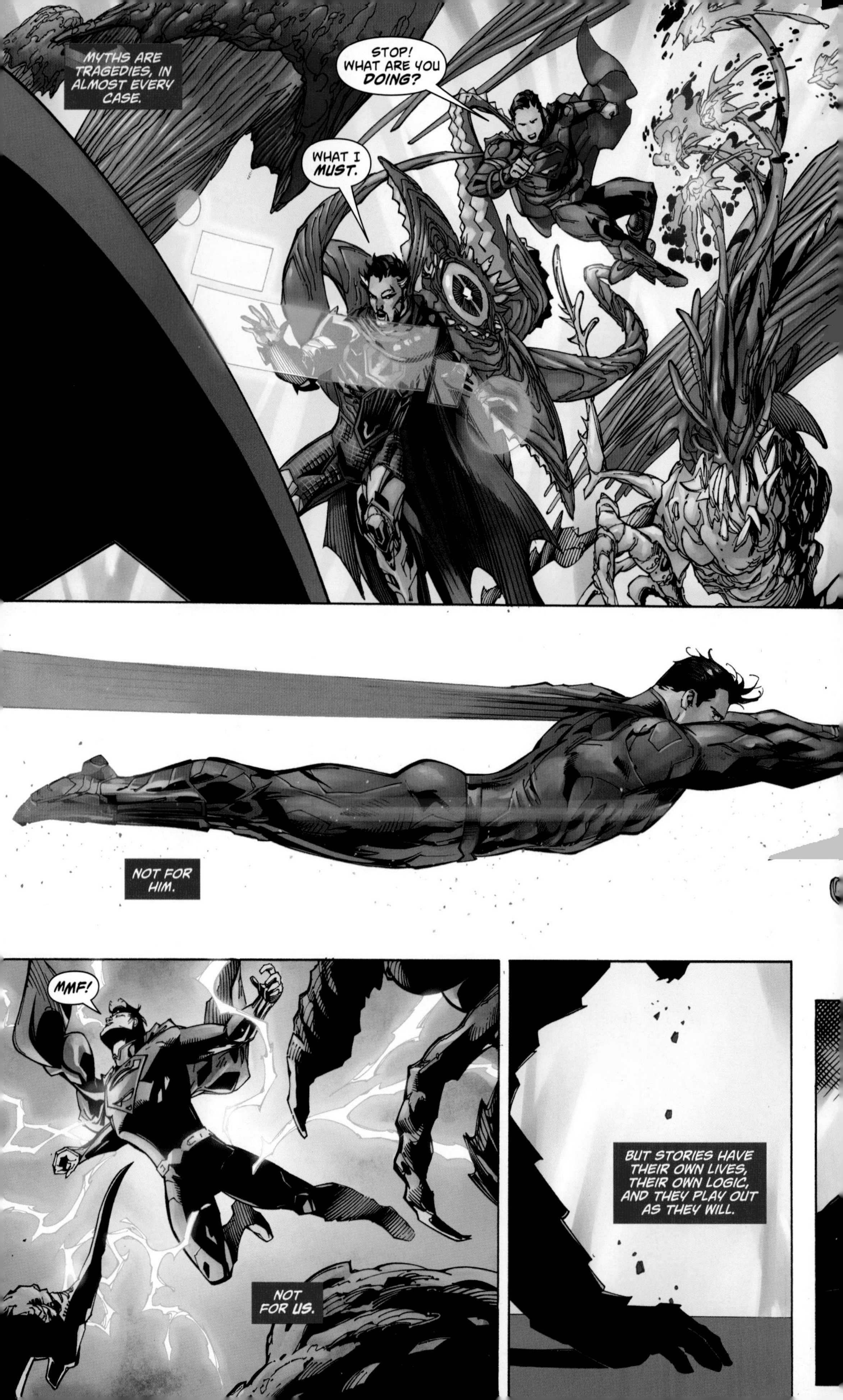
MYTHS ARE TRAGEDIES, IN ALMOST EVERY CASE.
STOP! WHAT ARE YOU DOING?
WHAT I MUST.
NOT FOR HIM.
MMF!
NOT FOR US.
BUT STORIES HAVE THEIR OWN LIVES, THEIR OWN LOGIC, AND THEY PLAY OUT AS THEY WILL.

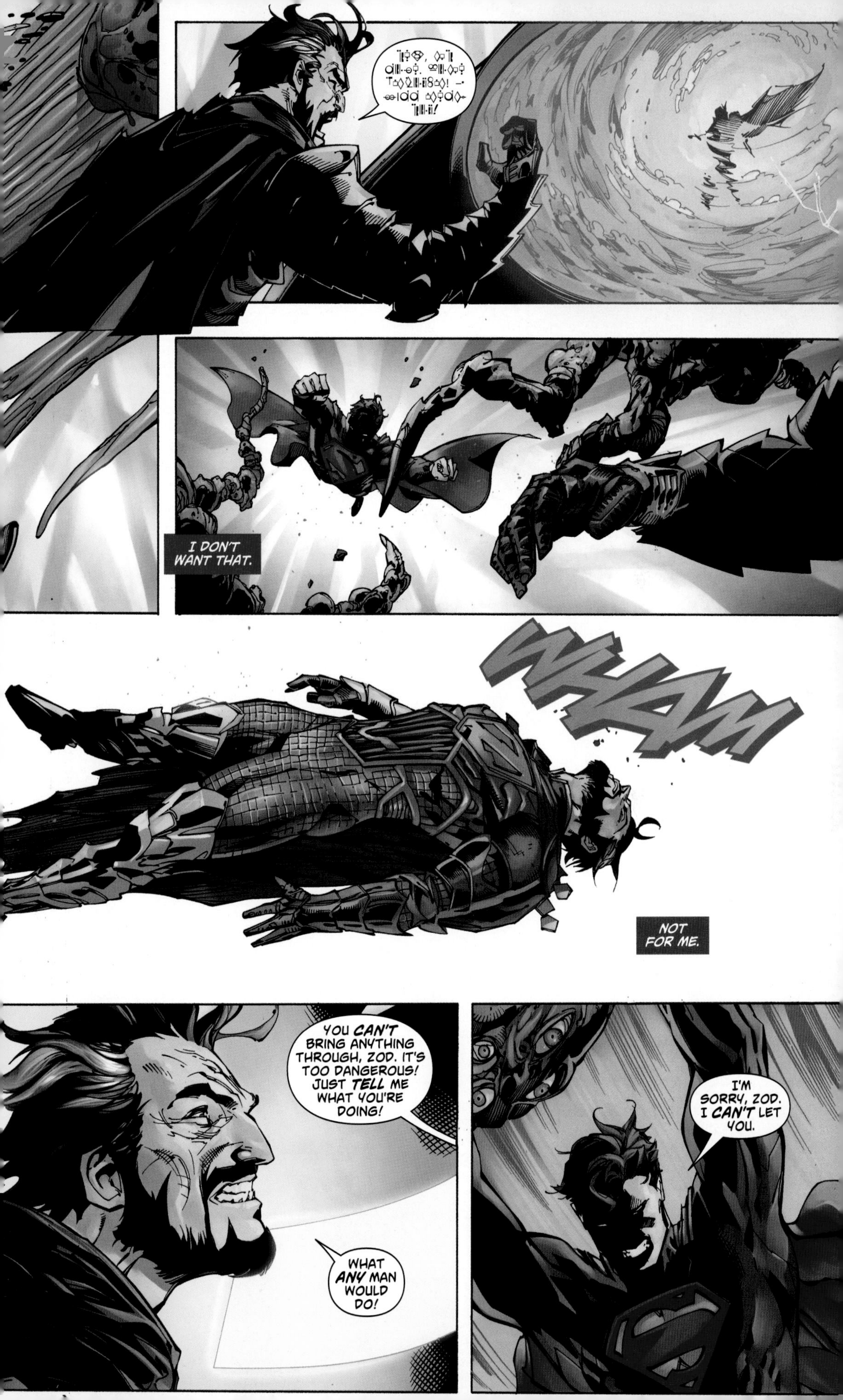
I DON'T WANT THAT.
WHAM
NOT FOR ME.
YOU CAN'T BRING ANYTHING THROUGH, ZOD. IT'S TOO DANGEROUS! JUST TELL ME WHAT YOU'RE DOING!
WHAT ANY MAN WOULD DO!
I'M SORRY, ZOD. I CAN'T LET YOU.

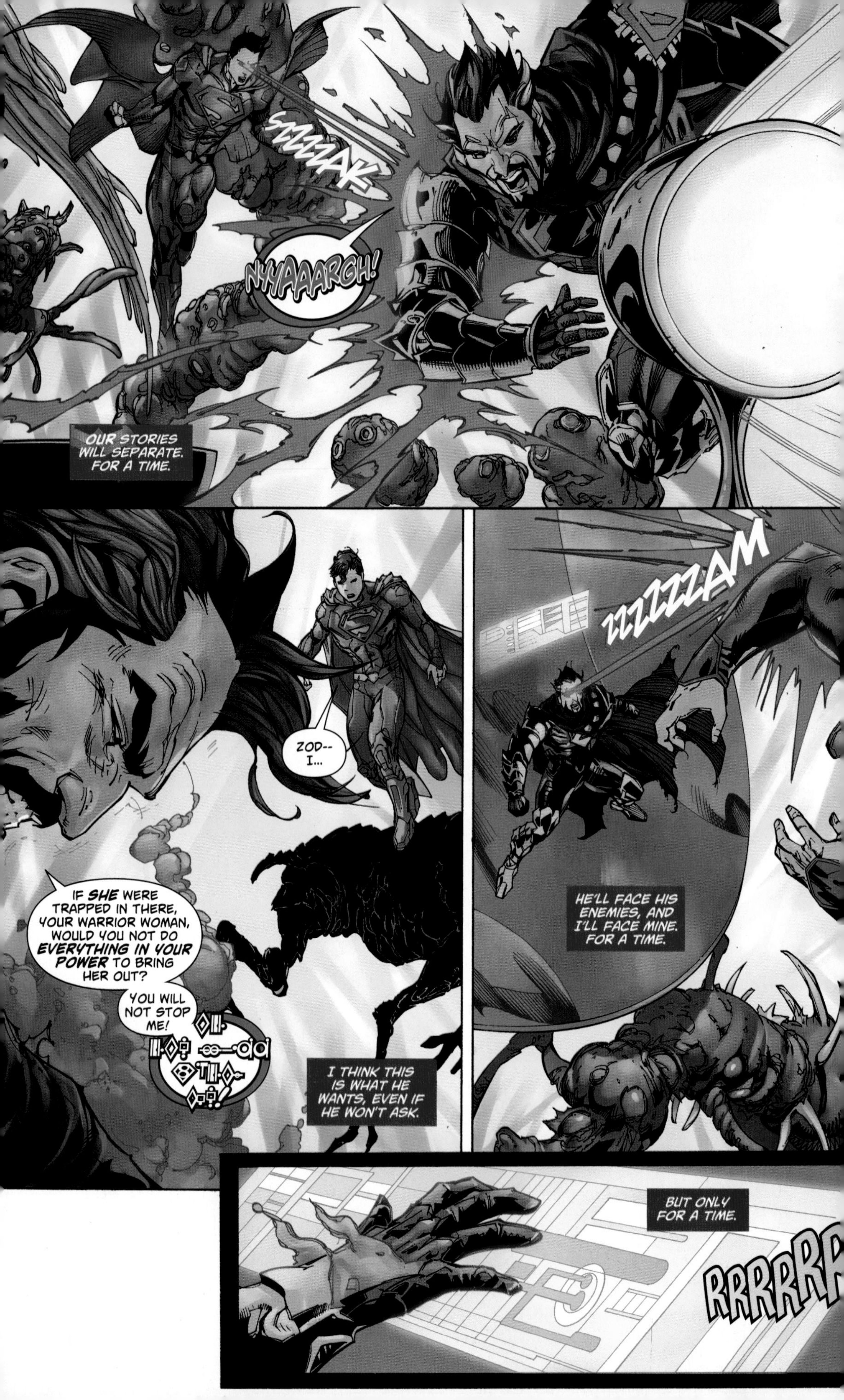
SCZZZAK
NYYAAARGH!
OUR STORIES WILL SEPARATE. FOR A TIME.
ZOD-- I...
IF SHE WERE TRAPPED IN THERE, YOUR WARRIOR WOMAN, WOULD YOU NOT DO EVERYTHING IN YOUR POWER TO BRING HER OUT?
YOU WILL NOT STOP ME!
I THINK THIS IS WHAT HE WANTS, EVEN IF HE WON'T ASK.
ZZZZZZAM
HE'LL FACE HIS ENEMIES, AND I'LL FACE MINE. FOR A TIME.
BUT ONLY FOR A TIME.
RRRRR

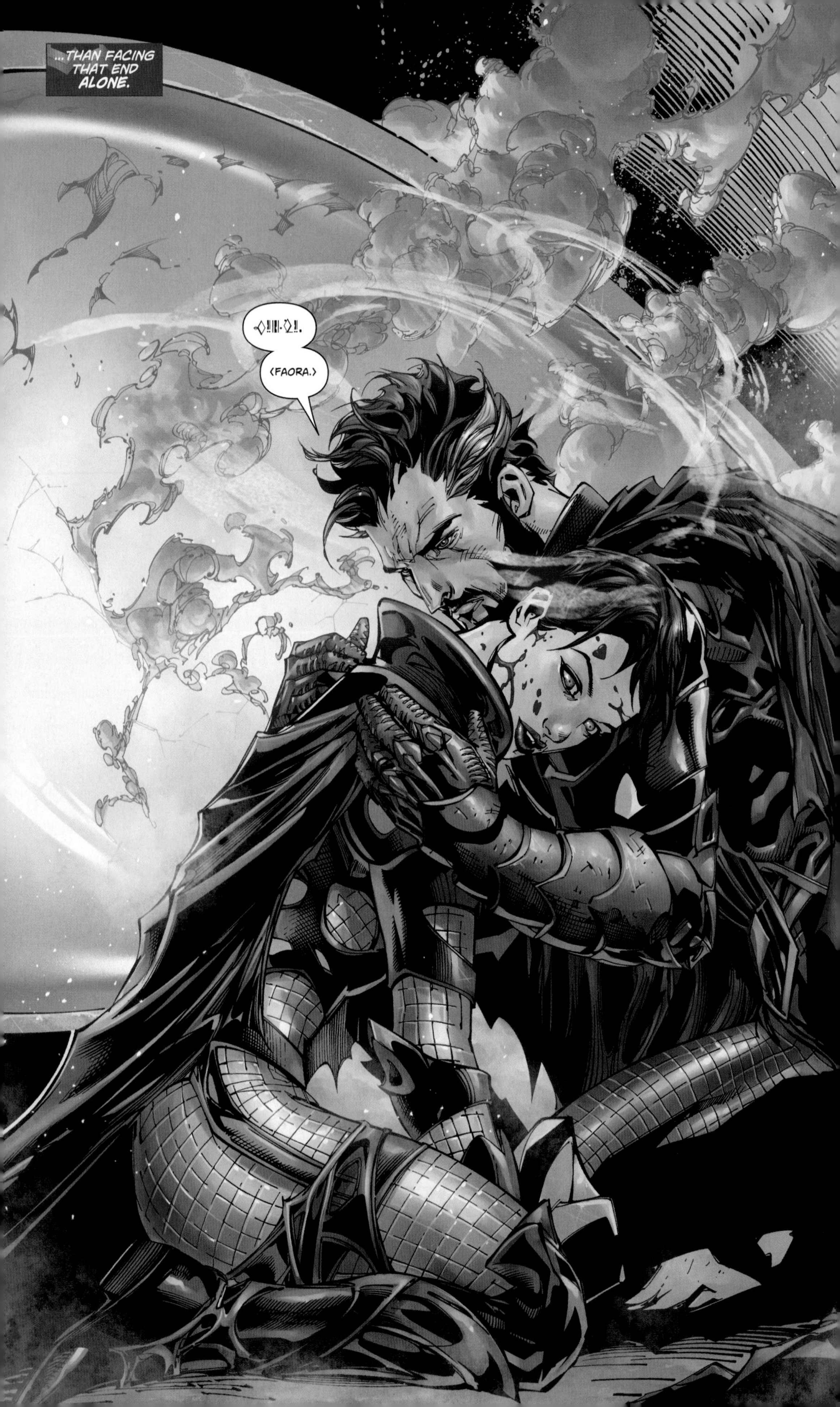
...THAN FACING THAT END ALONE.
<FAORA.>

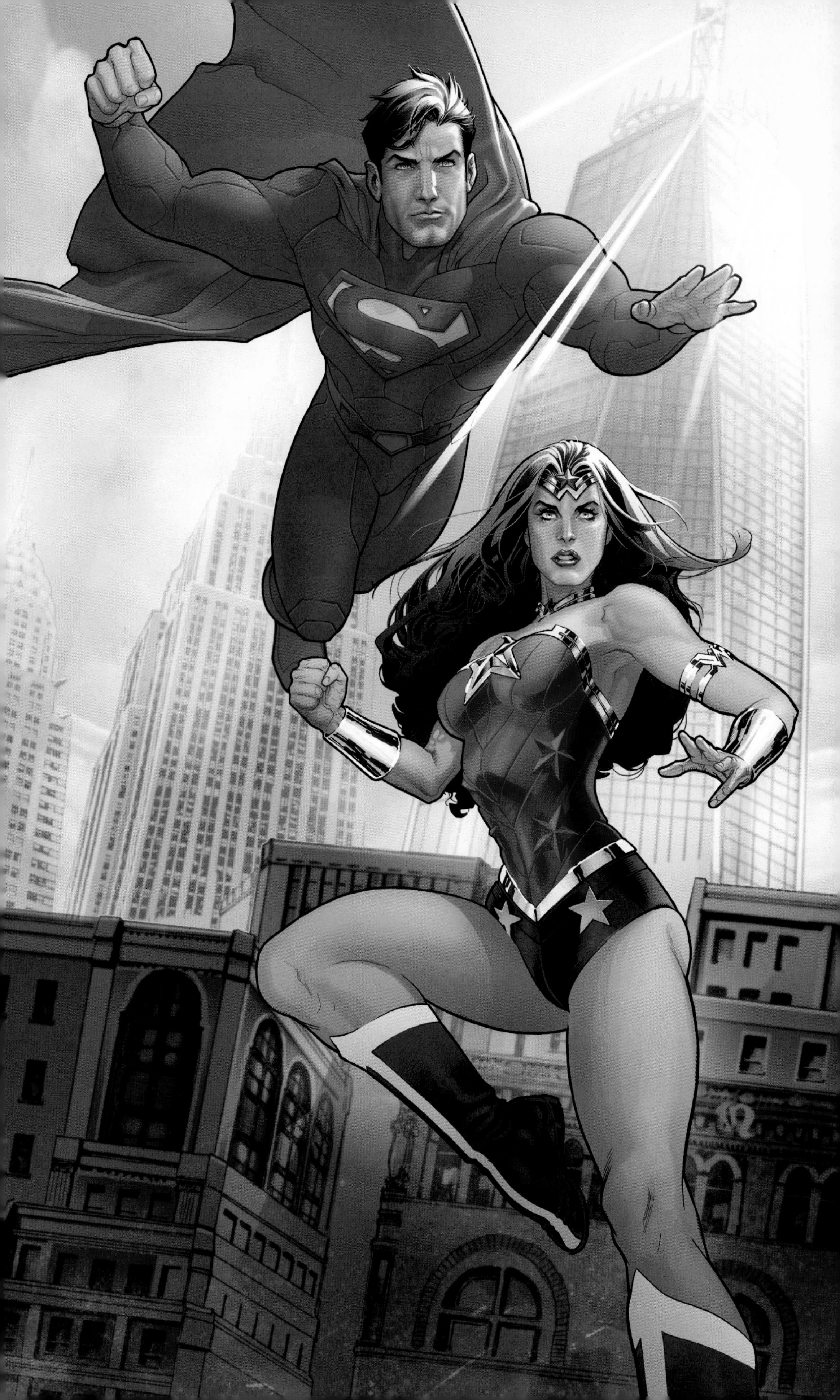

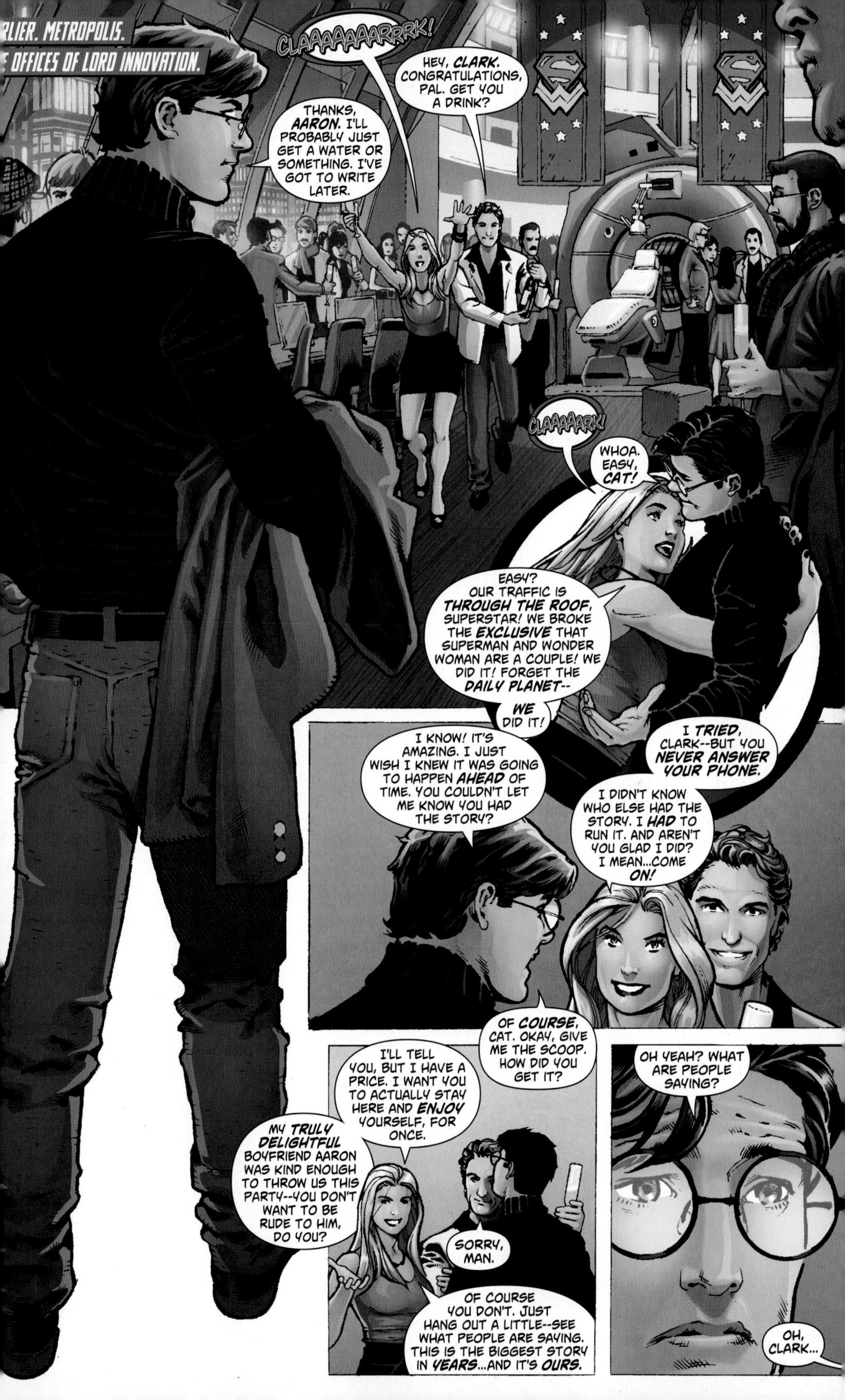
RLIER. METROPOLIS.
E OFFICES OF LORD INNOVATION.
CLAAAAAAARRRK!
HEY, CLARK. CONGRATULATIONS, PAL. GET YOU A DRINK?
THANKS, AARON. I'LL PROBABLY JUST GET A WATER OR SOMETHING. I'VE GOT TO WRITE LATER.
CLAAAAARK!
WHOA. EASY, CAT!
EASY? OUR TRAFFIC IS THROUGH THE ROOF, SUPERSTAR! WE BROKE THE EXCLUSIVE THAT SUPERMAN AND WONDER WOMAN ARE A COUPLE! WE DID IT! FORGET THE DAILY PLANET--
WE DID IT!
I KNOW! IT'S AMAZING. I JUST WISH I KNEW IT WAS GOING TO HAPPEN AHEAD OF TIME. YOU COULDN'T LET ME KNOW YOU HAD THE STORY?
I TRIED, CLARK--BUT YOU NEVER ANSWER YOUR PHONE.
I DIDN'T KNOW WHO ELSE HAD THE STORY. I HAD TO RUN IT. AND AREN'T YOU GLAD I DID? I MEAN...COME ON!
OF COURSE, CAT. OKAY, GIVE ME THE SCOOP. HOW DID YOU GET IT?
I'LL TELL YOU, BUT I HAVE A PRICE. I WANT YOU TO ACTUALLY STAY HERE AND ENJOY YOURSELF, FOR ONCE.
MY TRULY DELIGHTFUL BOYFRIEND AARON WAS KIND ENOUGH TO THROW US THIS PARTY--YOU DON'T WANT TO BE RUDE TO HIM, DO YOU?
SORRY, MAN.
OF COURSE YOU DON'T. JUST HANG OUT A LITTLE--SEE WHAT PEOPLE ARE SAYING. THIS IS THE BIGGEST STORY IN YEARS...AND IT'S OURS.
OH YEAH? WHAT ARE PEOPLE SAYING?
OH, CLARK...

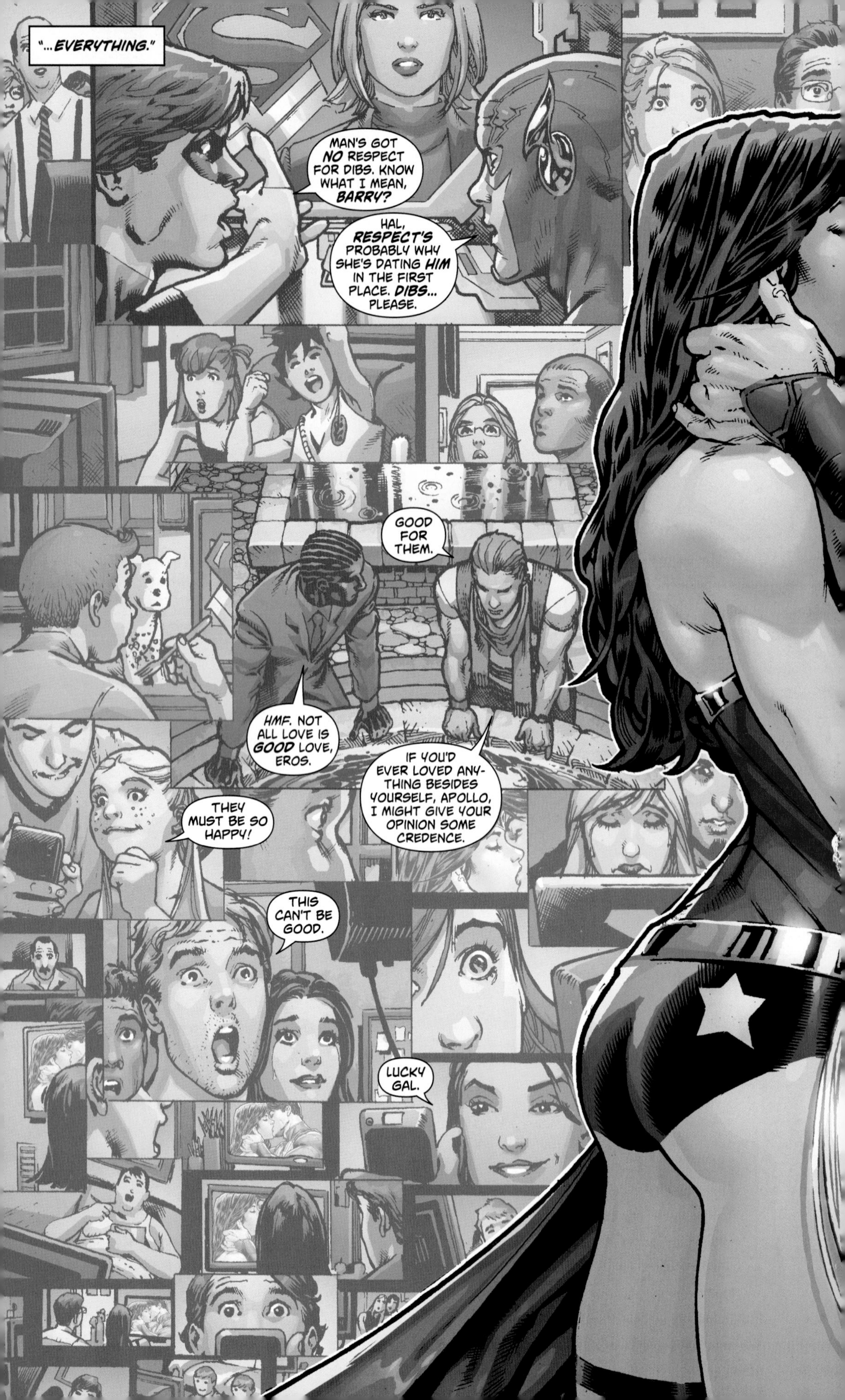
"...EVERYTHING."
MAN'S GOT NO RESPECT FOR DIBS. KNOW WHAT I MEAN, BARRY?
HAL, RESPECT'S PROBABLY WHY SHE'S DATING HIM IN THE FIRST PLACE. DIBS... PLEASE.
GOOD FOR THEM.
HMF. NOT ALL LOVE IS GOOD LOVE, EROS.
IF YOU'D EVER LOVED ANY-THING BESIDES YOURSELF, APOLLO, I MIGHT GIVE YOUR OPINION SOME CREDENCE.
THEY MUST BE SO HAPPY!
THIS CAN'T BE GOOD.
LUCKY GAL.

ALL FINISHED, **MR. LUTHOR?**

INDEED, GEORGE. YOU MAY TAKE THIS AWAY.

SURE THING. YOU HEAR THE NEWS?

NEWS? LOOK AT MY SURROUNDINGS, GEORGE. UNLESS YOU'VE TOLD ME SOMETHING, I DON'T KNOW IT.

SUPERMAN AND WONDER WOMAN--THEY'RE... Y'KNOW, **TOGETHER.** AN ITEM! DOIN' IT, I GUESS.

WHAT?

SEEMS KINDA NICE, YOU ASK ME. PEOPLE LIKE THAT--WHO ELSE ARE THEY GONNA BE WITH? MUST BE LONELY.

THAT'S JUST IT. THEY AREN'T PEOPLE AT ALL. THEY ARE POWER. UNPREDICTABLE, HORRENDOUS POWER, NOTHING MORE.

LEAVE ME ALONE, GEORGE. I NEED TO **THINK...**

I NEVER THOUGHT... OF COURSE, I **PLANNED** FOR THIS, BUT I NEVER ACTUALLY...

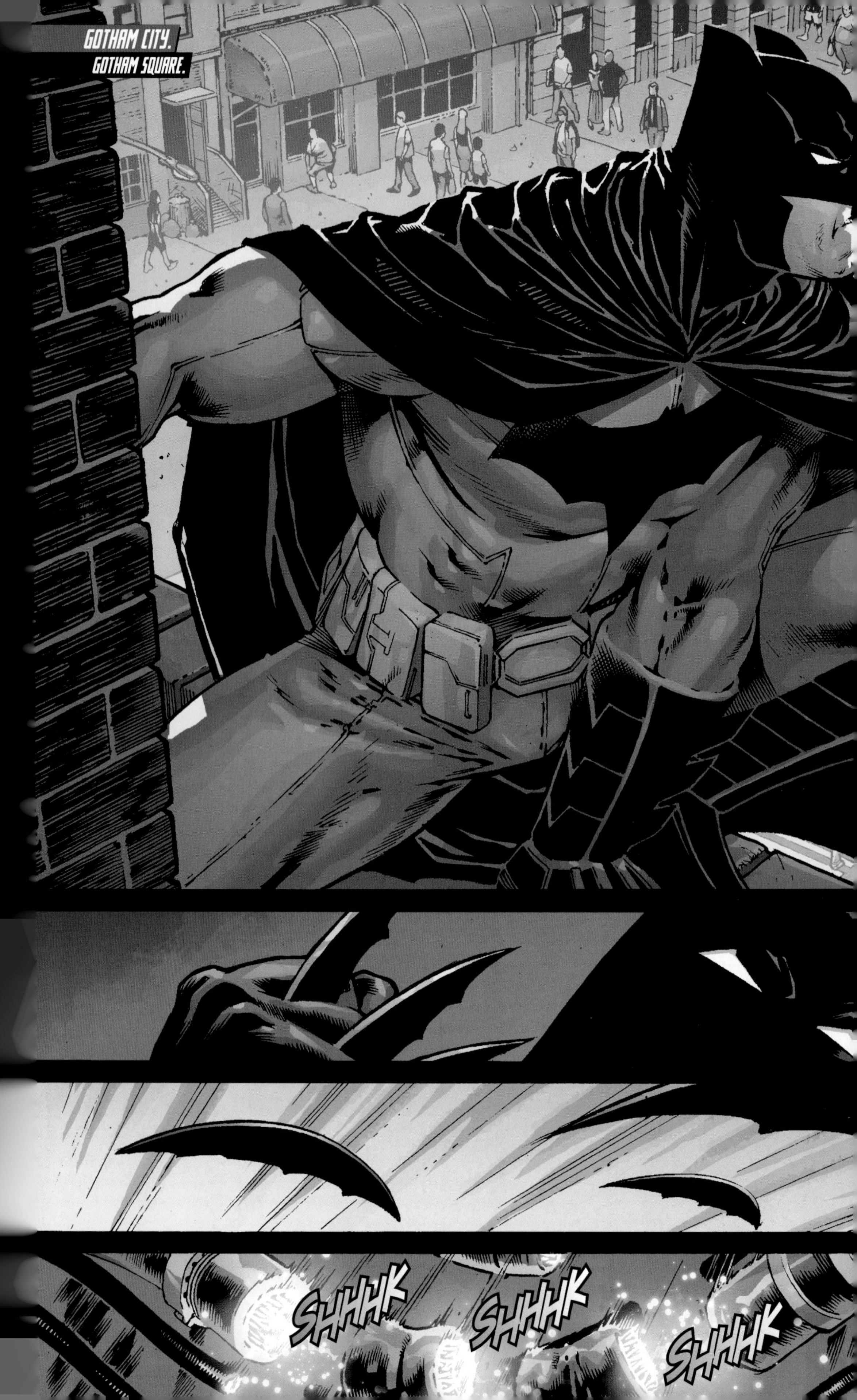
GOTHAM CITY.
GOTHAM SQUARE.
SHHHK
SHHHK
SHHHK

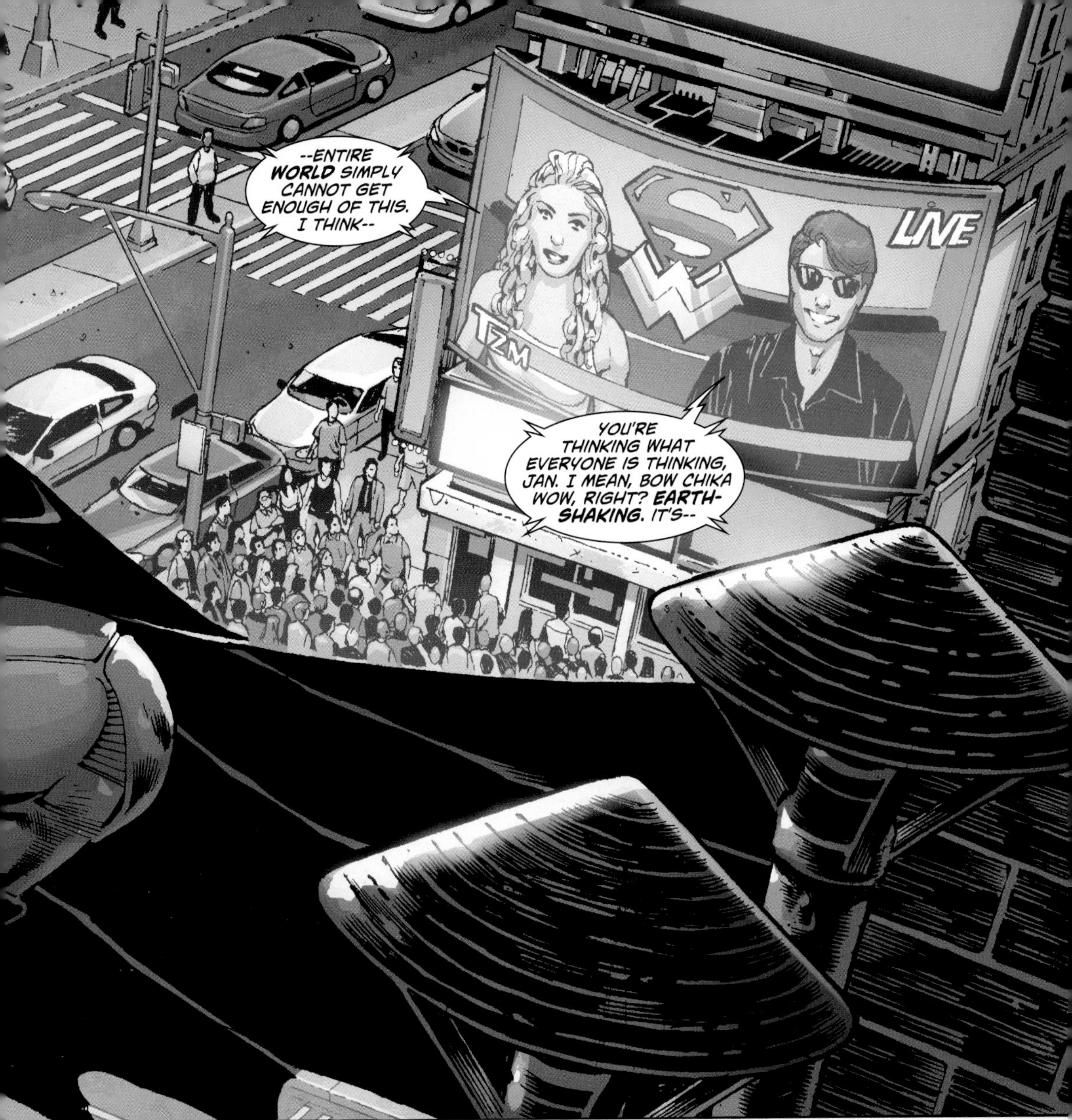
--ENTIRE WORLD SIMPLY CANNOT GET ENOUGH OF THIS. I THINK--
LIVE
TZM
YOU'RE THINKING WHAT EVERYONE IS THINKING, JAN. I MEAN, BOW CHIKA WOW, RIGHT? EARTH-SHAKING. IT'S--
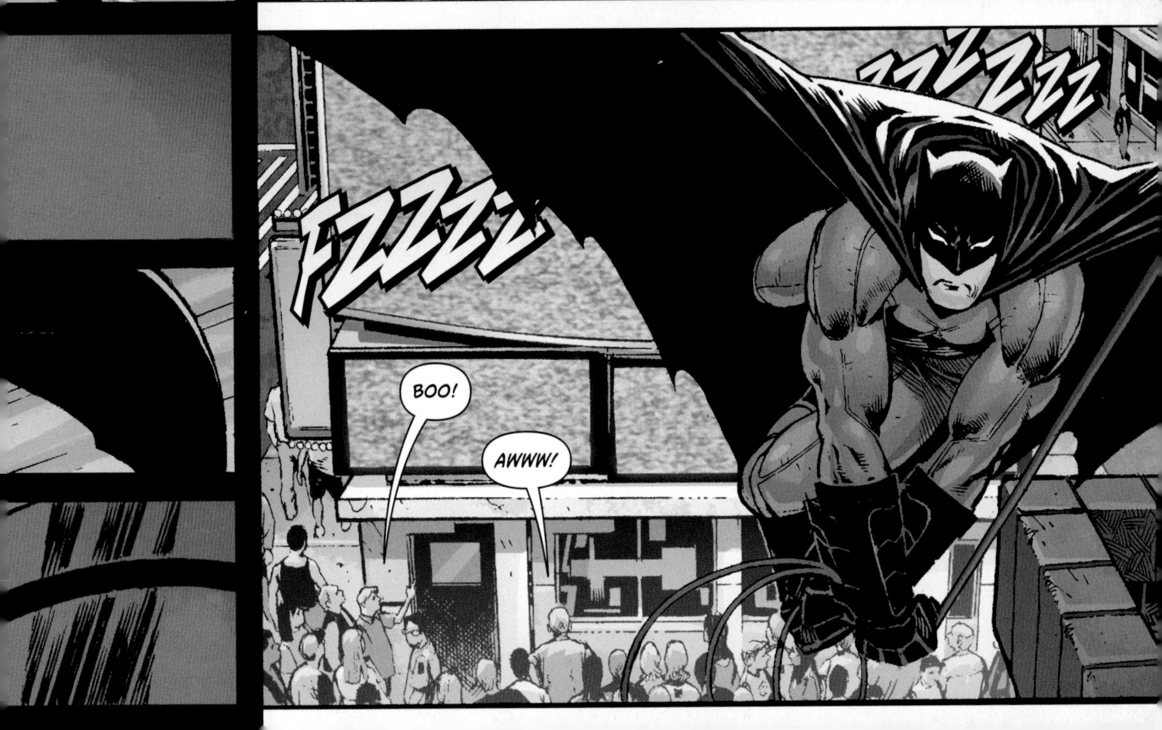
ZZZZZZ
FZZZZ
BOO!
AWWW!

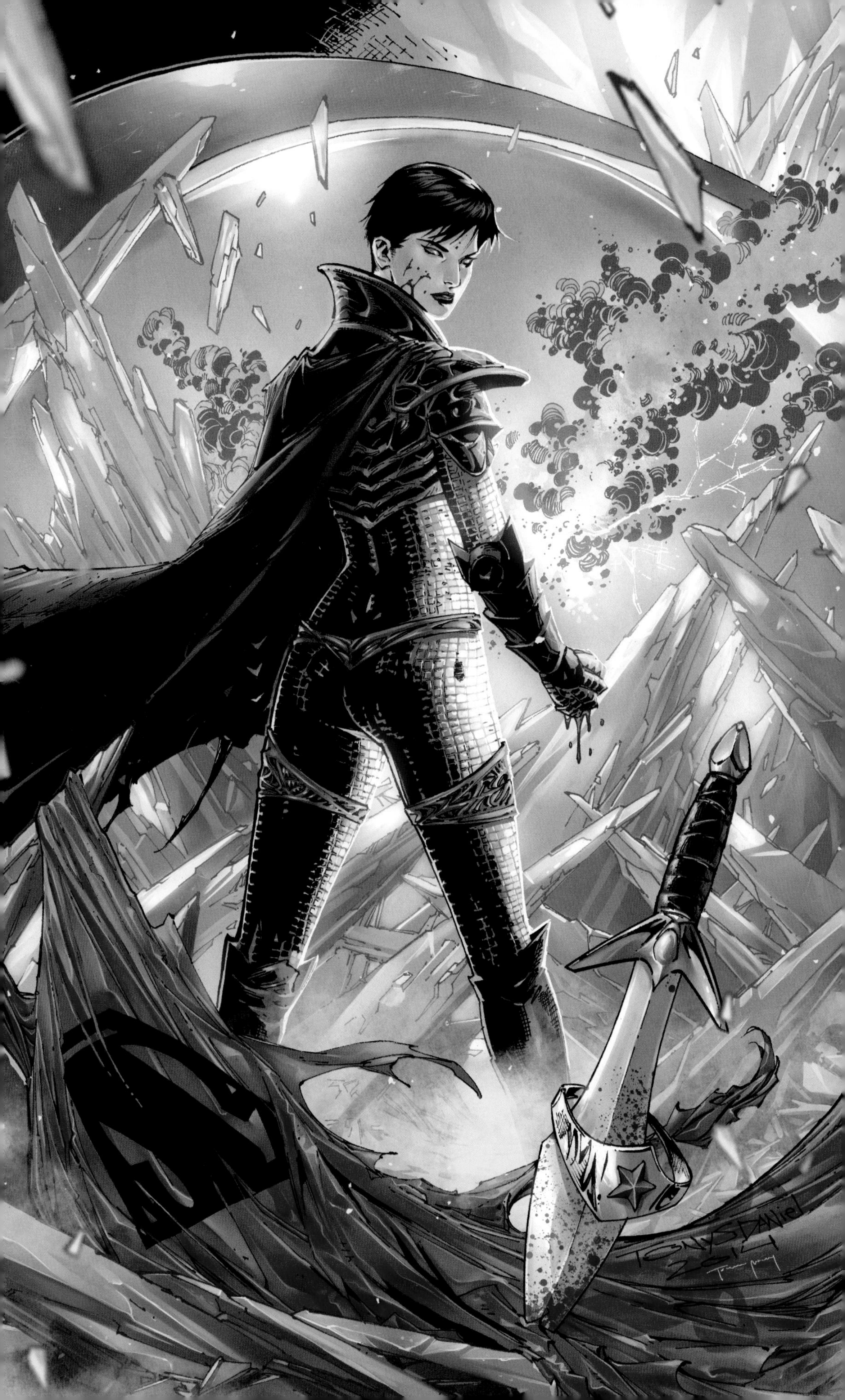
TONY S DANIEL 2014

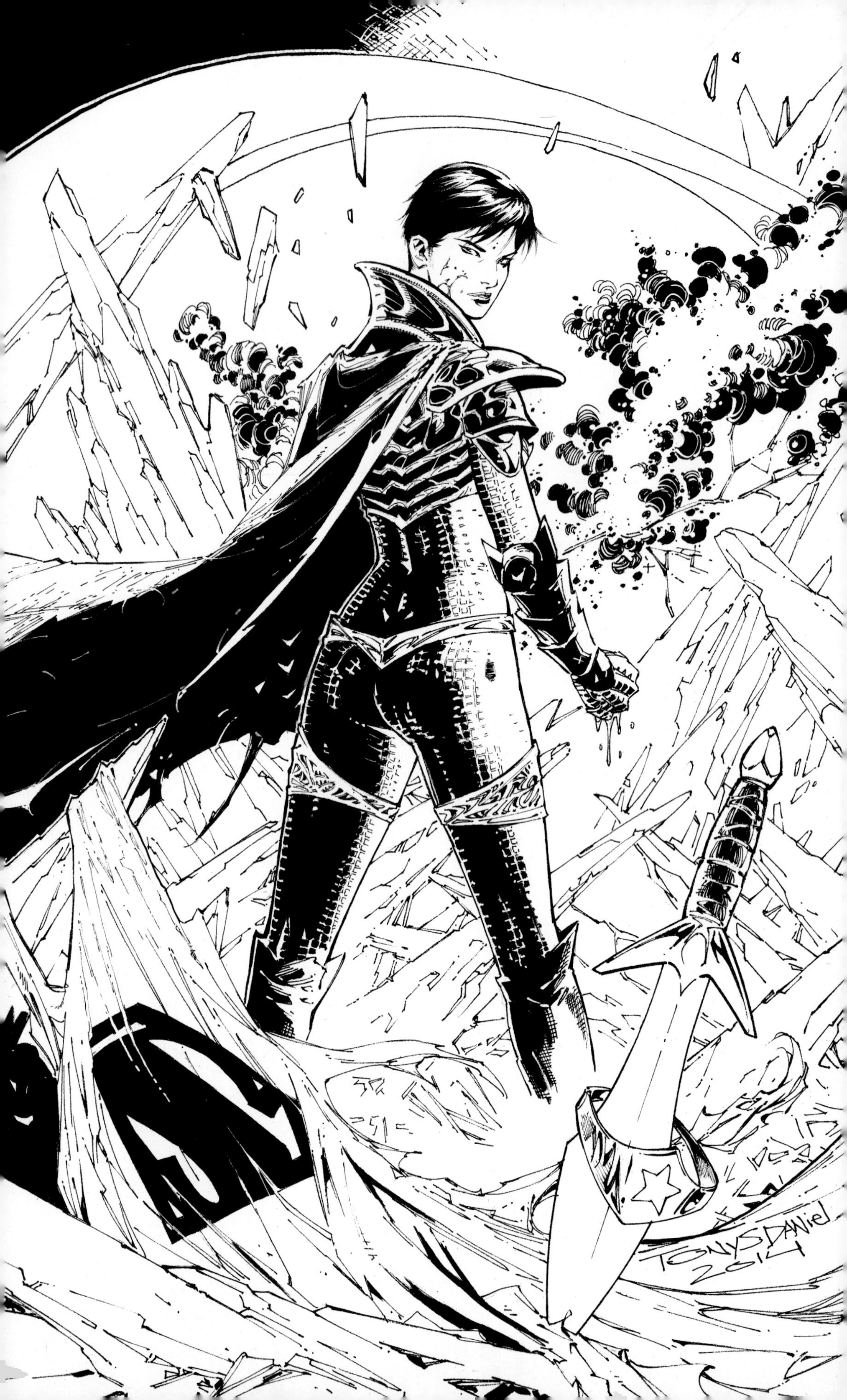
TONY S DANIEL
2014

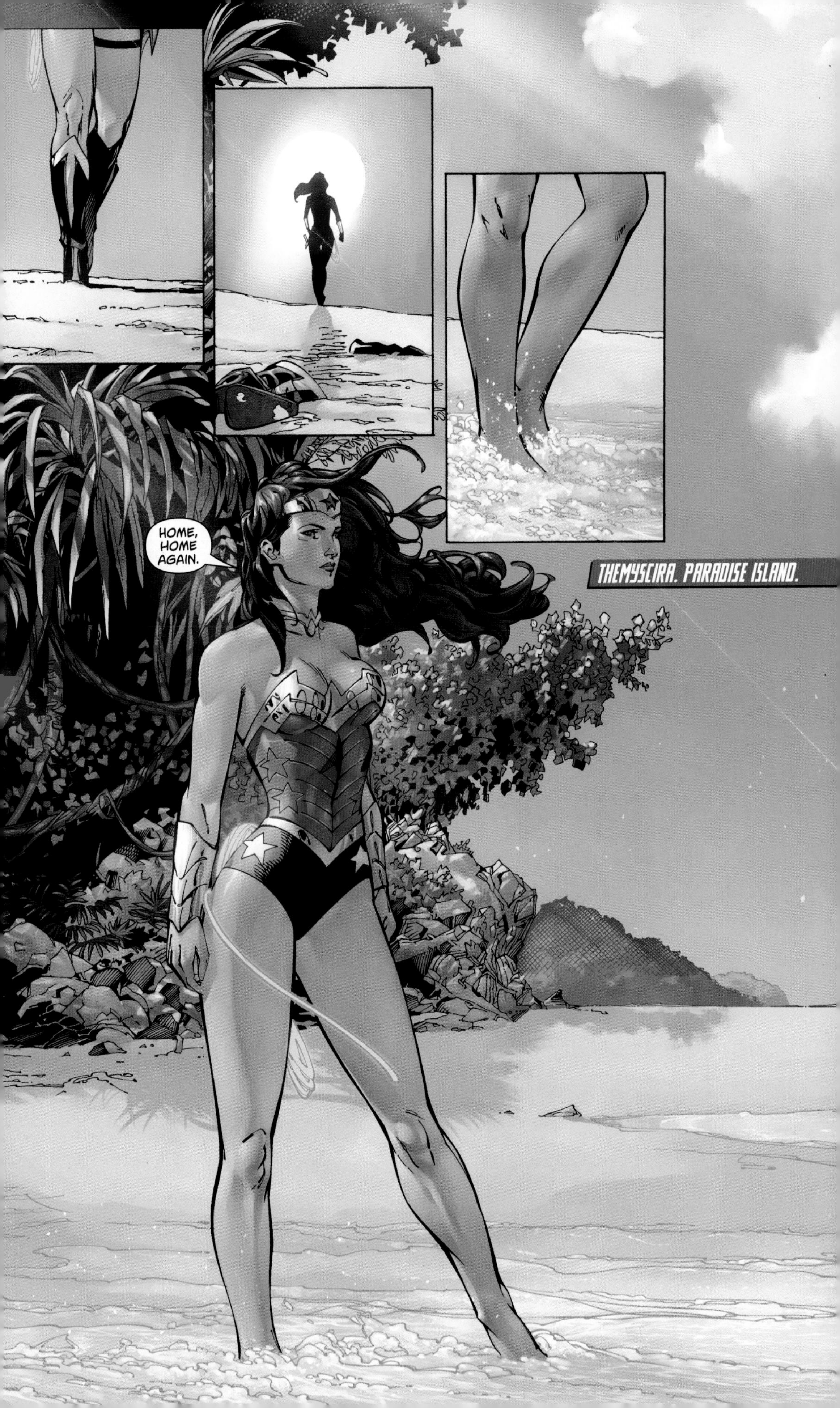
HOME, HOME AGAIN.
THEMYSCIRA. PARADISE ISLAND.

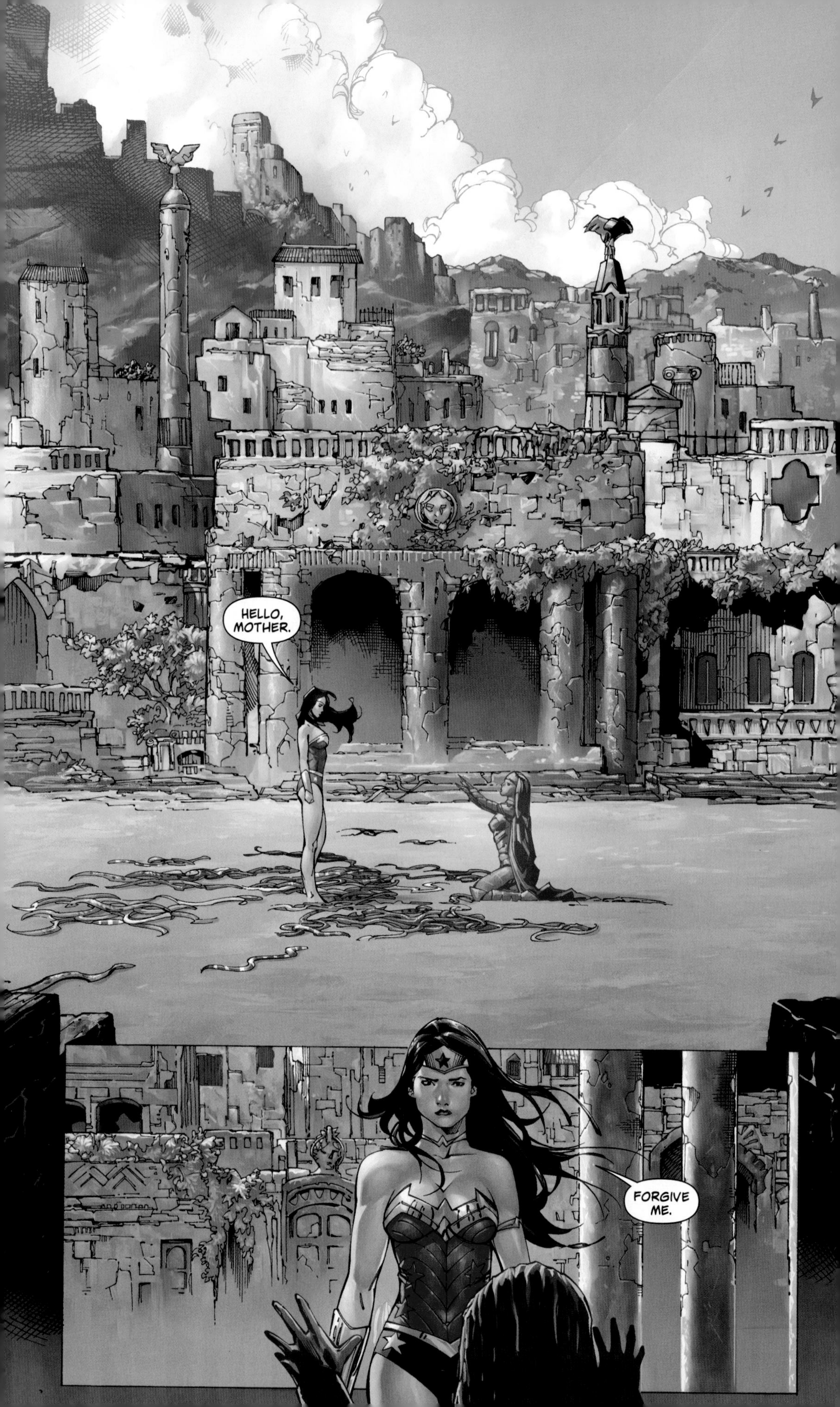
HELLO, MOTHER.
FORGIVE ME.

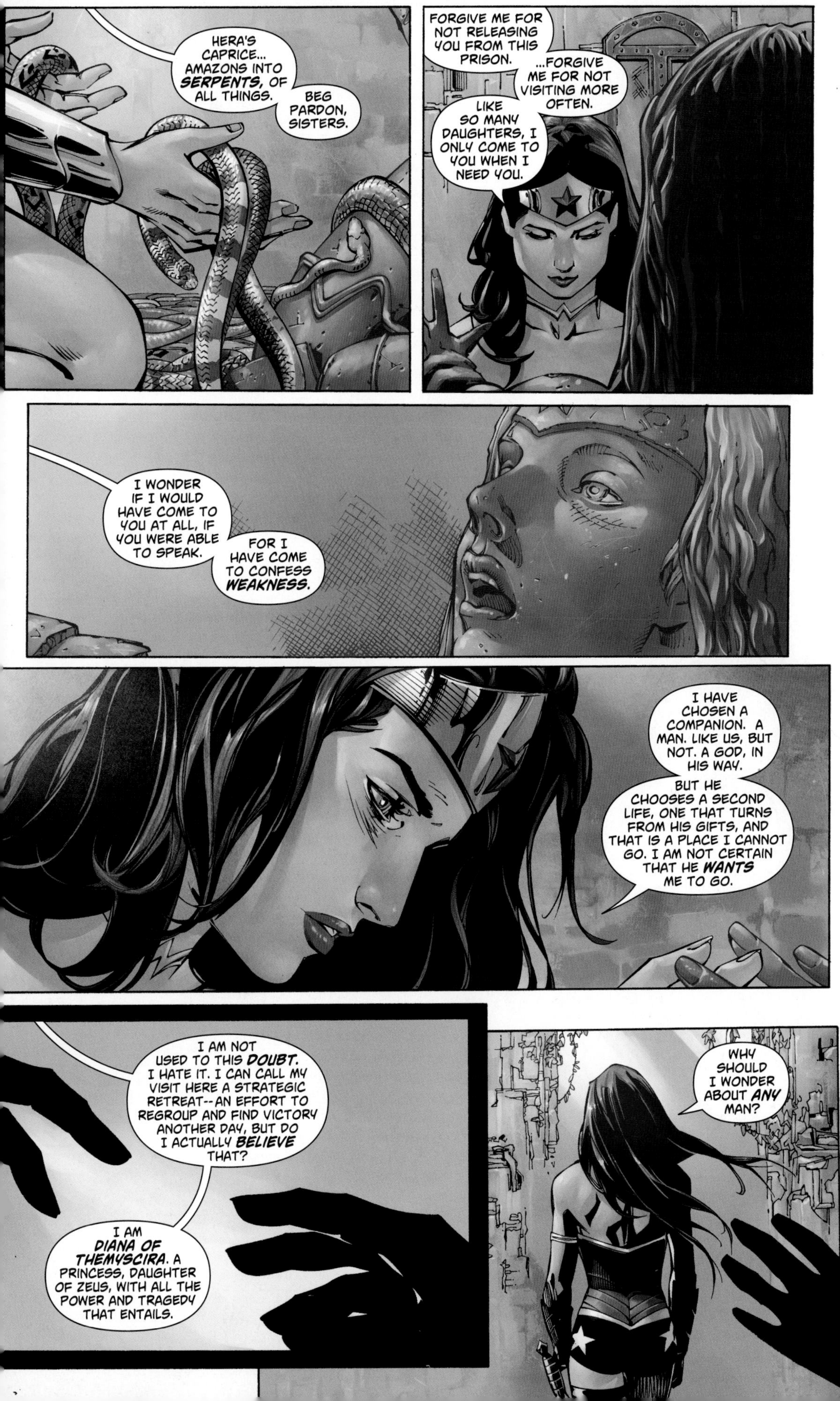
HERA'S CAPRICE... AMAZONS INTO SERPENTS, OF ALL THINGS.
BEG PARDON, SISTERS.
FORGIVE ME FOR NOT RELEASING YOU FROM THIS PRISON.
...FORGIVE ME FOR NOT VISITING MORE OFTEN.
LIKE SO MANY DAUGHTERS, I ONLY COME TO YOU WHEN I NEED YOU.
I WONDER IF I WOULD HAVE COME TO YOU AT ALL, IF YOU WERE ABLE TO SPEAK.
FOR I HAVE COME TO CONFESS WEAKNESS.
I HAVE CHOSEN A COMPANION. A MAN. LIKE US, BUT NOT. A GOD, IN HIS WAY.
BUT HE CHOOSES A SECOND LIFE, ONE THAT TURNS FROM HIS GIFTS, AND THAT IS A PLACE I CANNOT GO. I AM NOT CERTAIN THAT HE WANTS ME TO GO.
I AM NOT USED TO THIS DOUBT. I HATE IT. I CAN CALL MY VISIT HERE A STRATEGIC RETREAT--AN EFFORT TO REGROUP AND FIND VICTORY ANOTHER DAY, BUT DO I ACTUALLY BELIEVE THAT?
I AM DIANA OF THEMYSCIRA. A PRINCESS, DAUGHTER OF ZEUS, WITH ALL THE POWER AND TRAGEDY THAT ENTAILS.
WHY SHOULD I WONDER ABOUT ANY MAN?

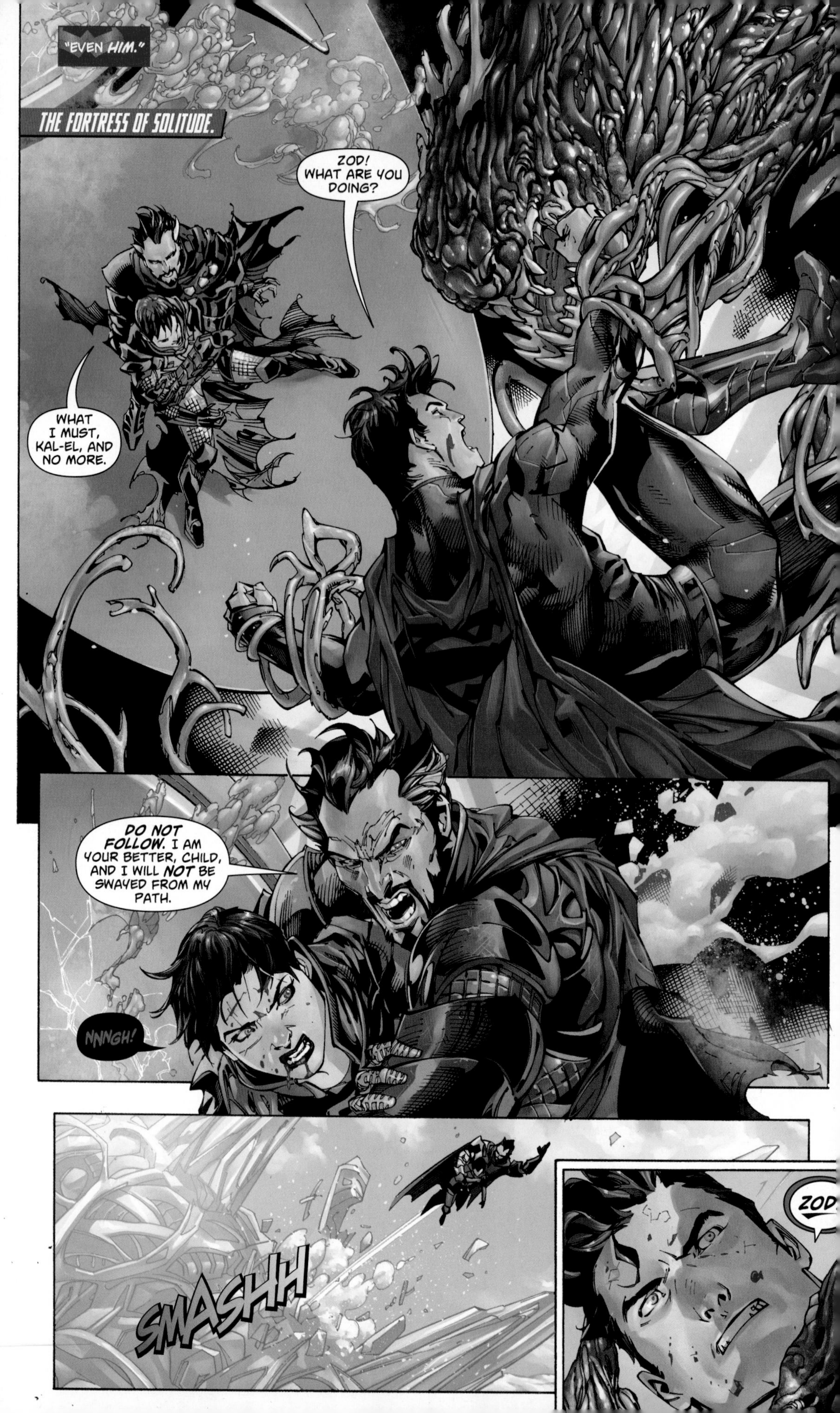
"EVEN HIM."
THE FORTRESS OF SOLITUDE.
ZOD! WHAT ARE YOU DOING?
WHAT I MUST, KAL-EL, AND NO MORE.
DO NOT FOLLOW. I AM YOUR BETTER, CHILD, AND I WILL NOT BE SWAYED FROM MY PATH.
NNNGH!
SMASHH
ZOD

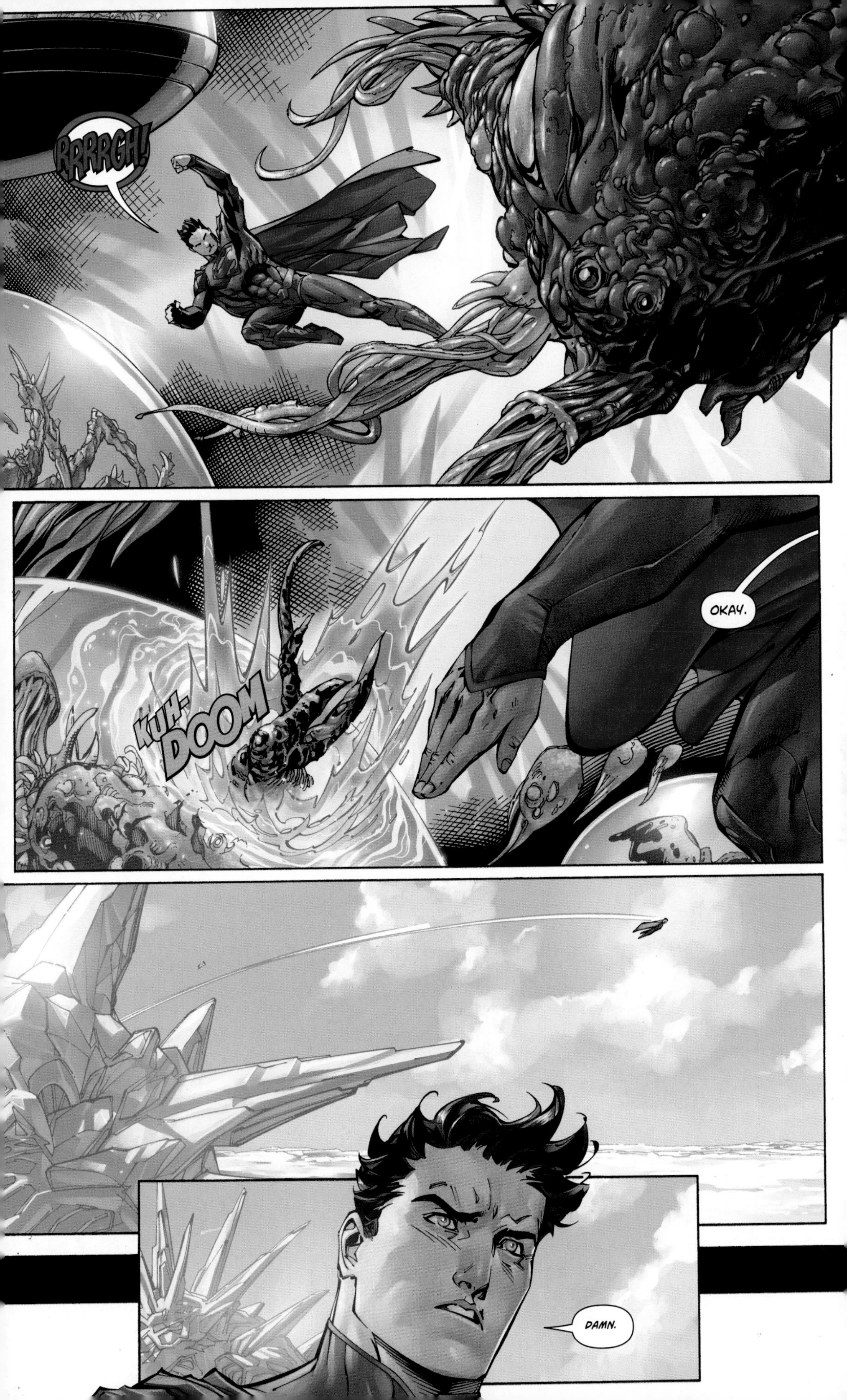
RRRRGH!
KUH-DOOM
OKAY.
DAMN.

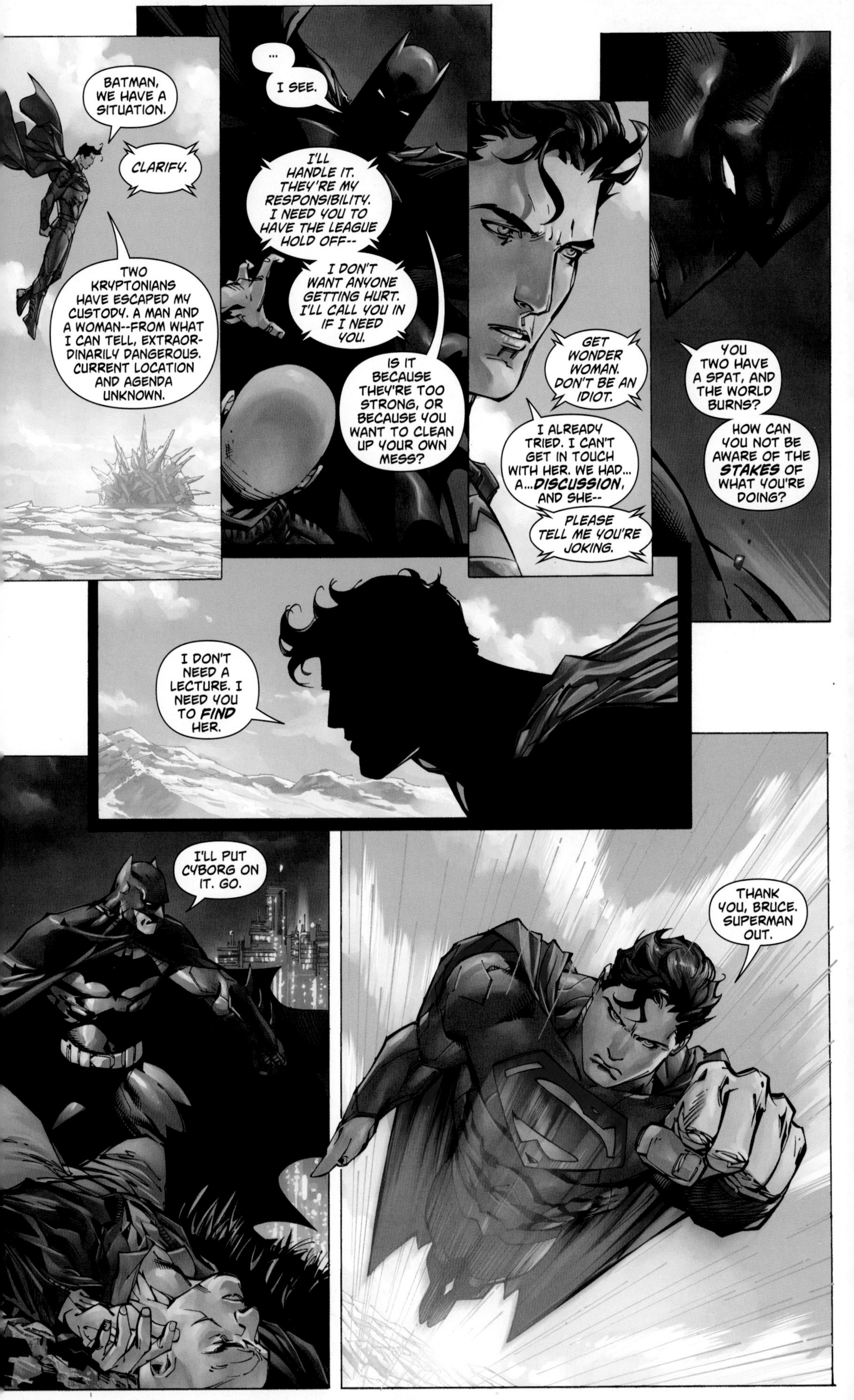

BATMAN, WE HAVE A SITUATION.
CLARIFY.
TWO KRYPTONIANS HAVE ESCAPED MY CUSTODY. A MAN AND A WOMAN--FROM WHAT I CAN TELL, EXTRAOR-DINARILY DANGEROUS. CURRENT LOCATION AND AGENDA UNKNOWN.
...
I SEE.
I'LL HANDLE IT. THEY'RE MY RESPONSIBILITY. I NEED YOU TO HAVE THE LEAGUE HOLD OFF--
I DON'T WANT ANYONE GETTING HURT. I'LL CALL YOU IN IF I NEED YOU.
IS IT BECAUSE THEY'RE TOO STRONG, OR BECAUSE YOU WANT TO CLEAN UP YOUR OWN MESS?
GET WONDER WOMAN. DON'T BE AN IDIOT.
I ALREADY TRIED. I CAN'T GET IN TOUCH WITH HER. WE HAD... A...DISCUSSION, AND SHE--
PLEASE TELL ME YOU'RE JOKING.
YOU TWO HAVE A SPAT, AND THE WORLD BURNS?
HOW CAN YOU NOT BE AWARE OF THE STAKES OF WHAT YOU'RE DOING?
I DON'T NEED A LECTURE. I NEED YOU TO FIND HER.
I'LL PUT CYBORG ON IT. GO.
THANK YOU, BRUCE. SUPERMAN OUT.

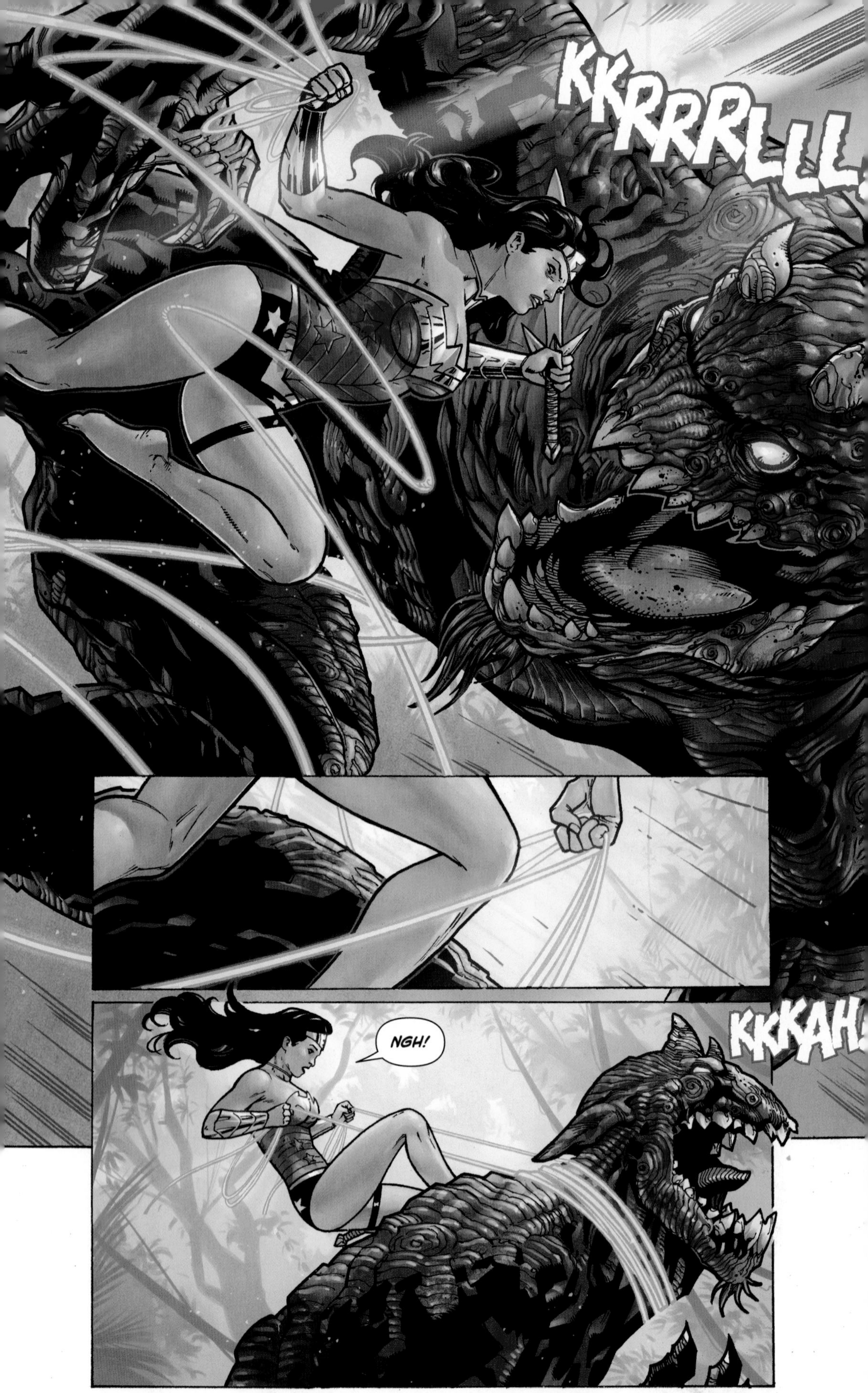

KKRRRLLL
NGH!
KKKAH

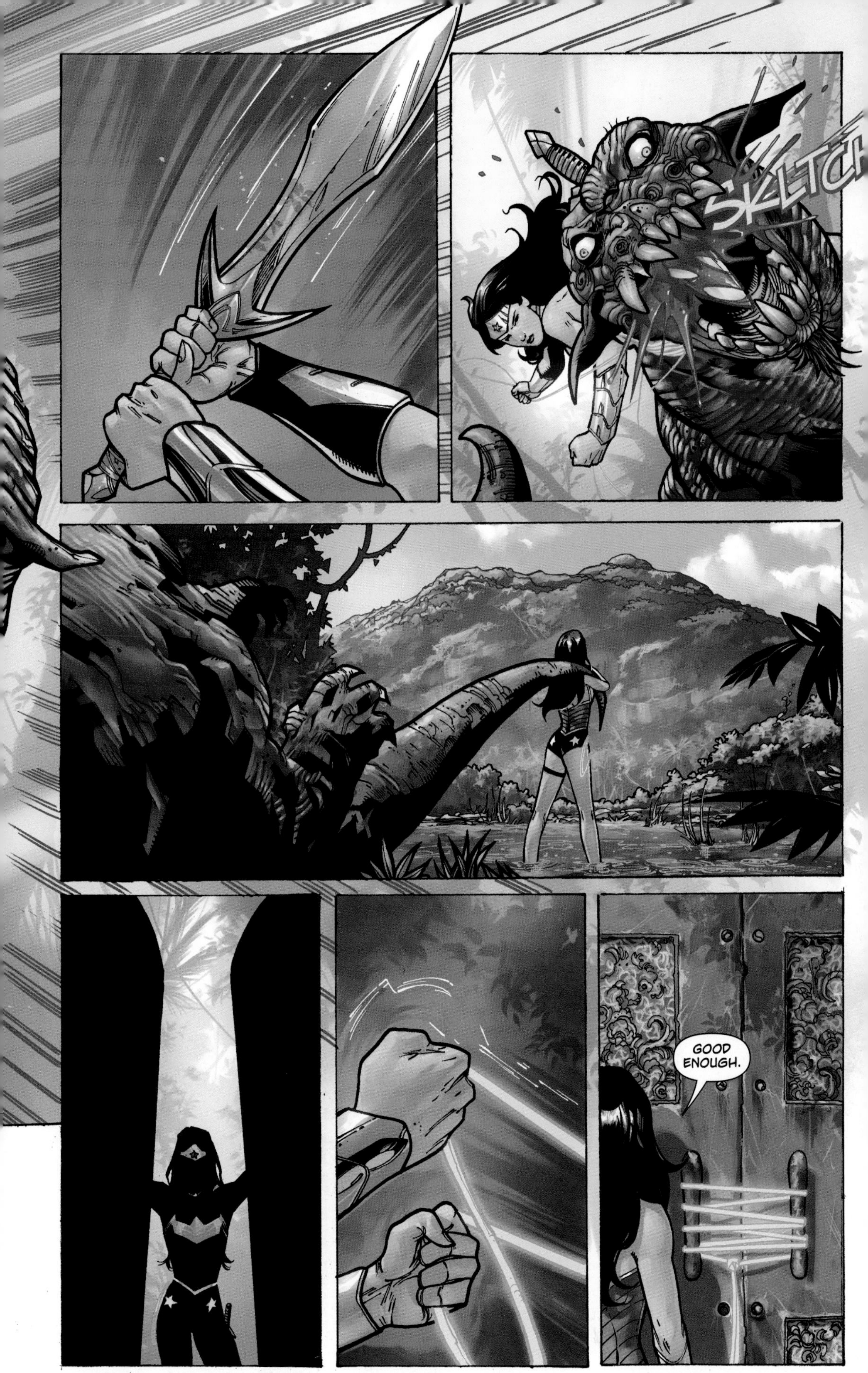
SKLTCH
GOOD ENOUGH.

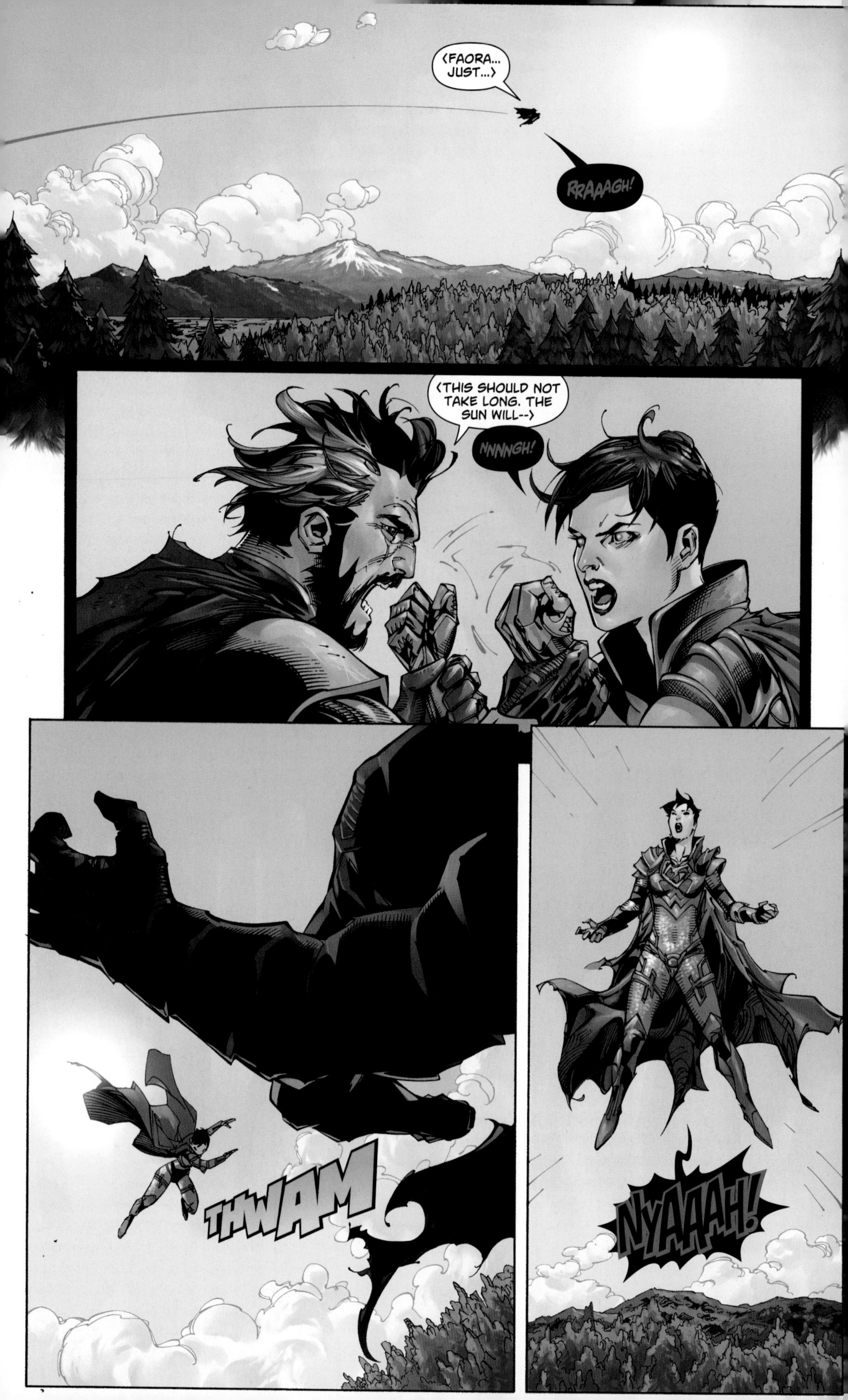
‹FAORA... JUST...›
RRAAAGH!
‹THIS SHOULD NOT TAKE LONG. THE SUN WILL--›
NNNNGH!
THWAM
NYAAAH!

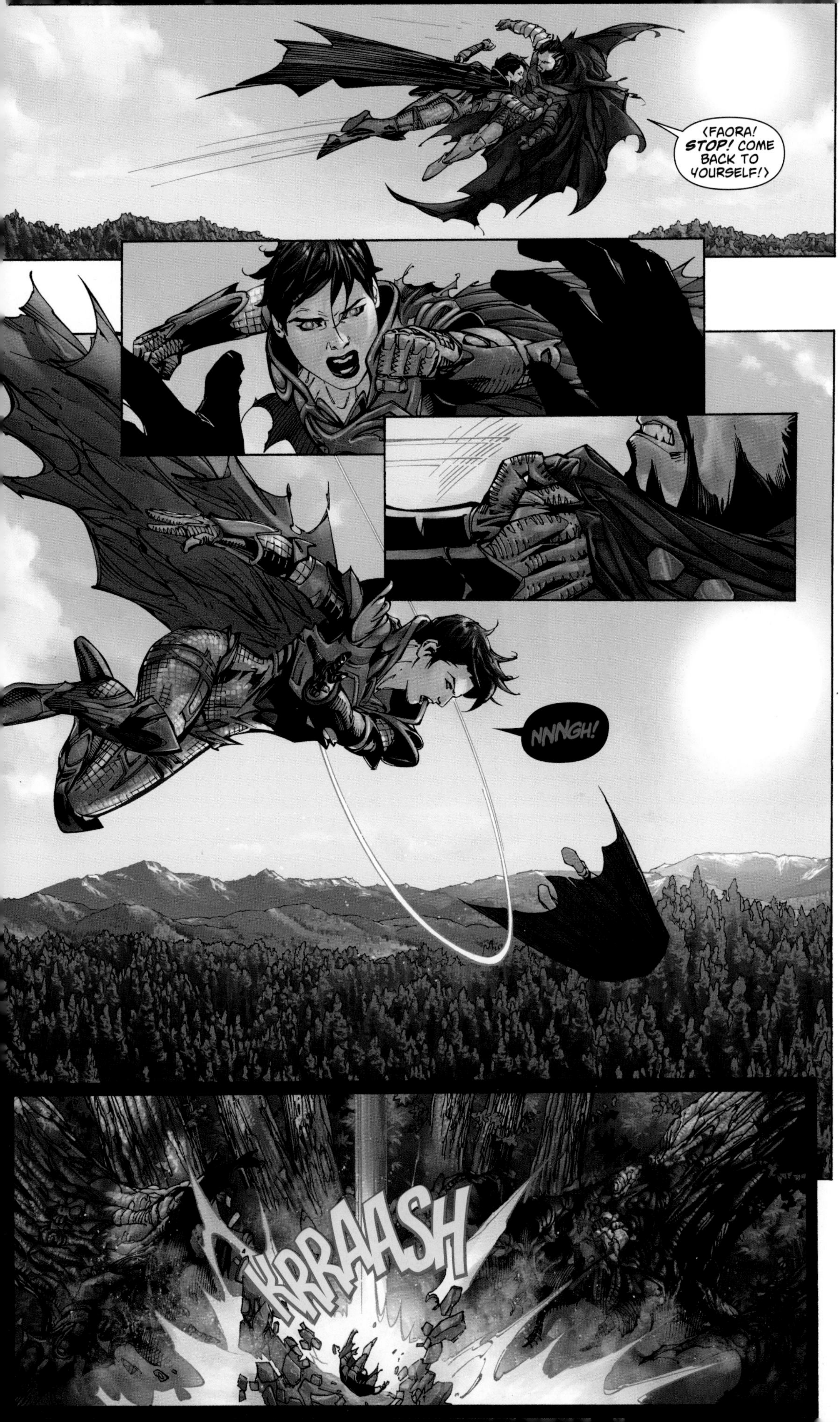
‹FAORA! STOP! COME BACK TO YOURSELF!›
NNNGH!
KRRAASH

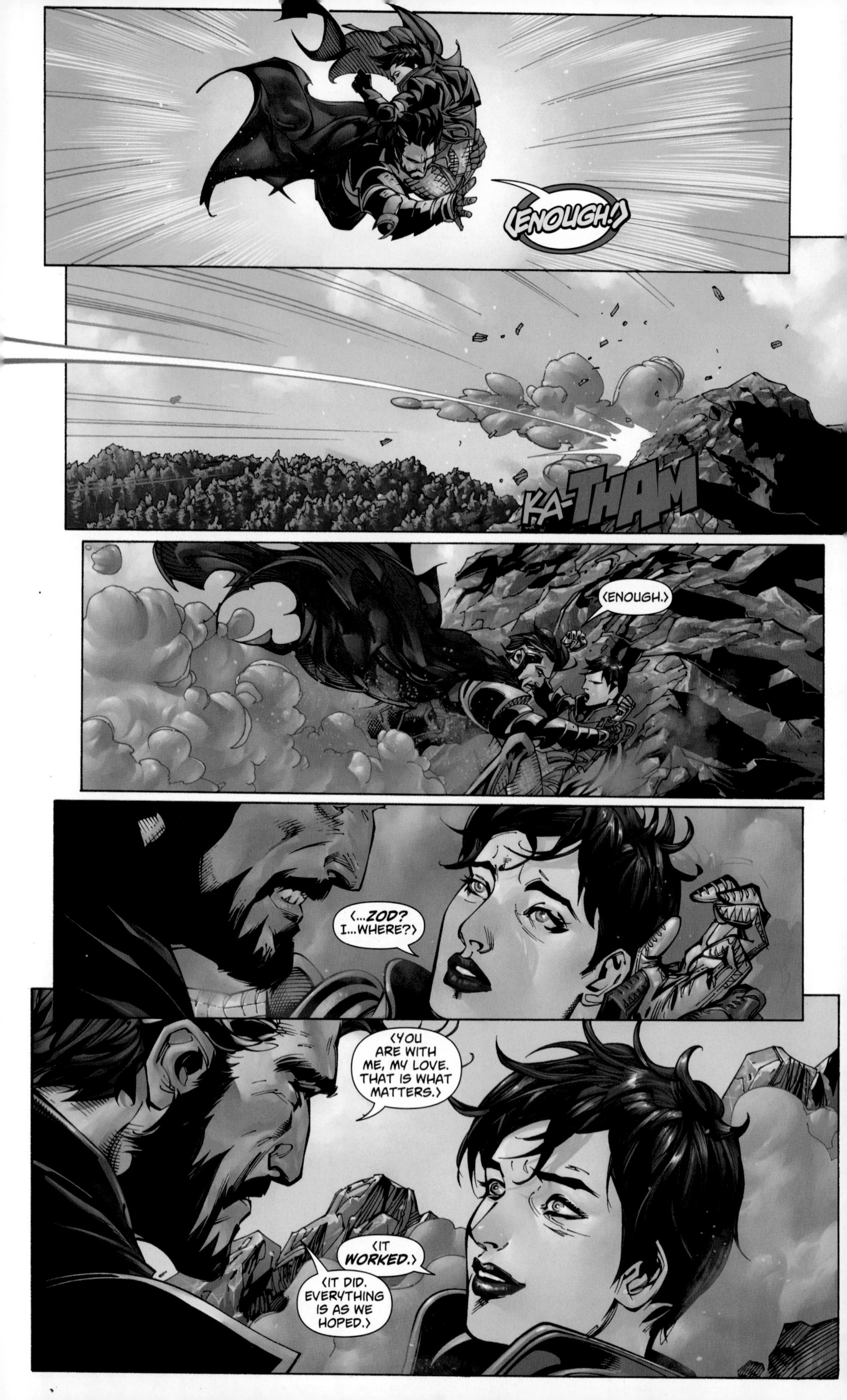

⟨ENOUGH!⟩
KA-THAM
⟨ENOUGH.⟩
⟨...ZOD? I...WHERE?⟩
⟨YOU ARE WITH ME, MY LOVE. THAT IS WHAT MATTERS.⟩
⟨IT WORKED.⟩
⟨IT DID. EVERYTHING IS AS WE HOPED.⟩

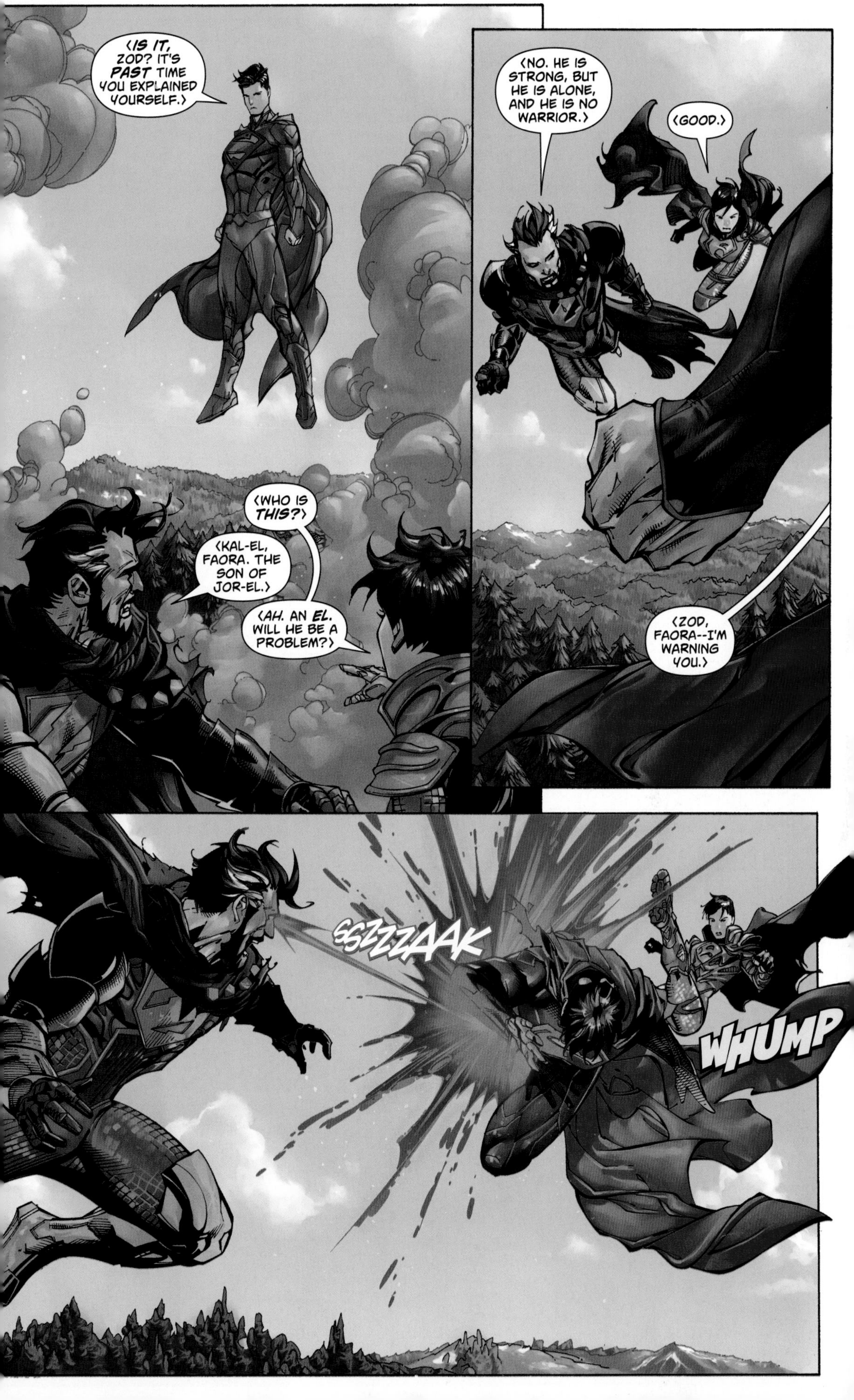
‹IS IT, ZOD? IT'S PAST TIME YOU EXPLAINED YOURSELF.›
‹WHO IS THIS?›
‹KAL-EL, FAORA. THE SON OF JOR-EL.›
‹AH. AN EL. WILL HE BE A PROBLEM?›
‹NO. HE IS STRONG, BUT HE IS ALONE, AND HE IS NO WARRIOR.›
‹GOOD.›
‹ZOD, FAORA--I'M WARNING YOU.›
SSZZZZAAK
WHUMP

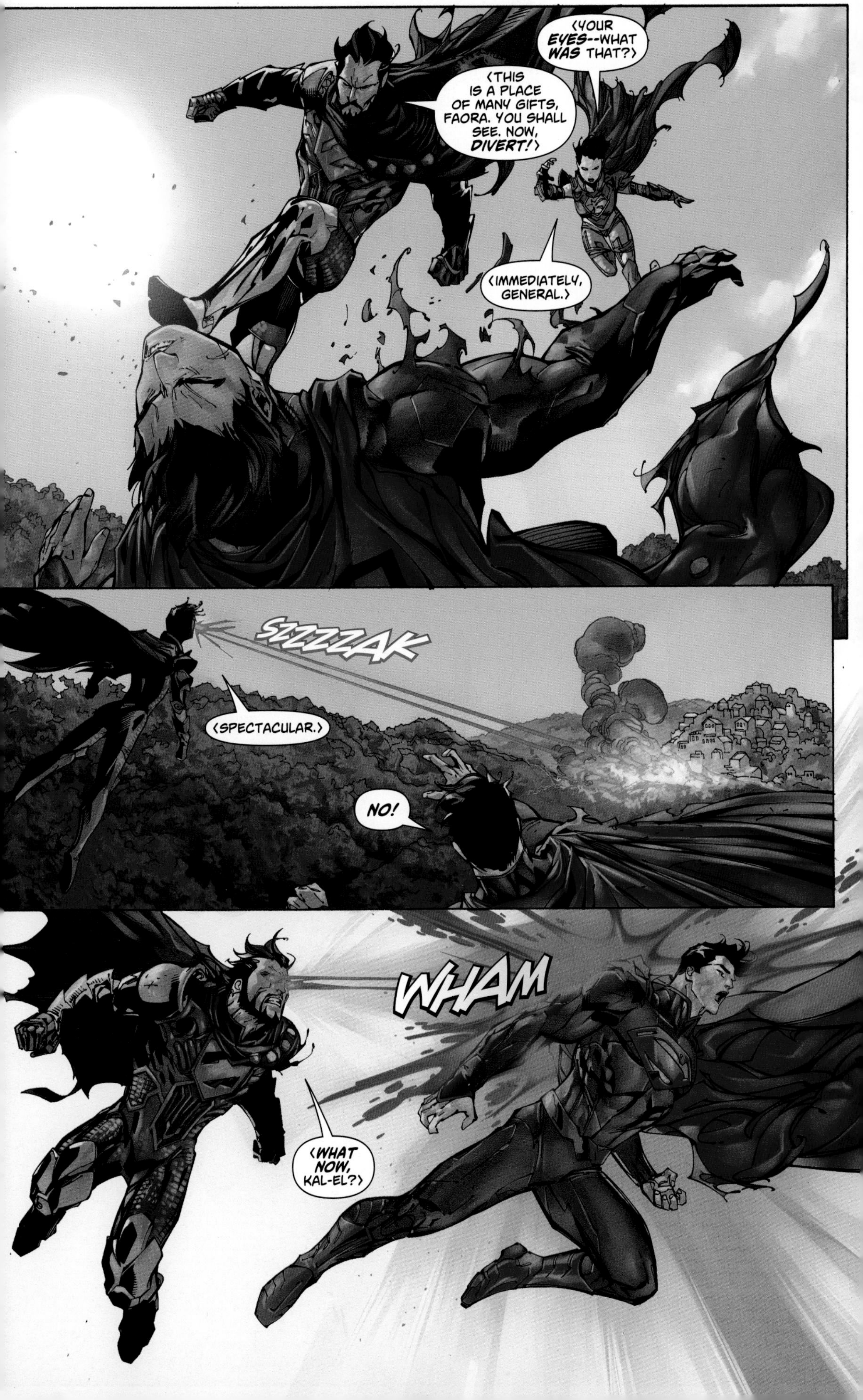

‹THIS IS A PLACE OF MANY GIFTS, FAORA. YOU SHALL SEE. NOW, DIVERT!›
‹YOUR EYES--WHAT WAS THAT?›
‹IMMEDIATELY, GENERAL.›
SZZZZAK
‹SPECTACULAR.›
NO!
WHAM
‹WHAT NOW, KAL-EL?›

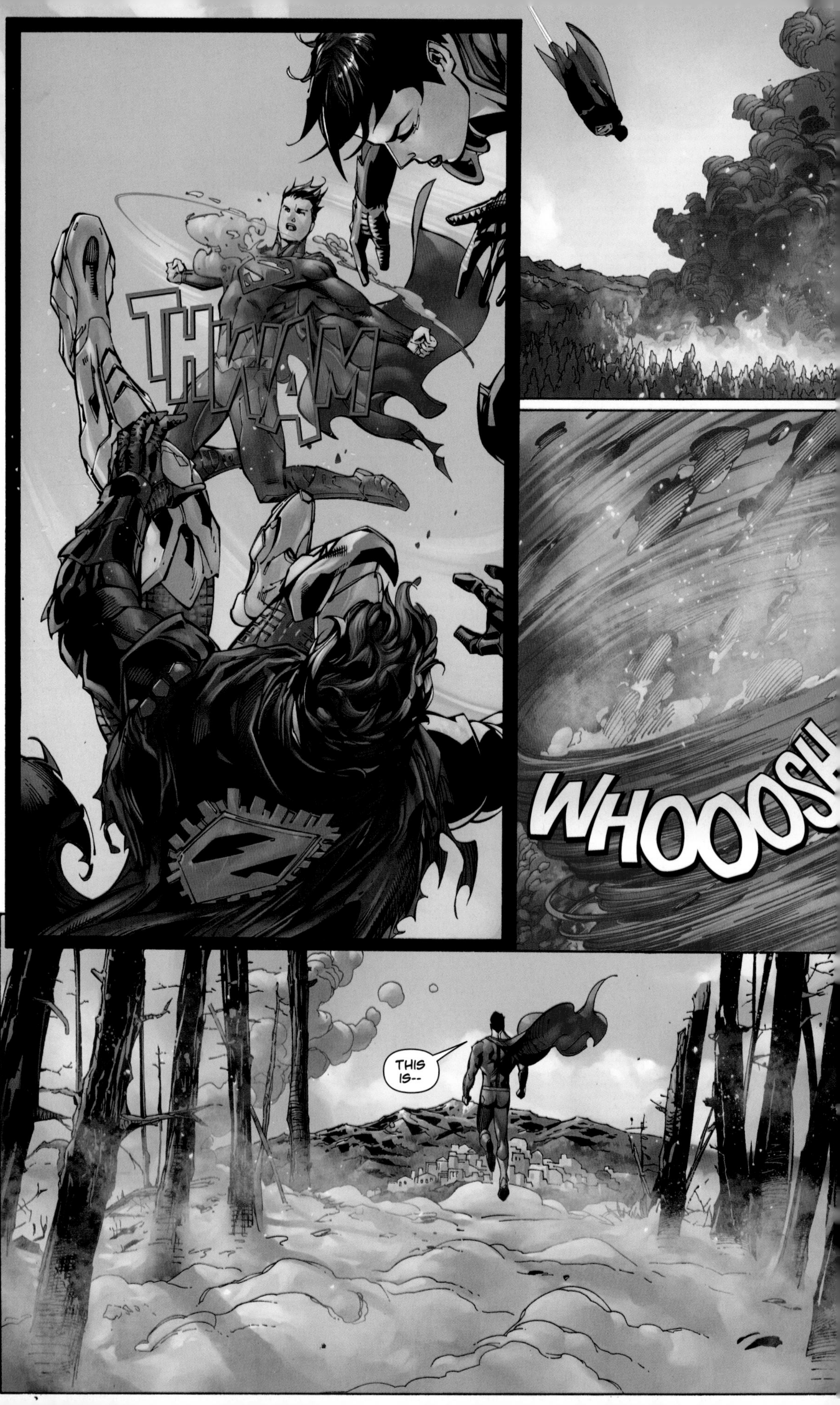
THWAM
WHOOOSH
THIS IS--

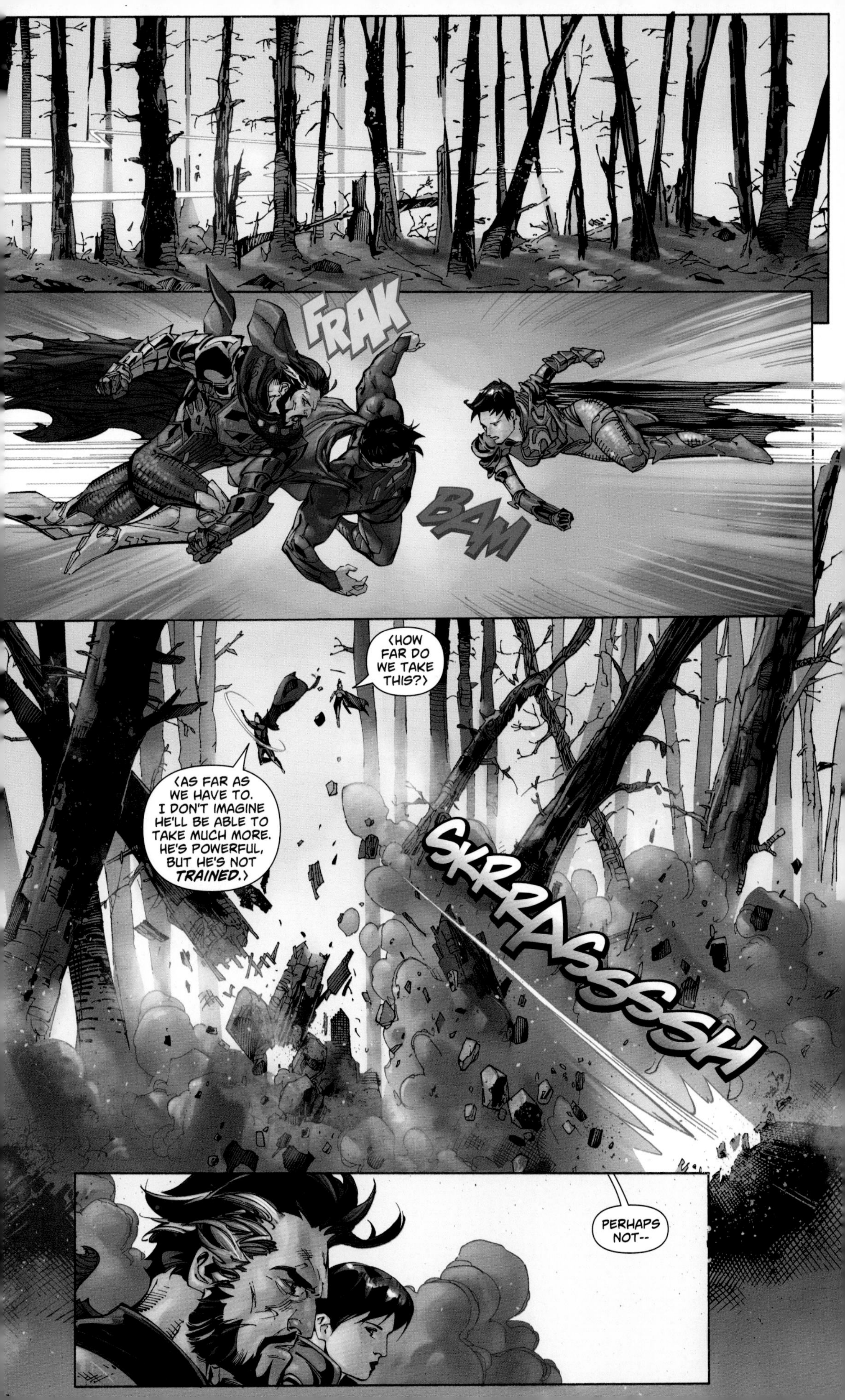
FRAK
BAM
‹HOW FAR DO WE TAKE THIS?›
‹AS FAR AS WE HAVE TO. I DON'T IMAGINE HE'LL BE ABLE TO TAKE MUCH MORE. HE'S POWERFUL, BUT HE'S NOT *TRAINED*.›
SKRASSSSH
PERHAPS NOT--

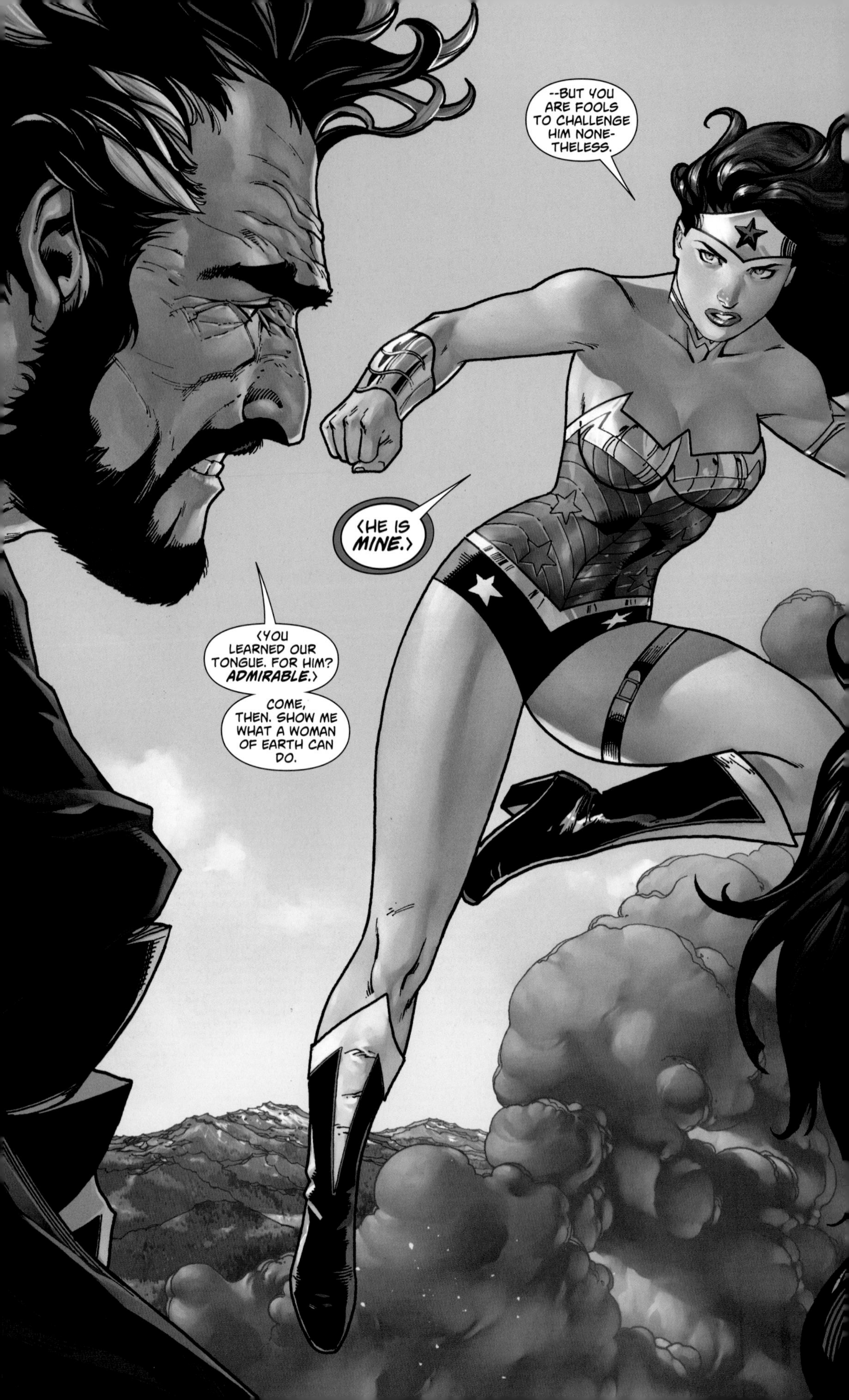
--BUT YOU ARE FOOLS TO CHALLENGE HIM NONE-THELESS.
<HE IS *MINE.*>
<YOU LEARNED OUR TONGUE. FOR HIM? ***ADMIRABLE.***>
COME, THEN. SHOW ME WHAT A WOMAN OF EARTH CAN DO.

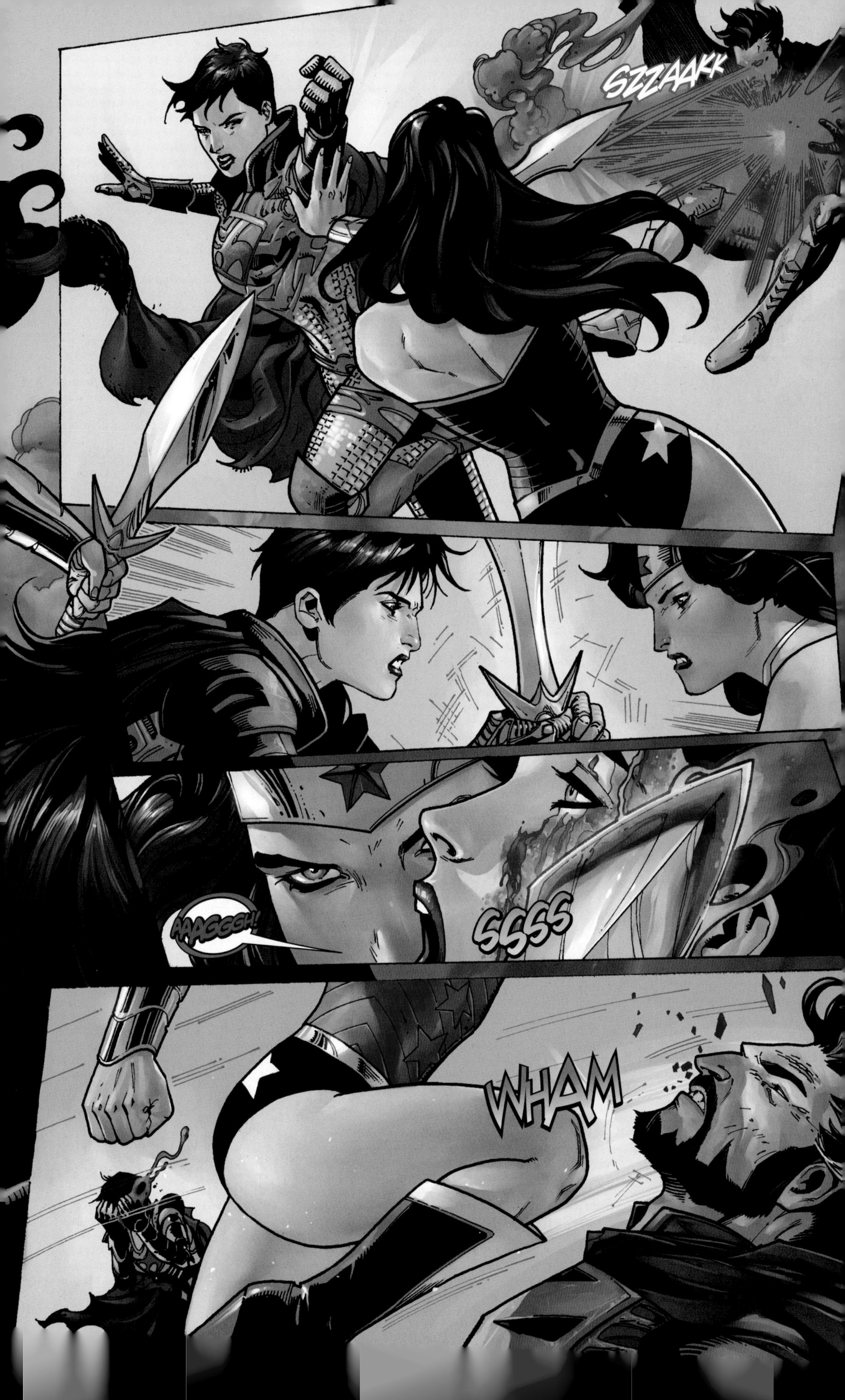
SZZAAKK
AAAGGGH!
SSSS
WHAM

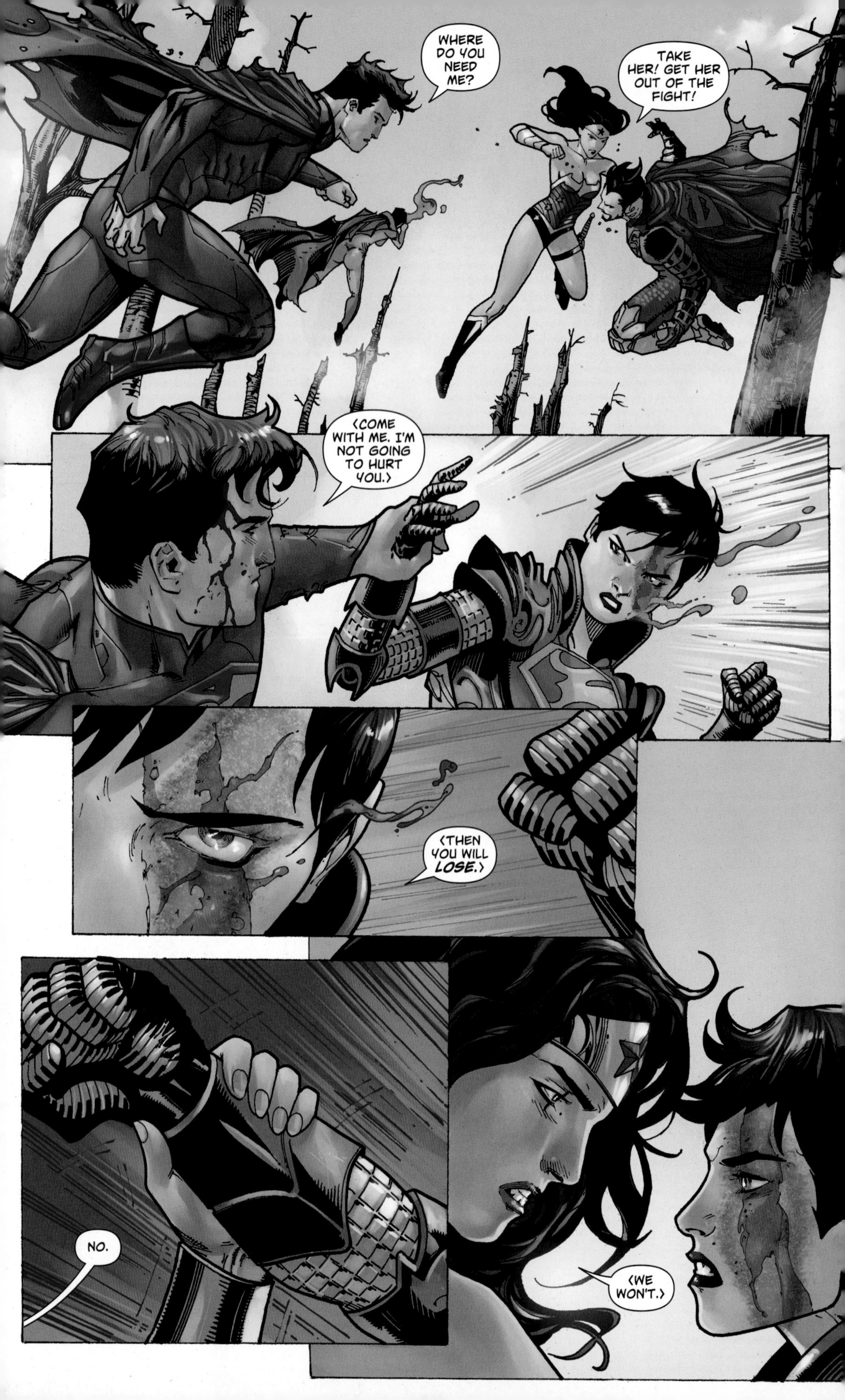
WHERE DO YOU NEED ME?
TAKE HER! GET HER OUT OF THE FIGHT!
<COME WITH ME. I'M NOT GOING TO HURT YOU.>
<THEN YOU WILL *LOSE*.>
NO.
<WE WON'T.>

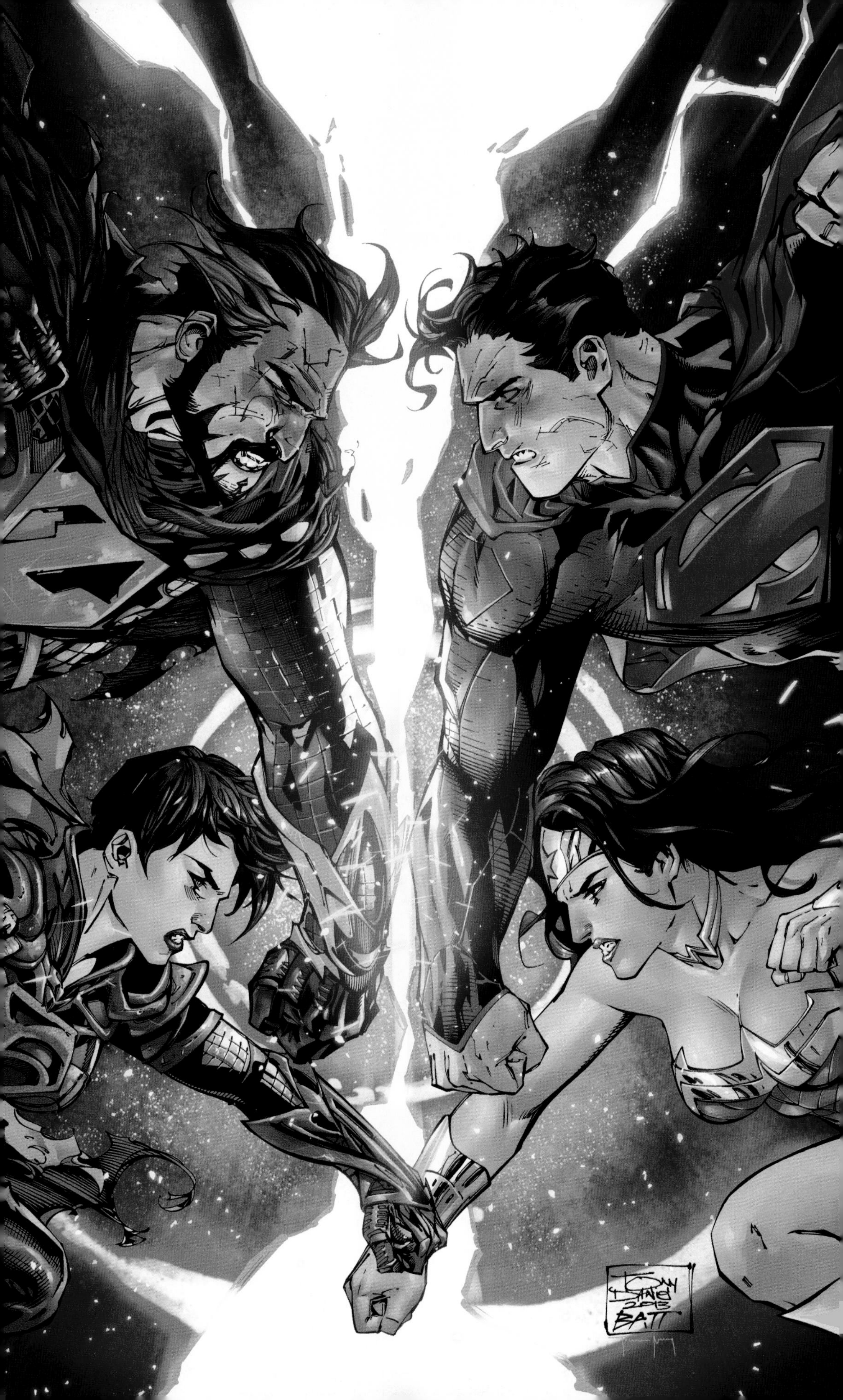

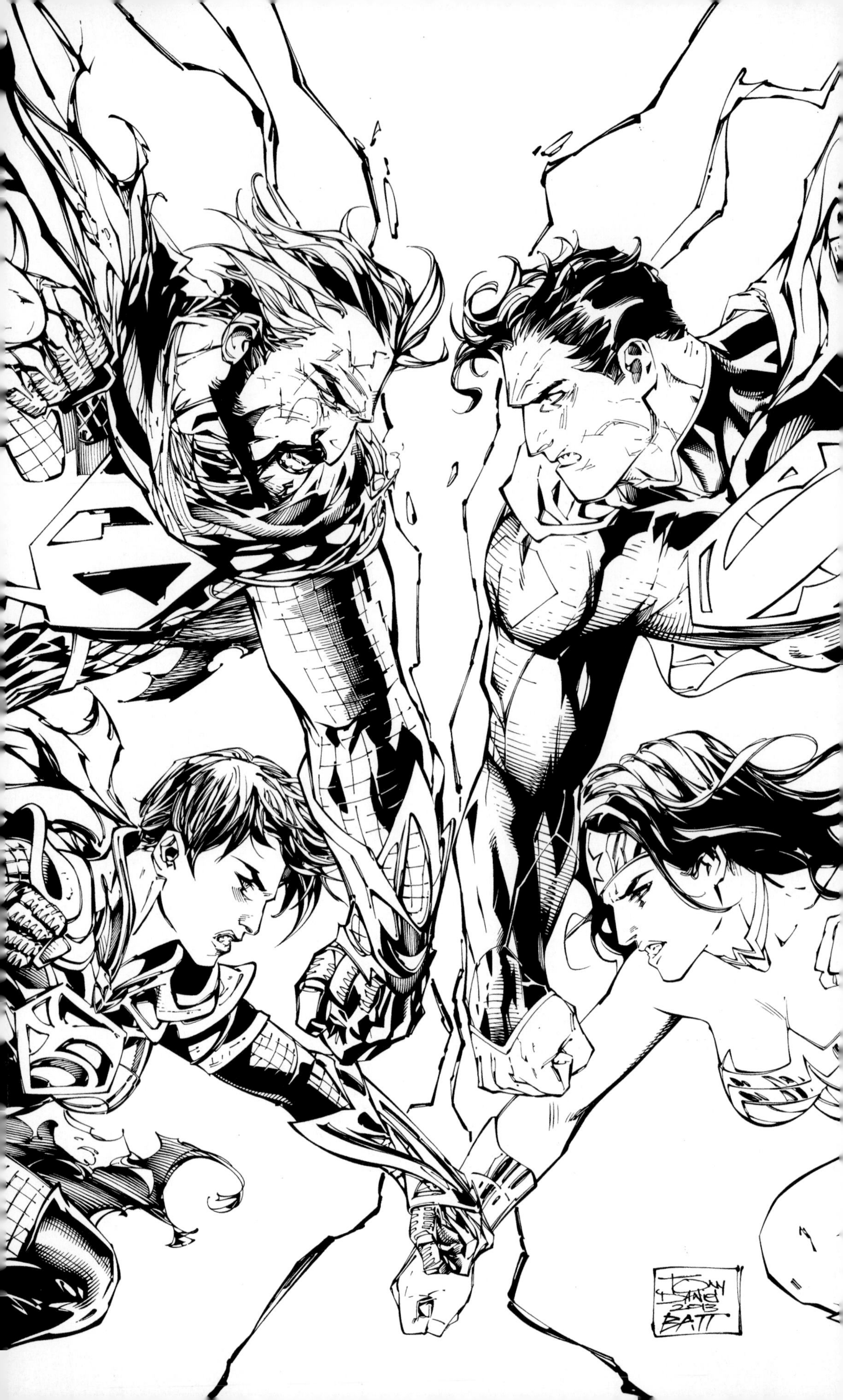

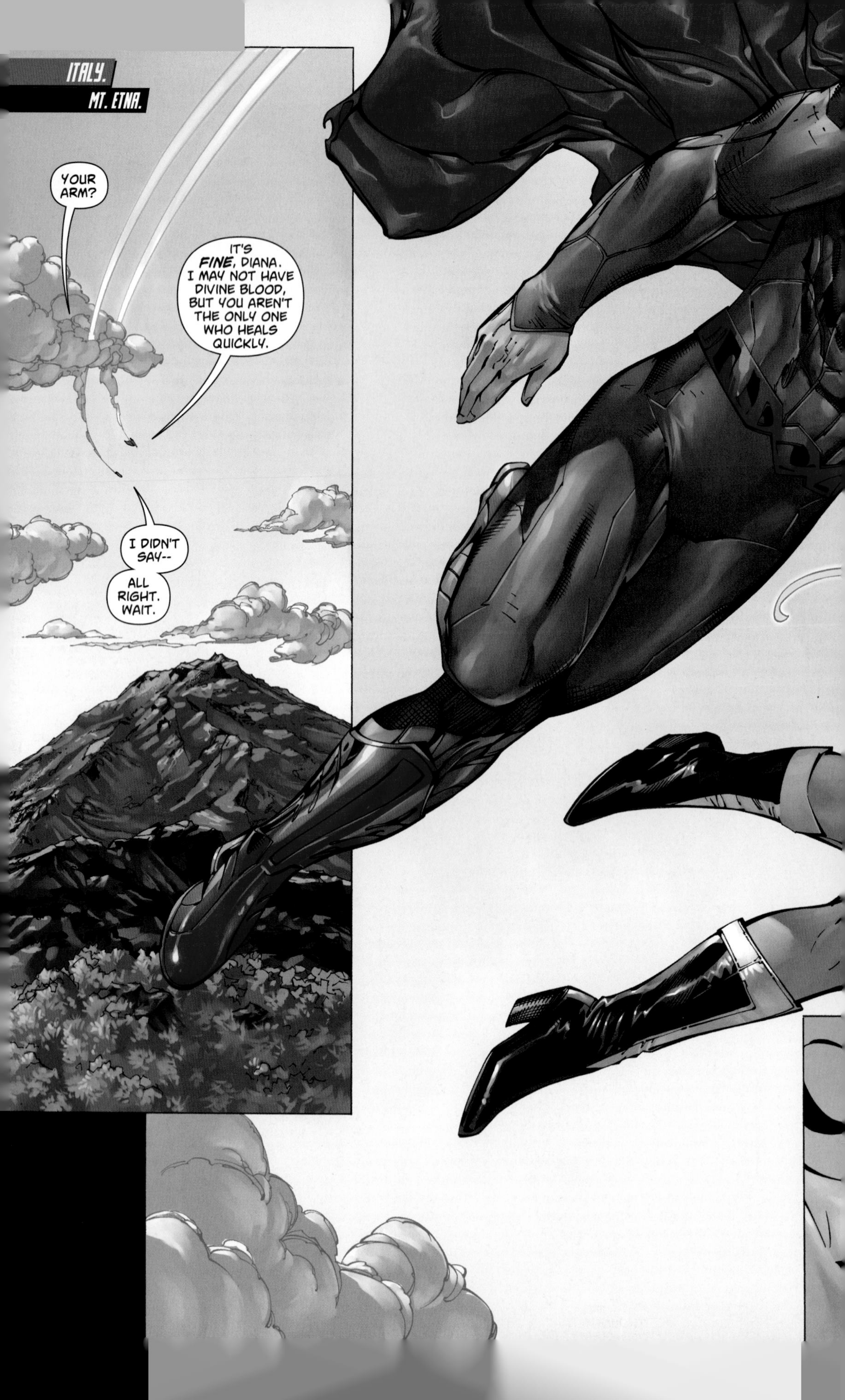
ITALY.
MT. ETNA.
YOUR ARM?
IT'S FINE, DIANA. I MAY NOT HAVE DIVINE BLOOD, BUT YOU AREN'T THE ONLY ONE WHO HEALS QUICKLY.
I DIDN'T SAY--
ALL RIGHT. WAIT.

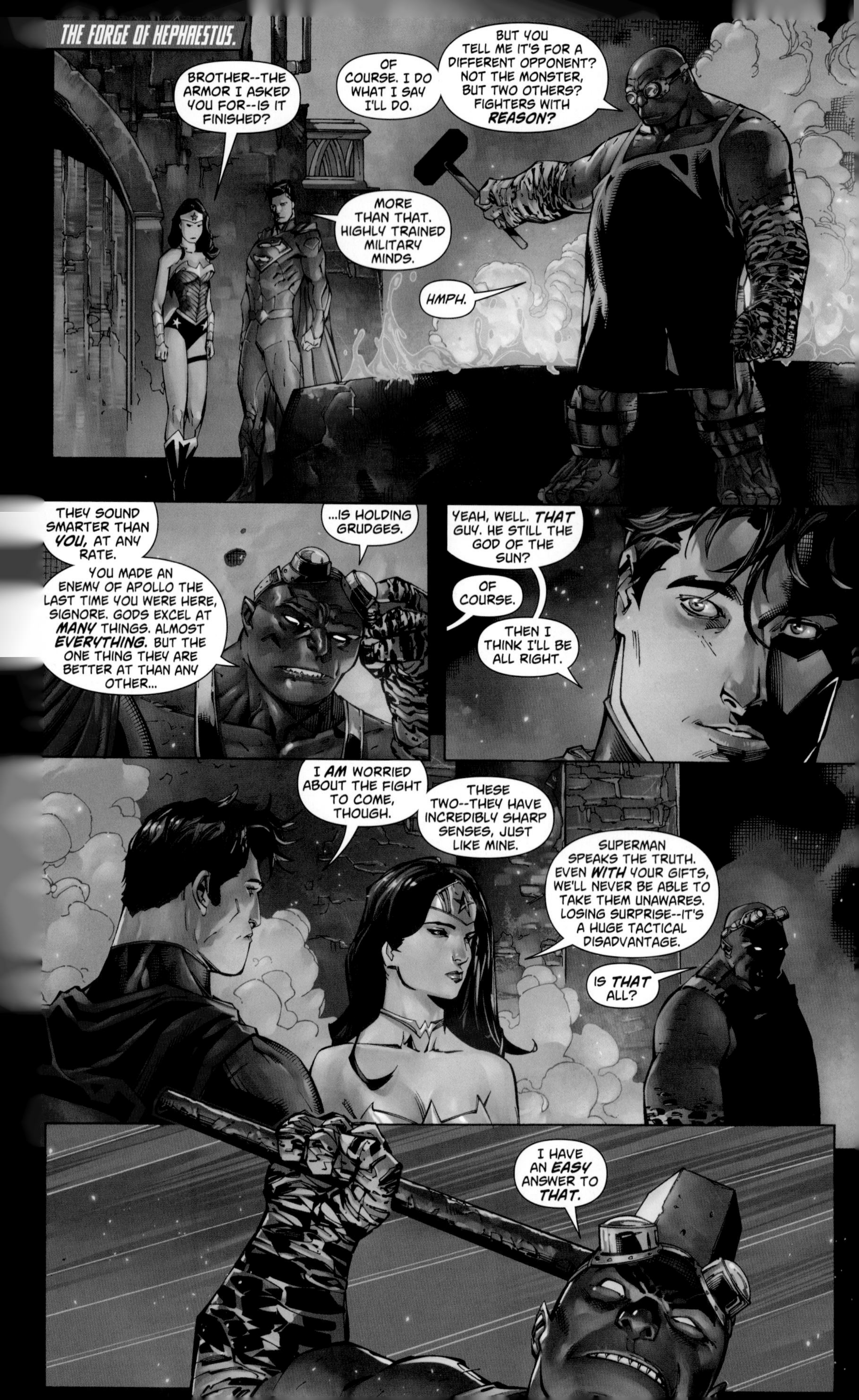

THE FORGE OF HEPHAESTUS.
BROTHER--THE ARMOR I ASKED YOU FOR--IS IT FINISHED?
OF COURSE. I DO WHAT I SAY I'LL DO.
BUT YOU TELL ME IT'S FOR A DIFFERENT OPPONENT? NOT THE MONSTER, BUT TWO OTHERS? FIGHTERS WITH REASON?
MORE THAN THAT. HIGHLY TRAINED MILITARY MINDS.
HMPH.
THEY SOUND SMARTER THAN YOU, AT ANY RATE.
YOU MADE AN ENEMY OF APOLLO THE LAST TIME YOU WERE HERE, SIGNORE. GODS EXCEL AT MANY THINGS. ALMOST EVERYTHING. BUT THE ONE THING THEY ARE BETTER AT THAN ANY OTHER...
...IS HOLDING GRUDGES.
YEAH, WELL. THAT GUY. HE STILL THE GOD OF THE SUN?
OF COURSE.
THEN I THINK I'LL BE ALL RIGHT.
I AM WORRIED ABOUT THE FIGHT TO COME, THOUGH.
THESE TWO--THEY HAVE INCREDIBLY SHARP SENSES, JUST LIKE MINE.
SUPERMAN SPEAKS THE TRUTH. EVEN WITH YOUR GIFTS, WE'LL NEVER BE ABLE TO TAKE THEM UNAWARES. LOSING SURPRISE--IT'S A HUGE TACTICAL DISADVANTAGE.
IS THAT ALL?
I HAVE AN EASY ANSWER TO THAT.

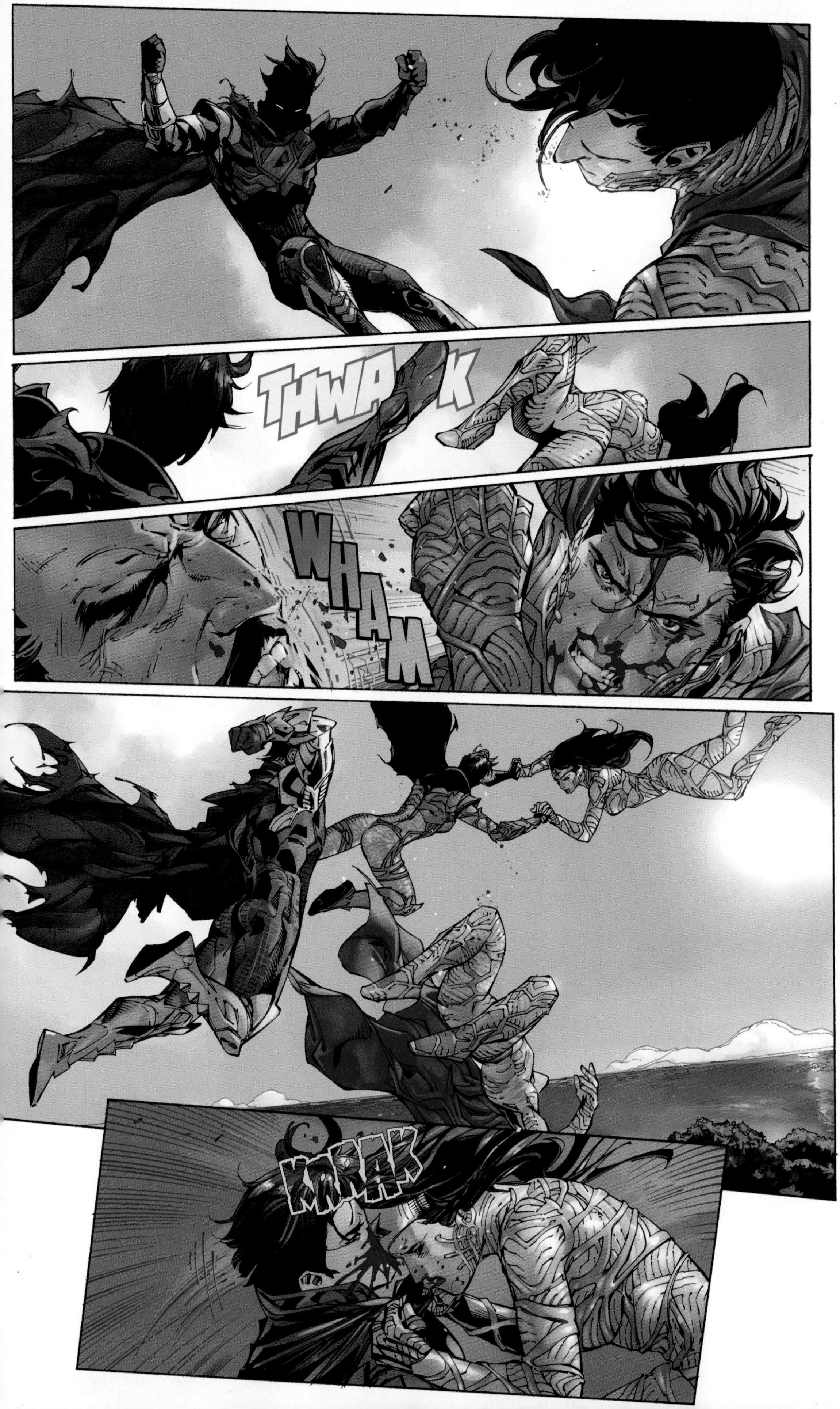
THWA K
WHAM
KRRAK

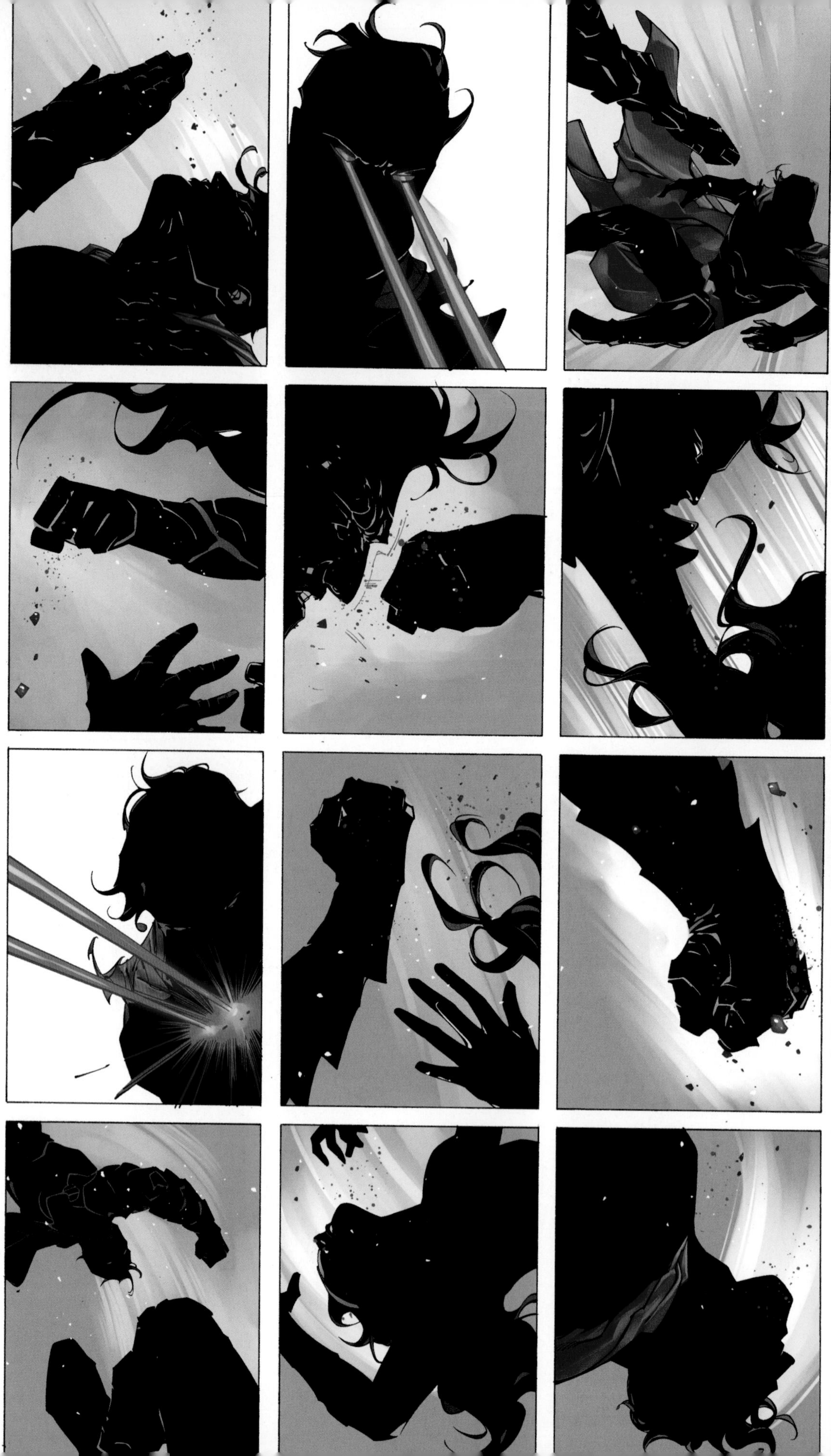

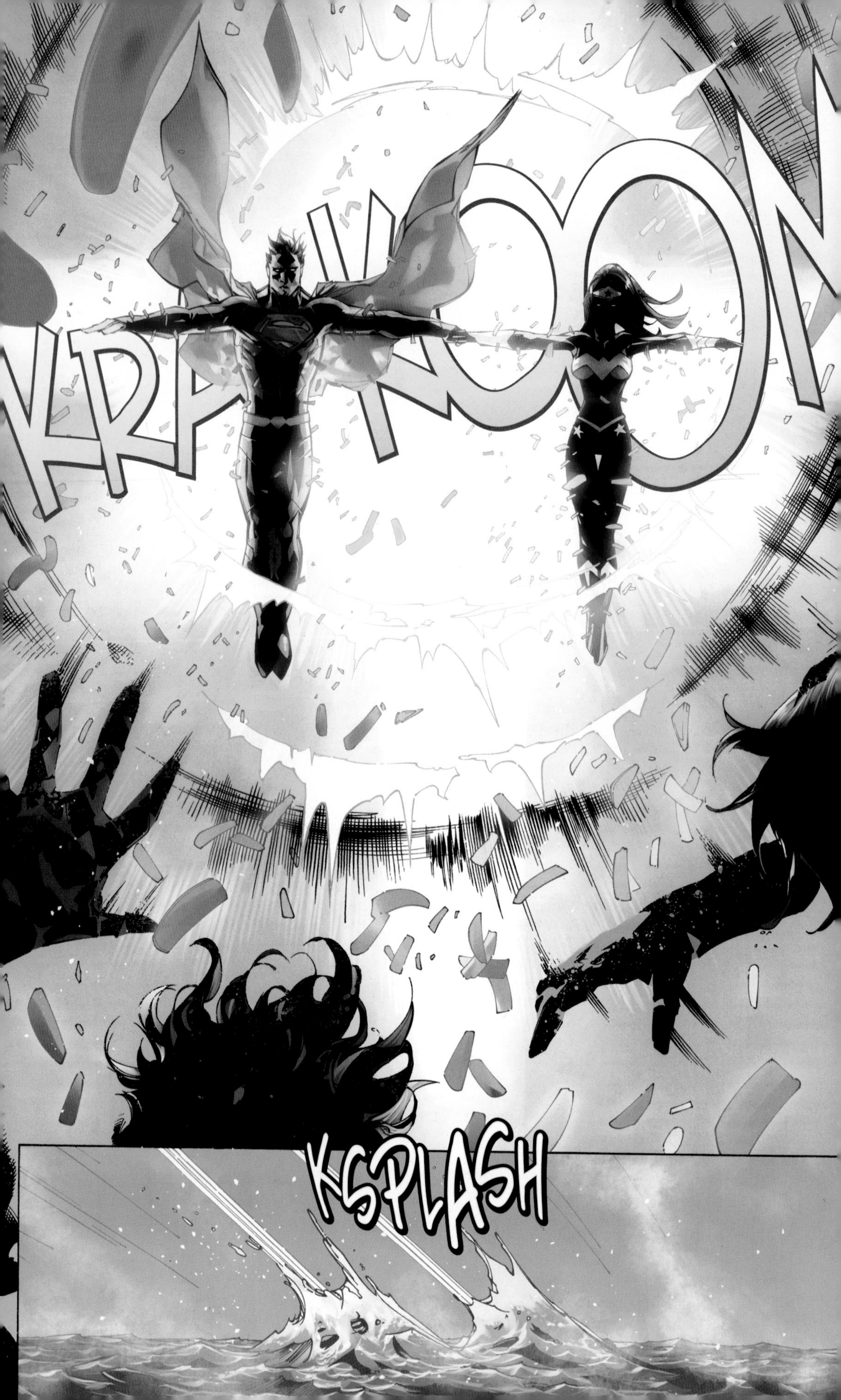
KRAKOOM
KSPLASH

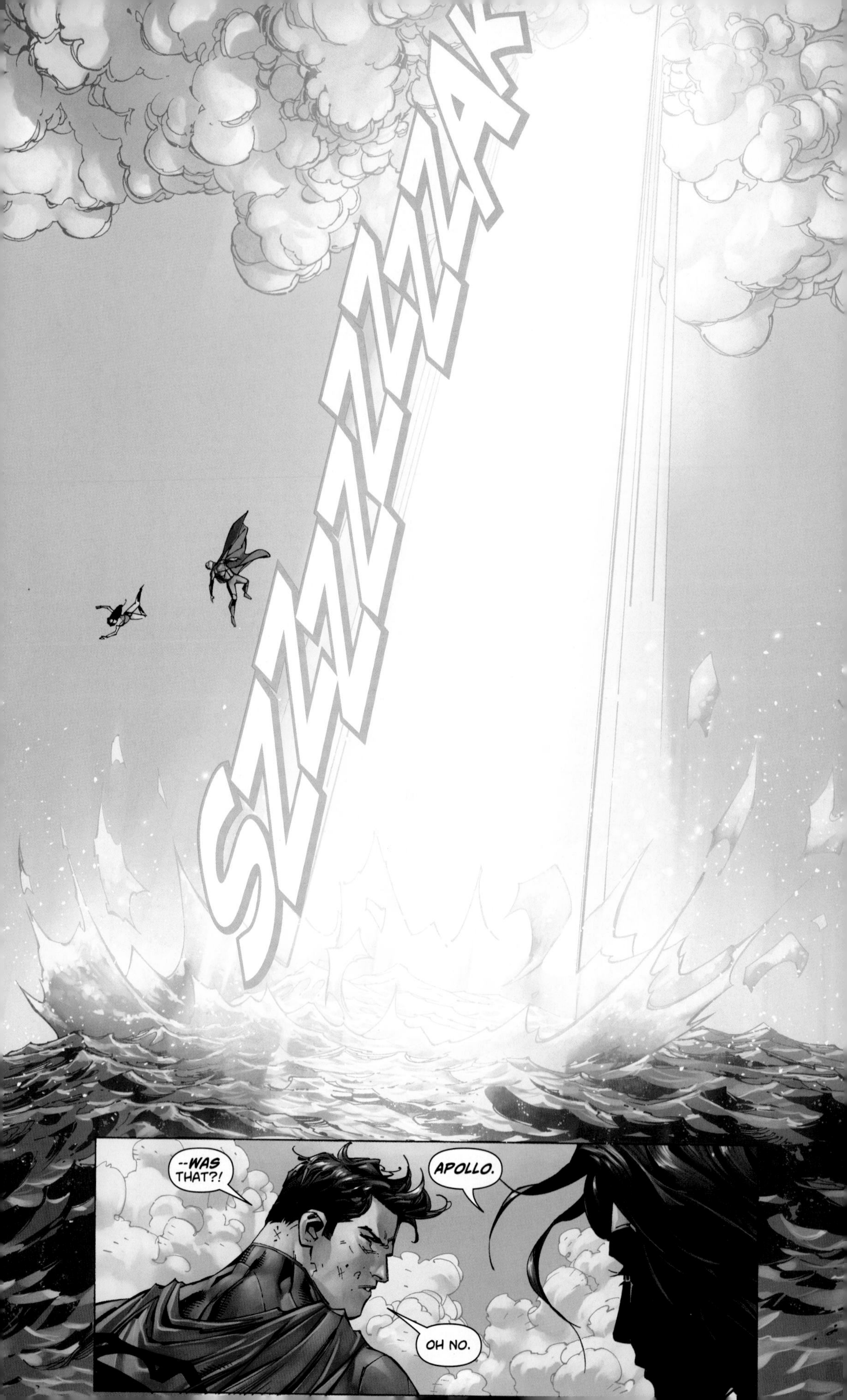
SZZZZZZZZZAK
--WAS THAT?!
APOLLO.
OH NO.

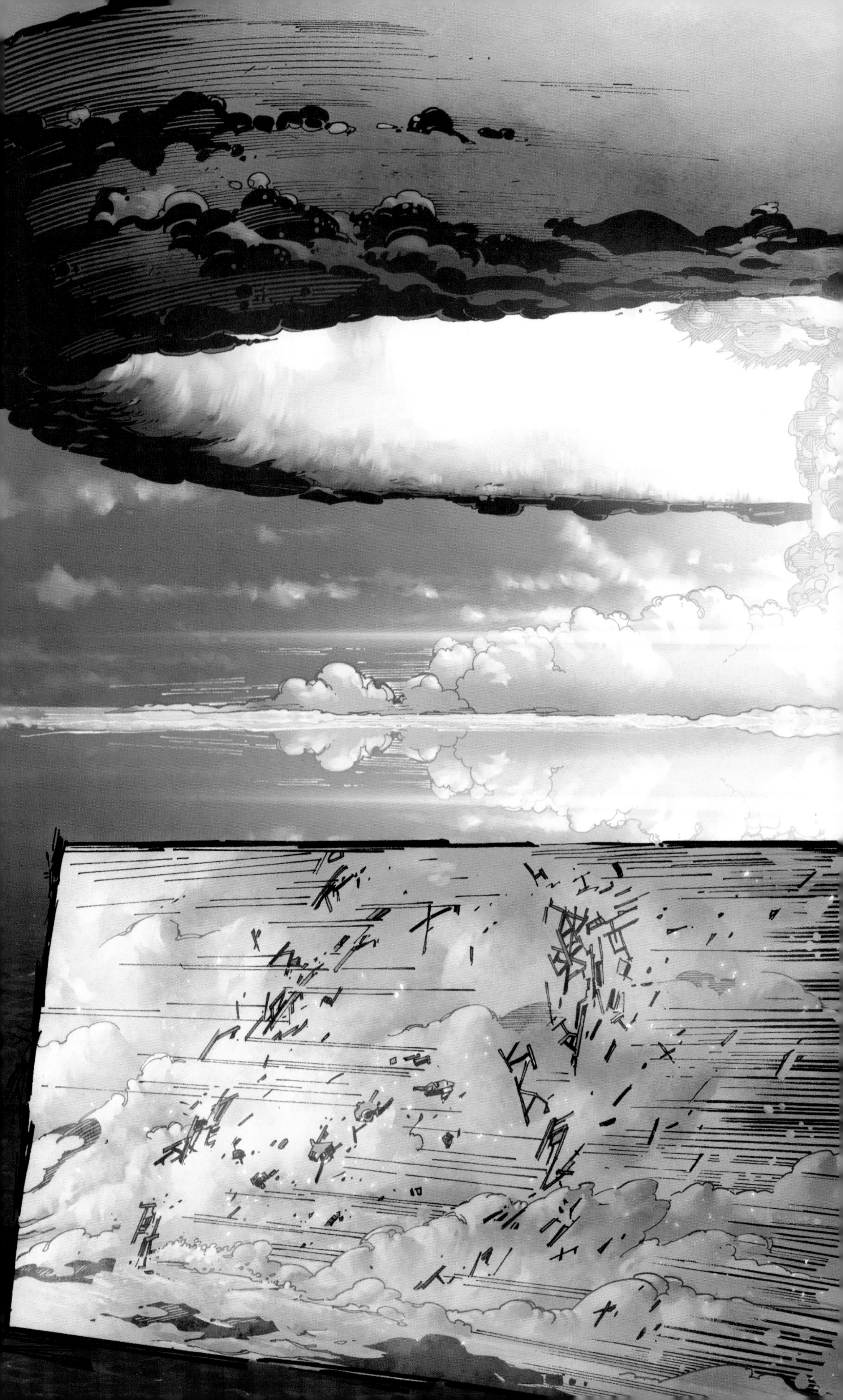

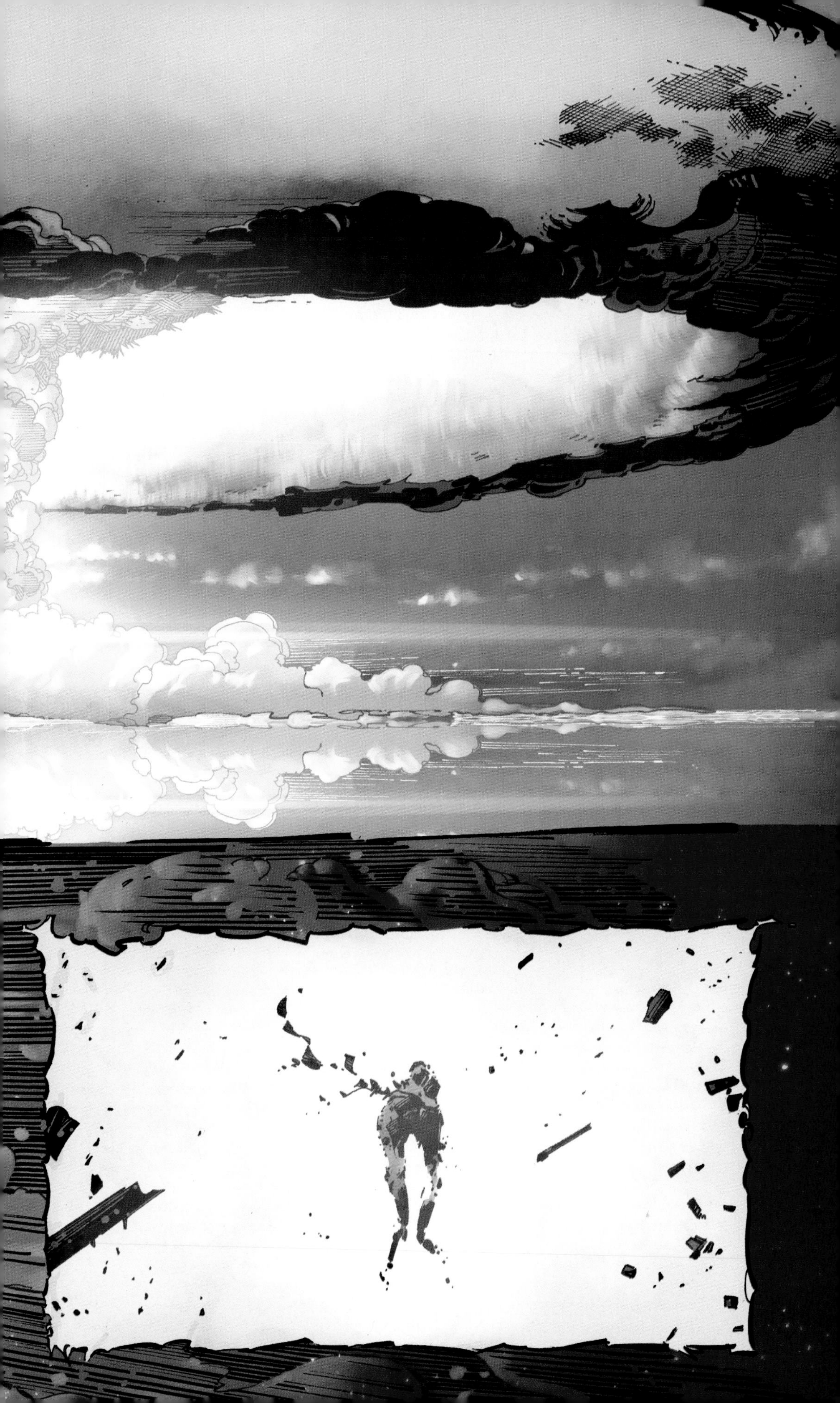

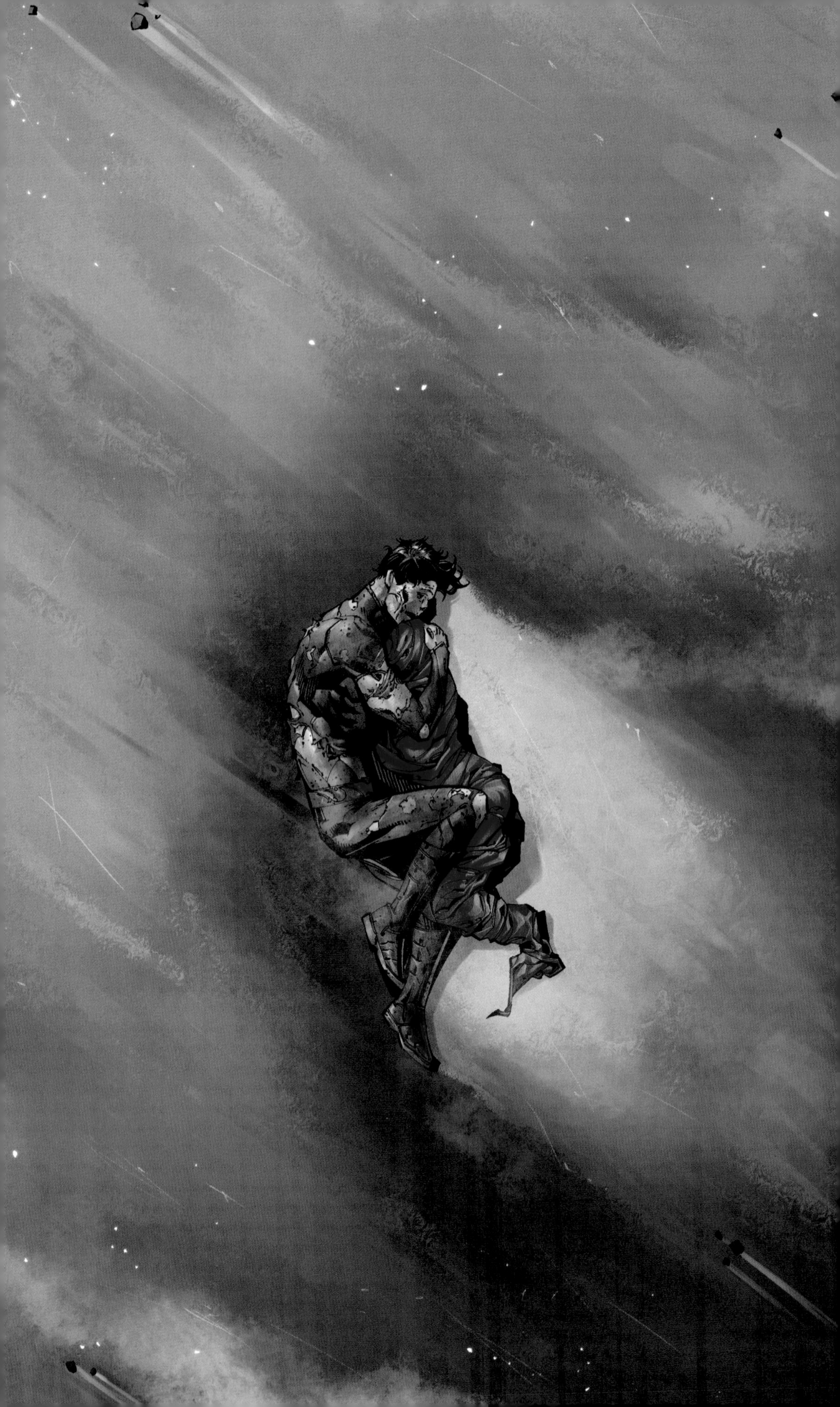

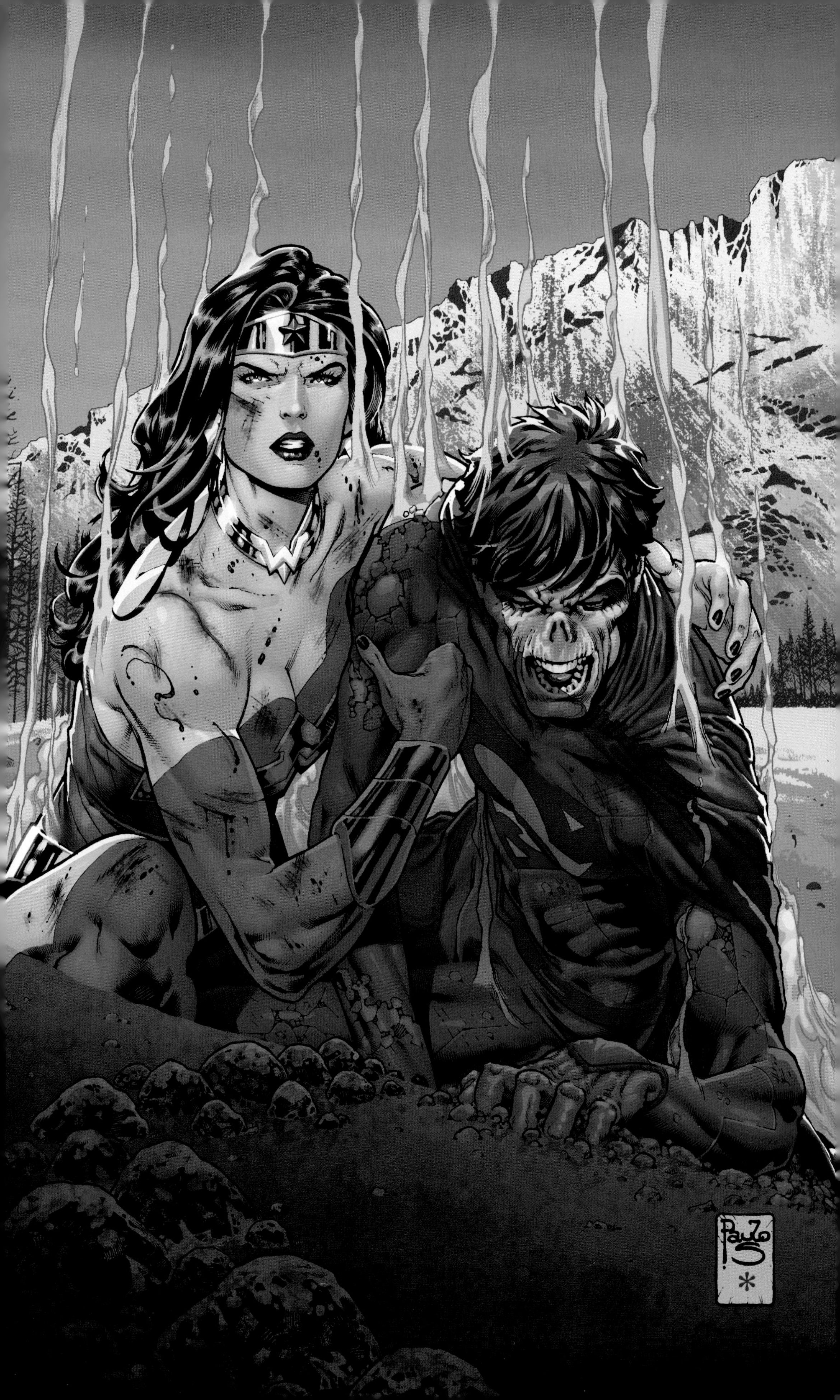

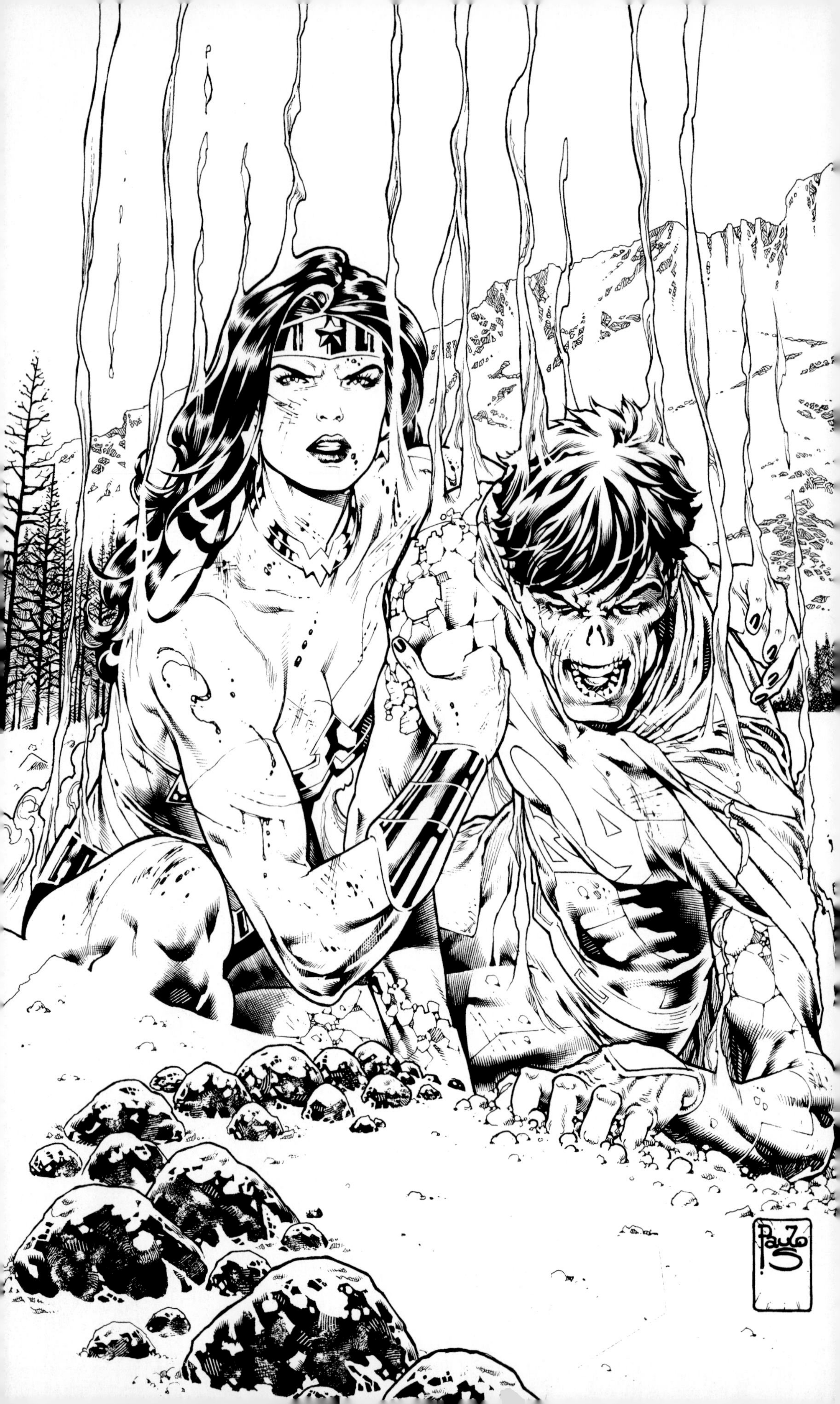

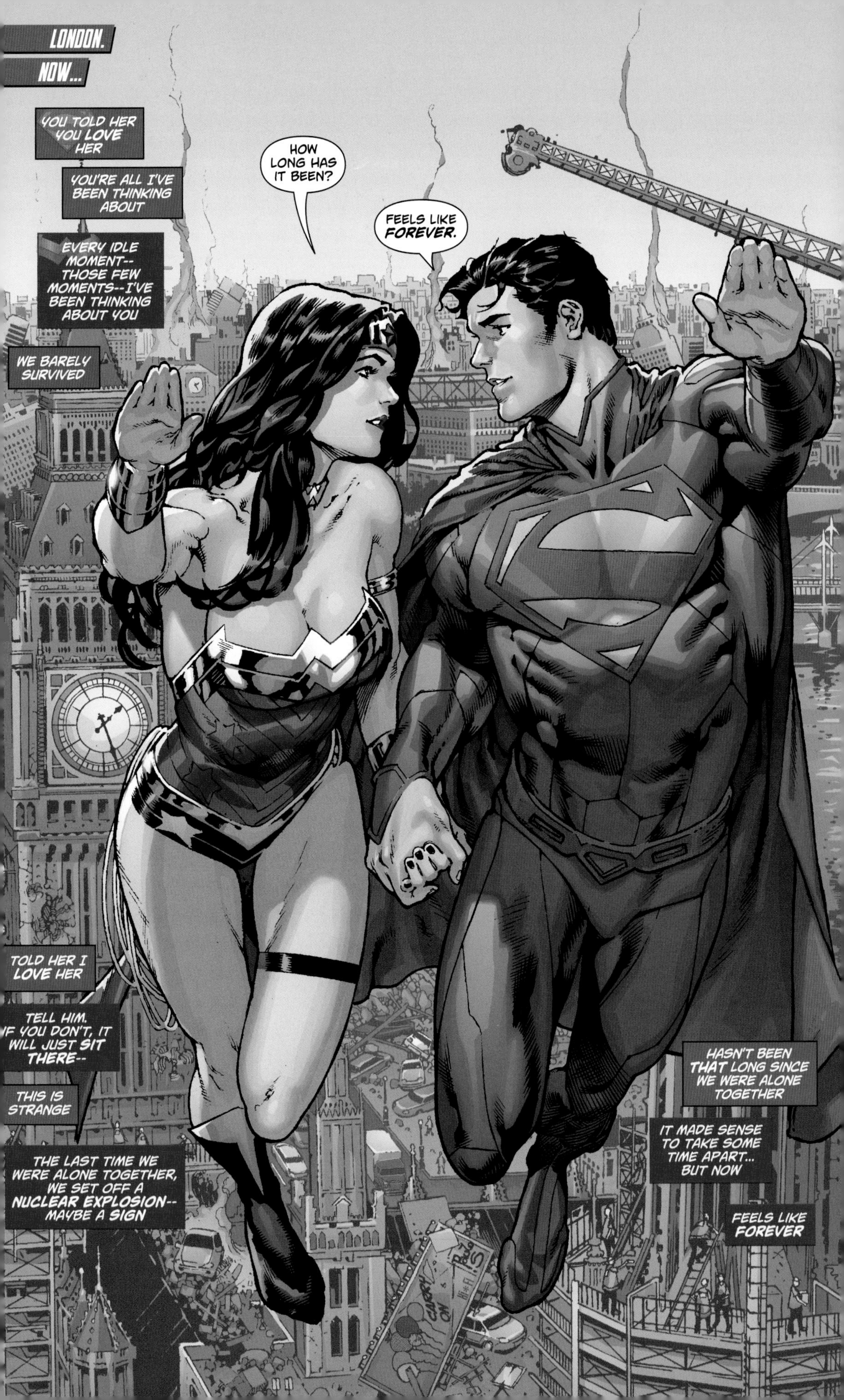
LONDON.
NOW...
YOU TOLD HER YOU LOVE HER
YOU'RE ALL I'VE BEEN THINKING ABOUT
EVERY IDLE MOMENT-- THOSE FEW MOMENTS--I'VE BEEN THINKING ABOUT YOU
WE BARELY SURVIVED
HOW LONG HAS IT BEEN?
FEELS LIKE FOREVER.
TOLD HER I LOVE HER
TELL HIM. IF YOU DON'T, IT WILL JUST SIT THERE--
THIS IS STRANGE
THE LAST TIME WE WERE ALONE TOGETHER, WE SET OFF A NUCLEAR EXPLOSION-- MAYBE A SIGN
HASN'T BEEN THAT LONG SINCE WE WERE ALONE TOGETHER
IT MADE SENSE TO TAKE SOME TIME APART... BUT NOW
FEELS LIKE FOREVER

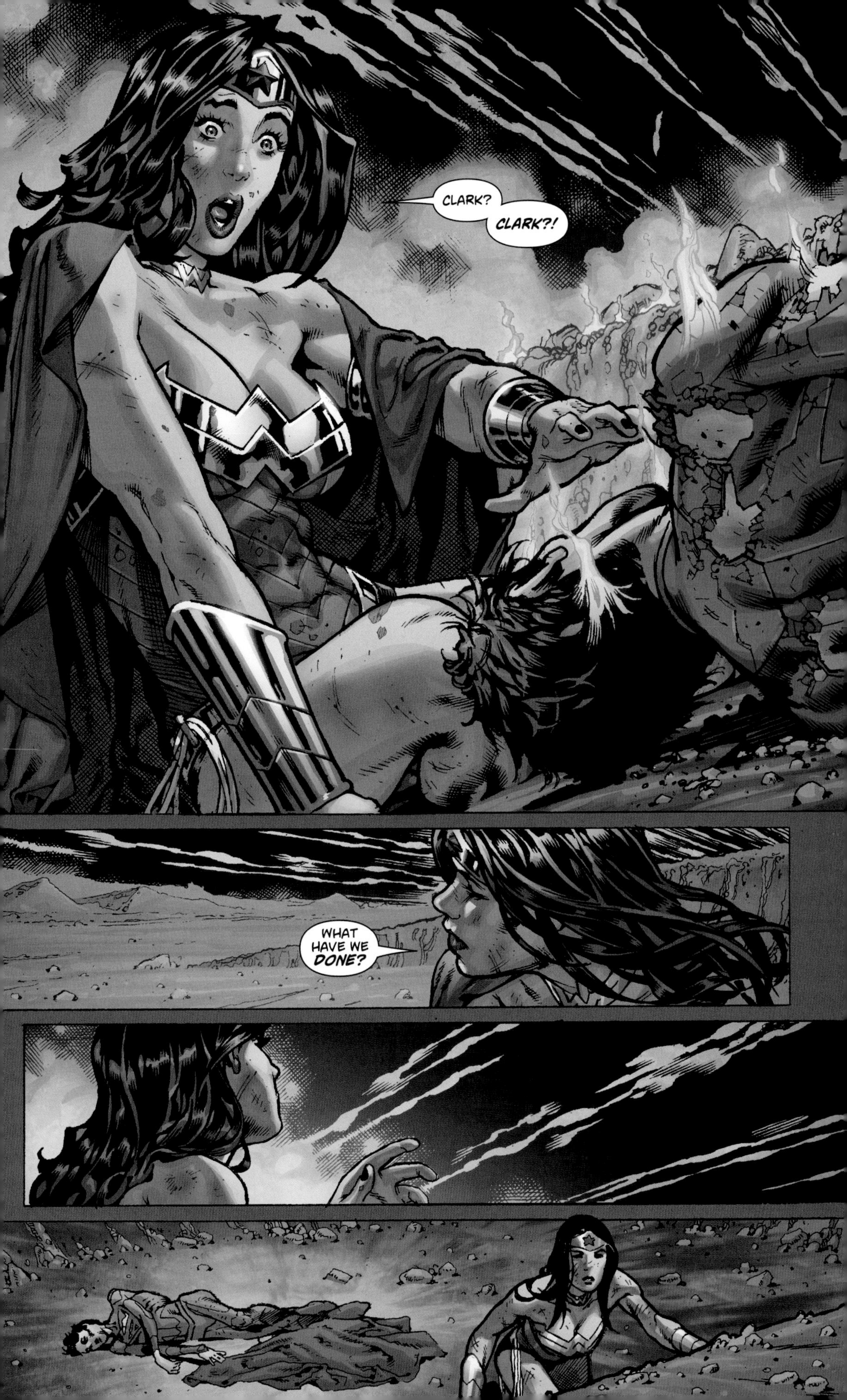
CLARK?
CLARK?!
WHAT HAVE WE DONE?

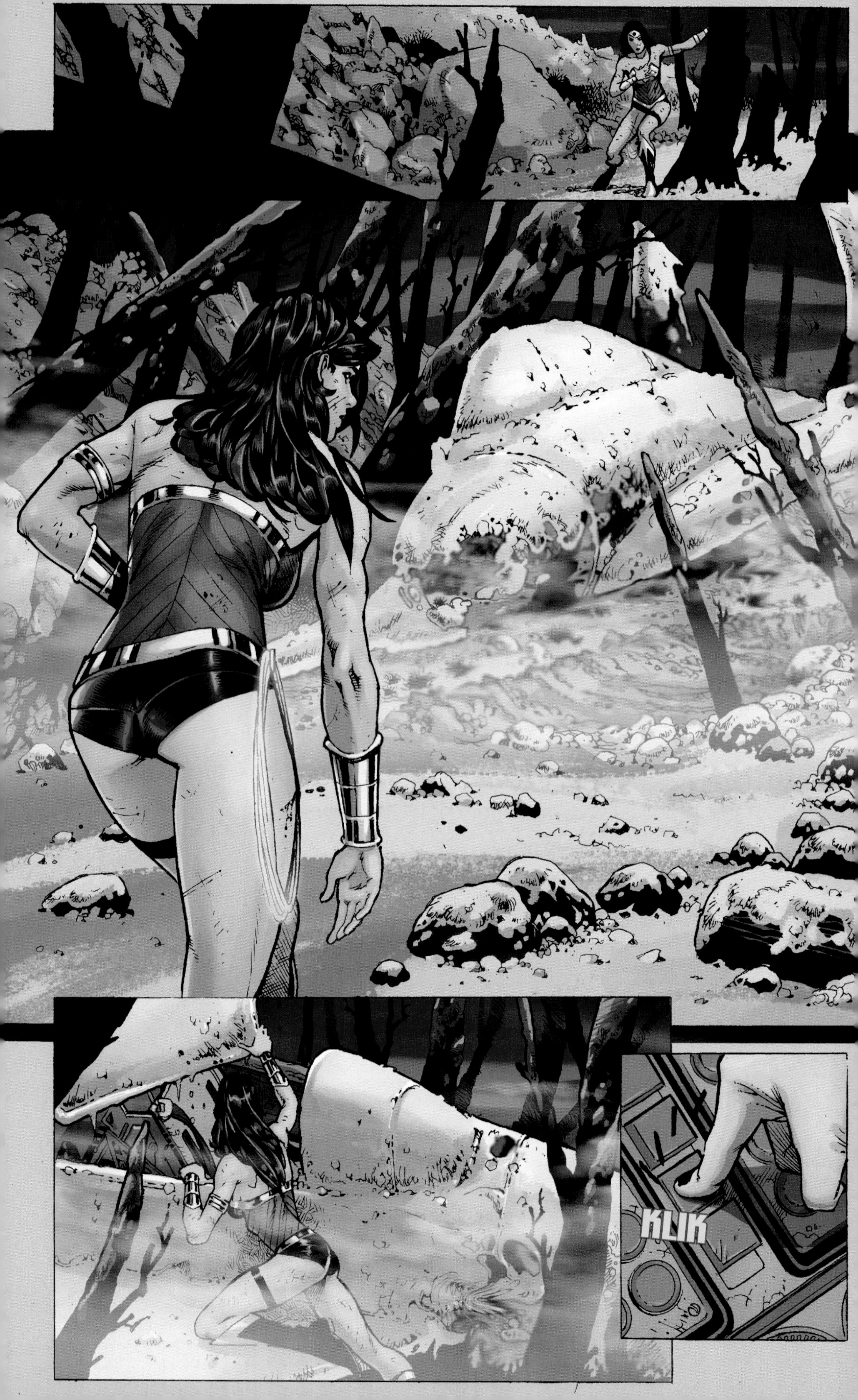
KLIK

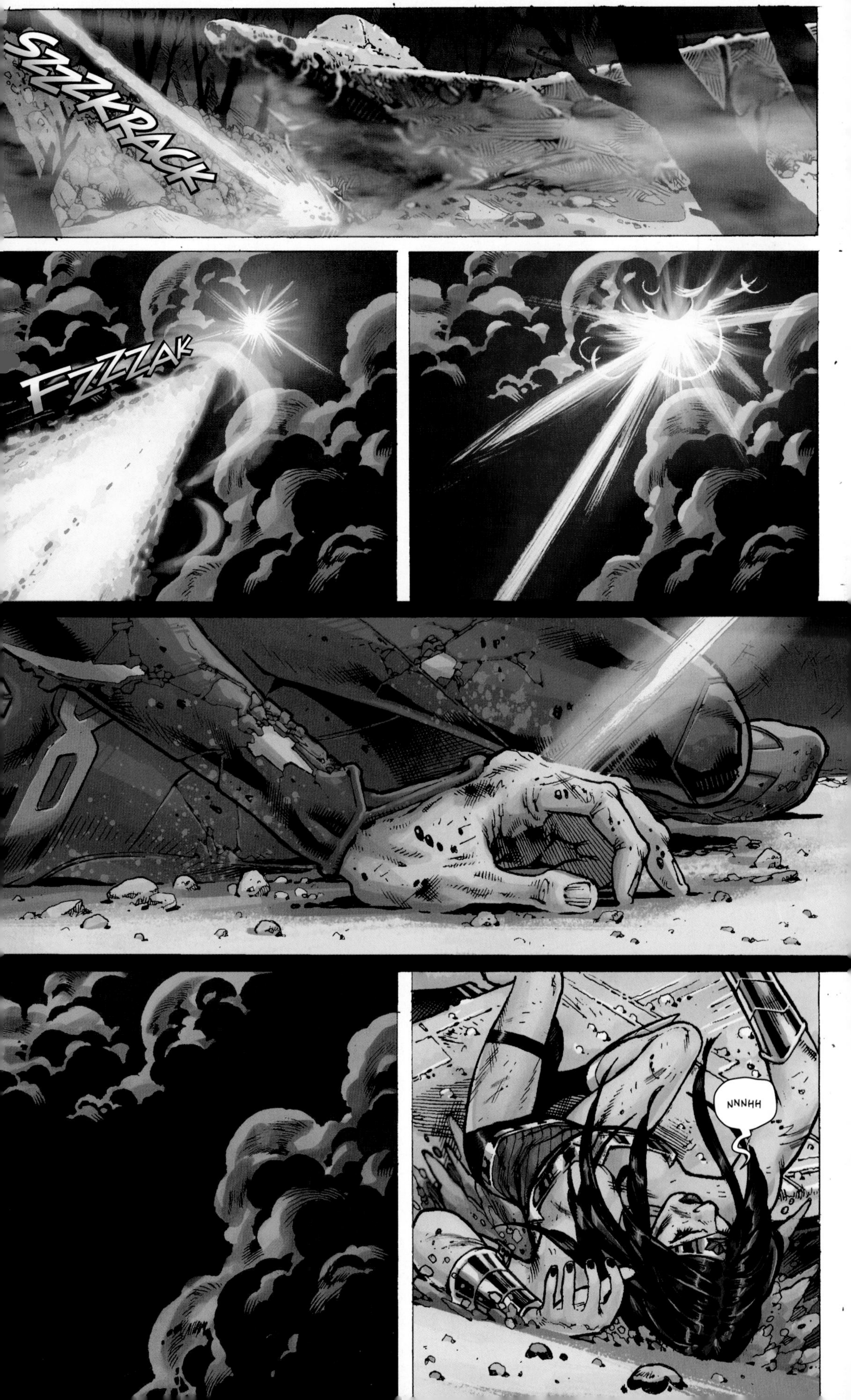
SSZZKRACK
FZZZZAK
NNNHH

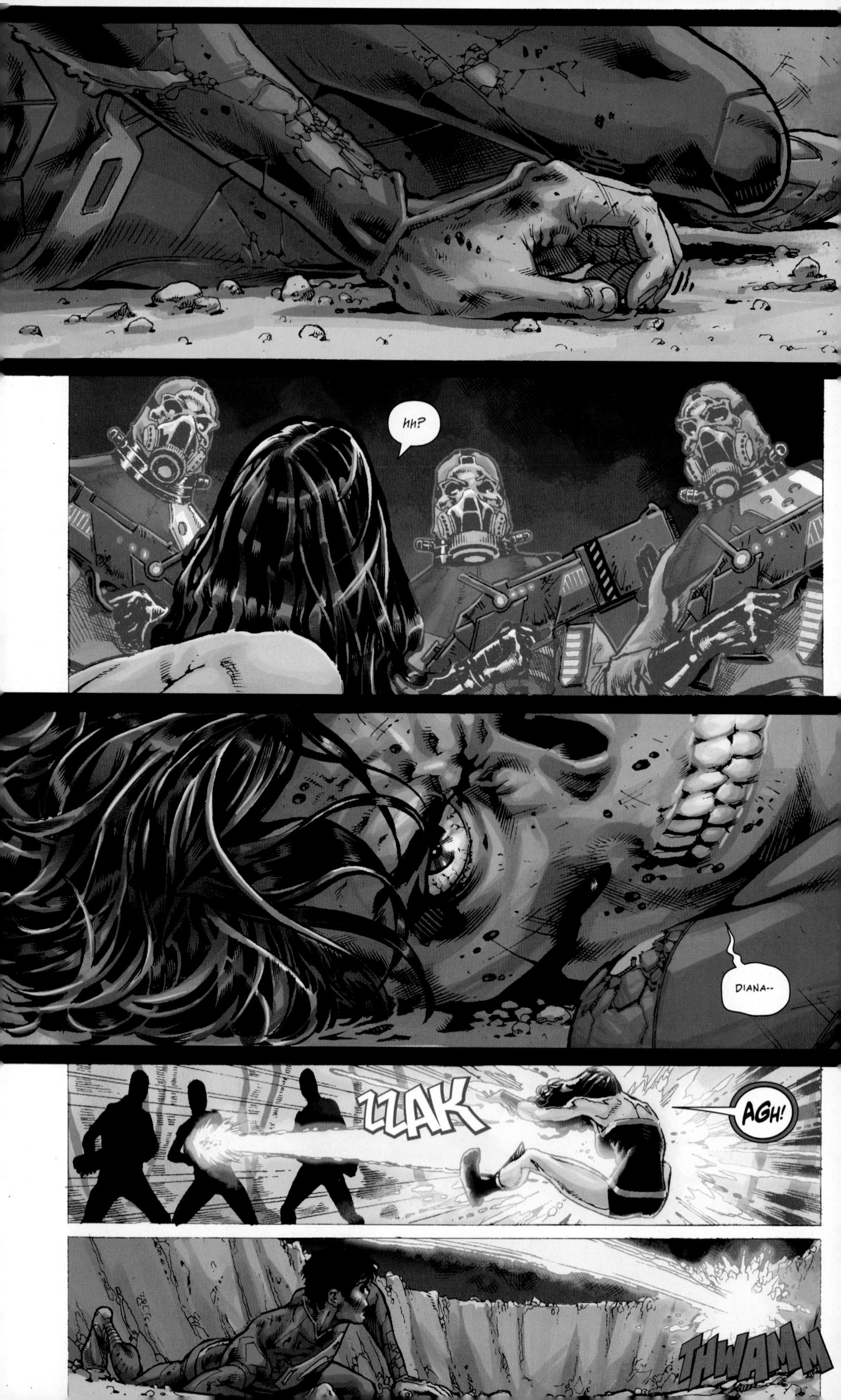
hh?
DIANA--
ZZAK
AGH!
THWAMM

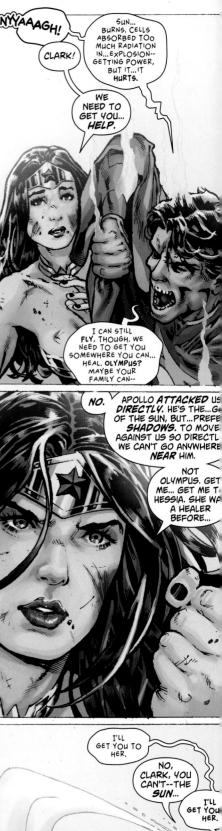

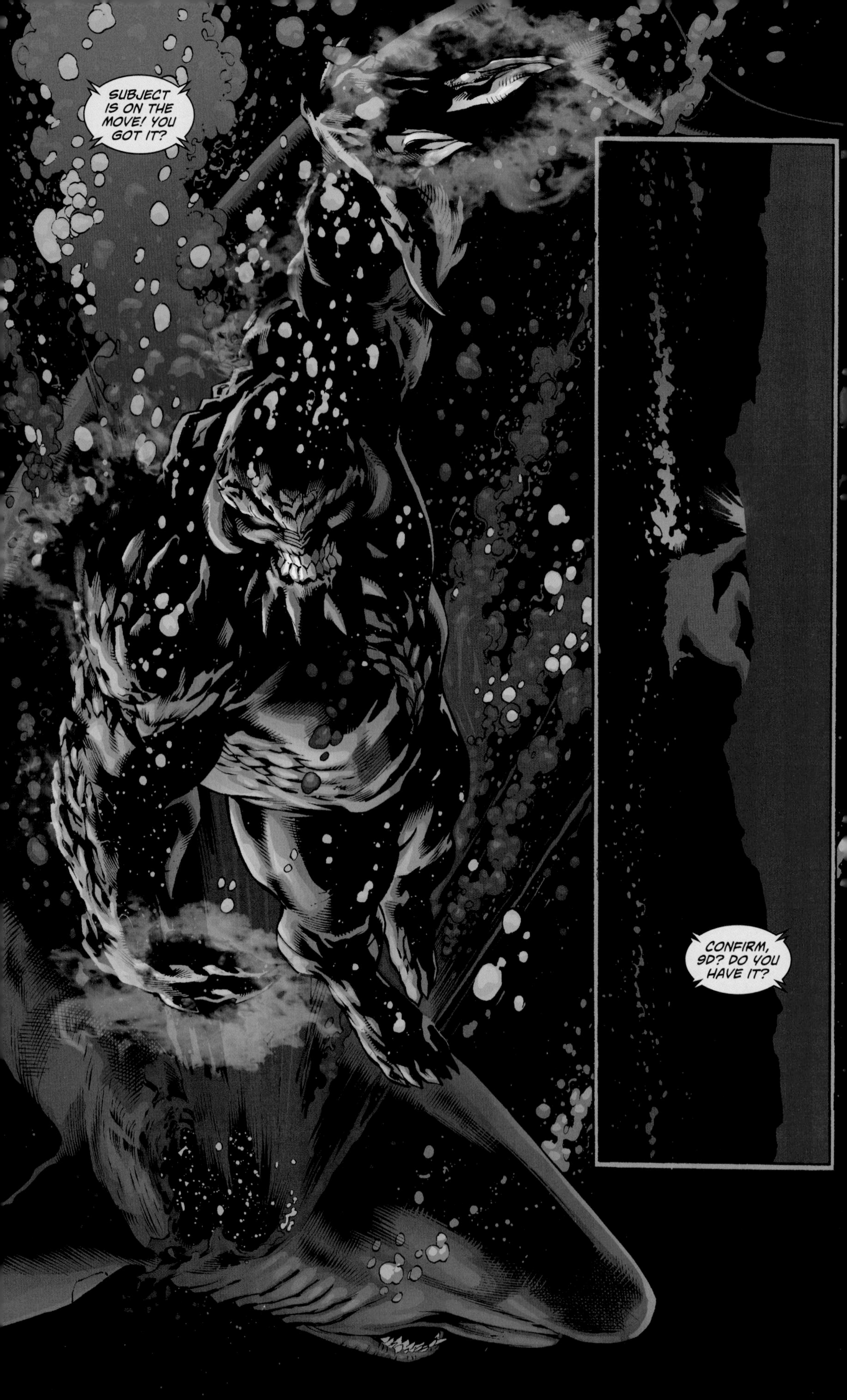
SUBJECT IS ON THE MOVE! YOU GOT IT?
CONFIRM, 9D? DO YOU HAVE IT?

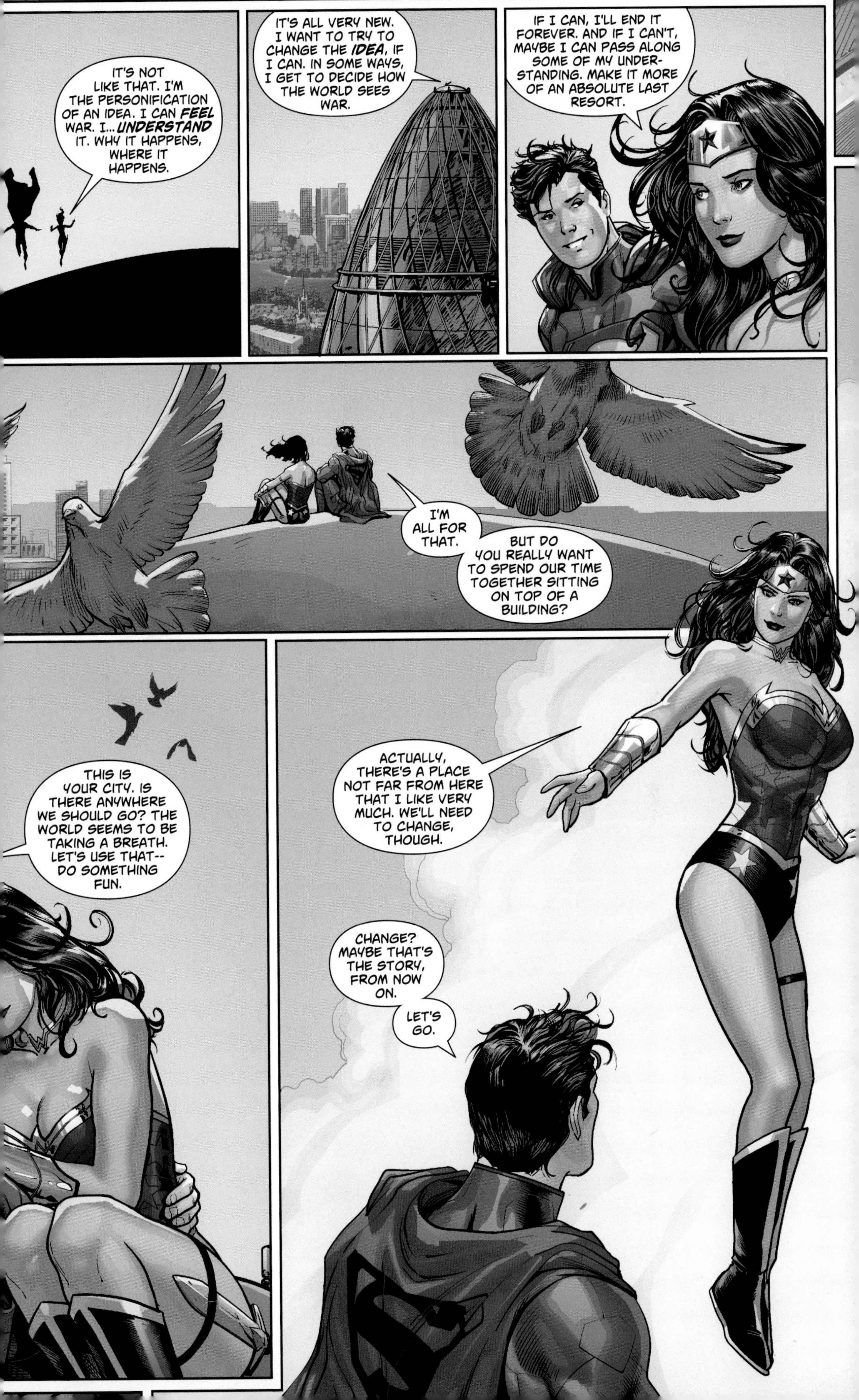
IT'S NOT LIKE THAT. I'M THE PERSONIFICATION OF AN IDEA. I CAN FEEL WAR. I...UNDERSTAND IT. WHY IT HAPPENS, WHERE IT HAPPENS.
IT'S ALL VERY NEW. I WANT TO TRY TO CHANGE THE IDEA, IF I CAN. IN SOME WAYS, I GET TO DECIDE HOW THE WORLD SEES WAR.
IF I CAN, I'LL END IT FOREVER. AND IF I CAN'T, MAYBE I CAN PASS ALONG SOME OF MY UNDER-STANDING. MAKE IT MORE OF AN ABSOLUTE LAST RESORT.
I'M ALL FOR THAT.
BUT DO YOU REALLY WANT TO SPEND OUR TIME TOGETHER SITTING ON TOP OF A BUILDING?
THIS IS YOUR CITY. IS THERE ANYWHERE WE SHOULD GO? THE WORLD SEEMS TO BE TAKING A BREATH. LET'S USE THAT-- DO SOMETHING FUN.
ACTUALLY, THERE'S A PLACE NOT FAR FROM HERE THAT I LIKE VERY MUCH. WE'LL NEED TO CHANGE, THOUGH.
CHANGE? MAYBE THAT'S THE STORY, FROM NOW ON.
LET'S GO.

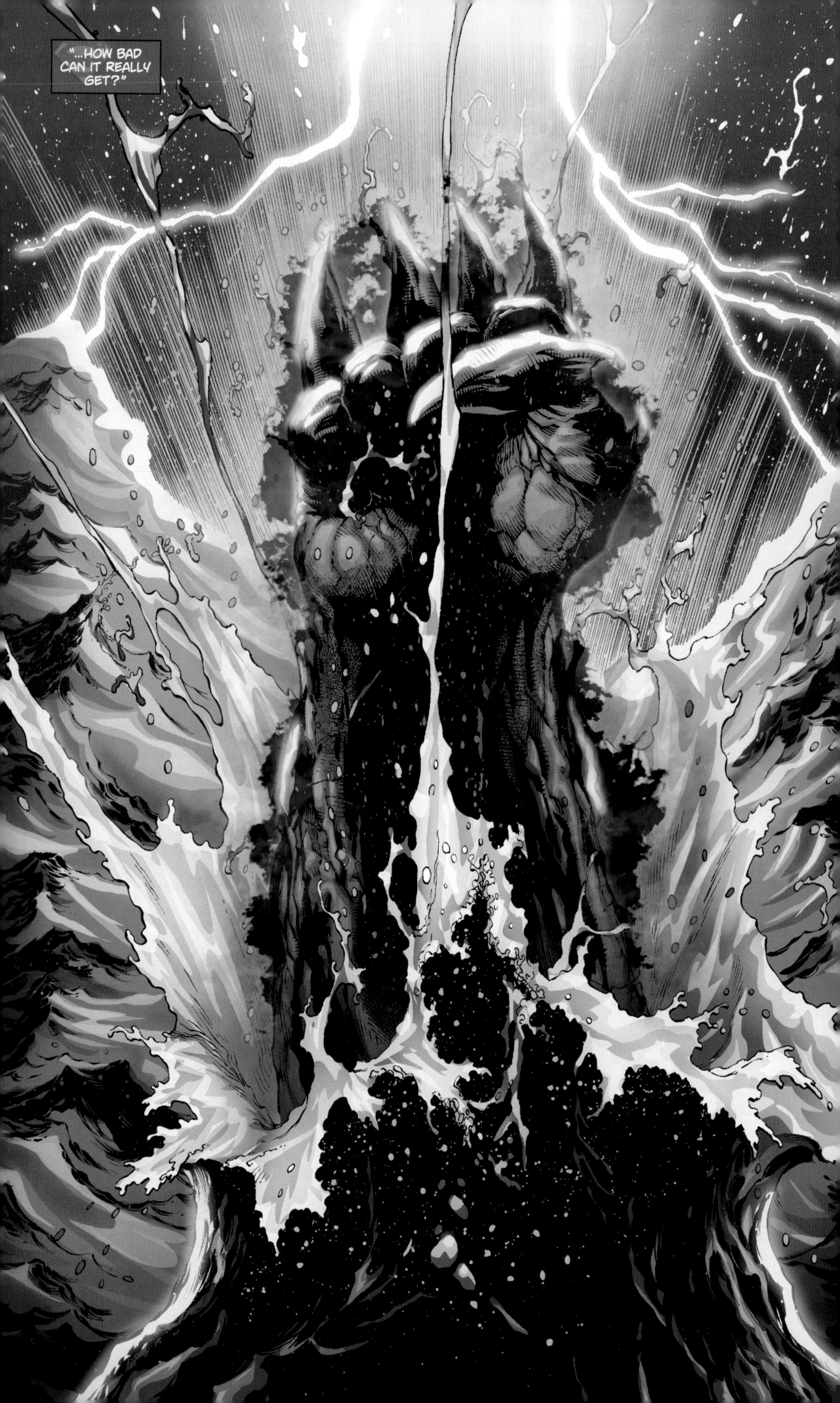
"...HOW BAD CAN IT REALLY GET?"

VARIANT COVER GALLERY

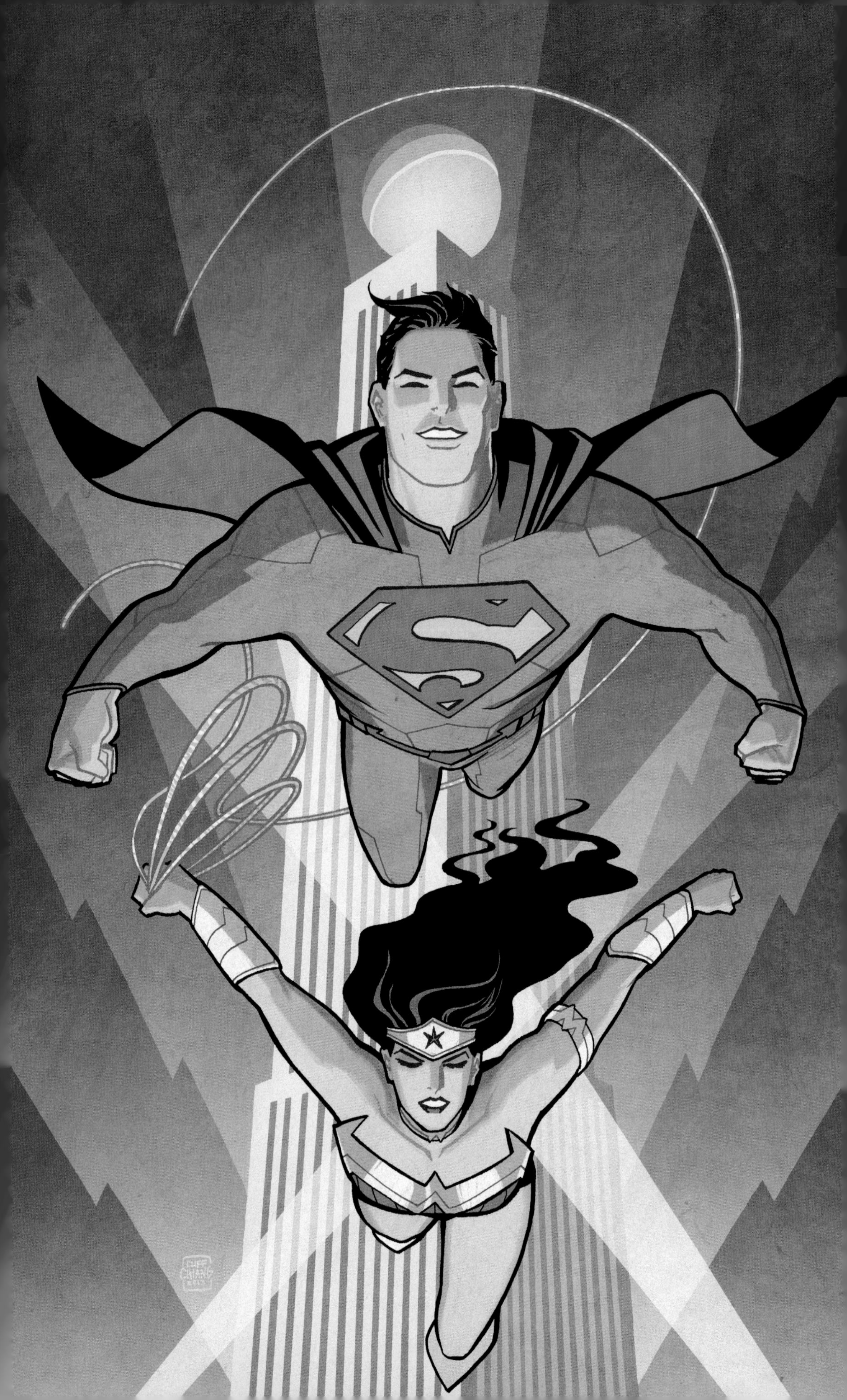
CLIFF CHIANG

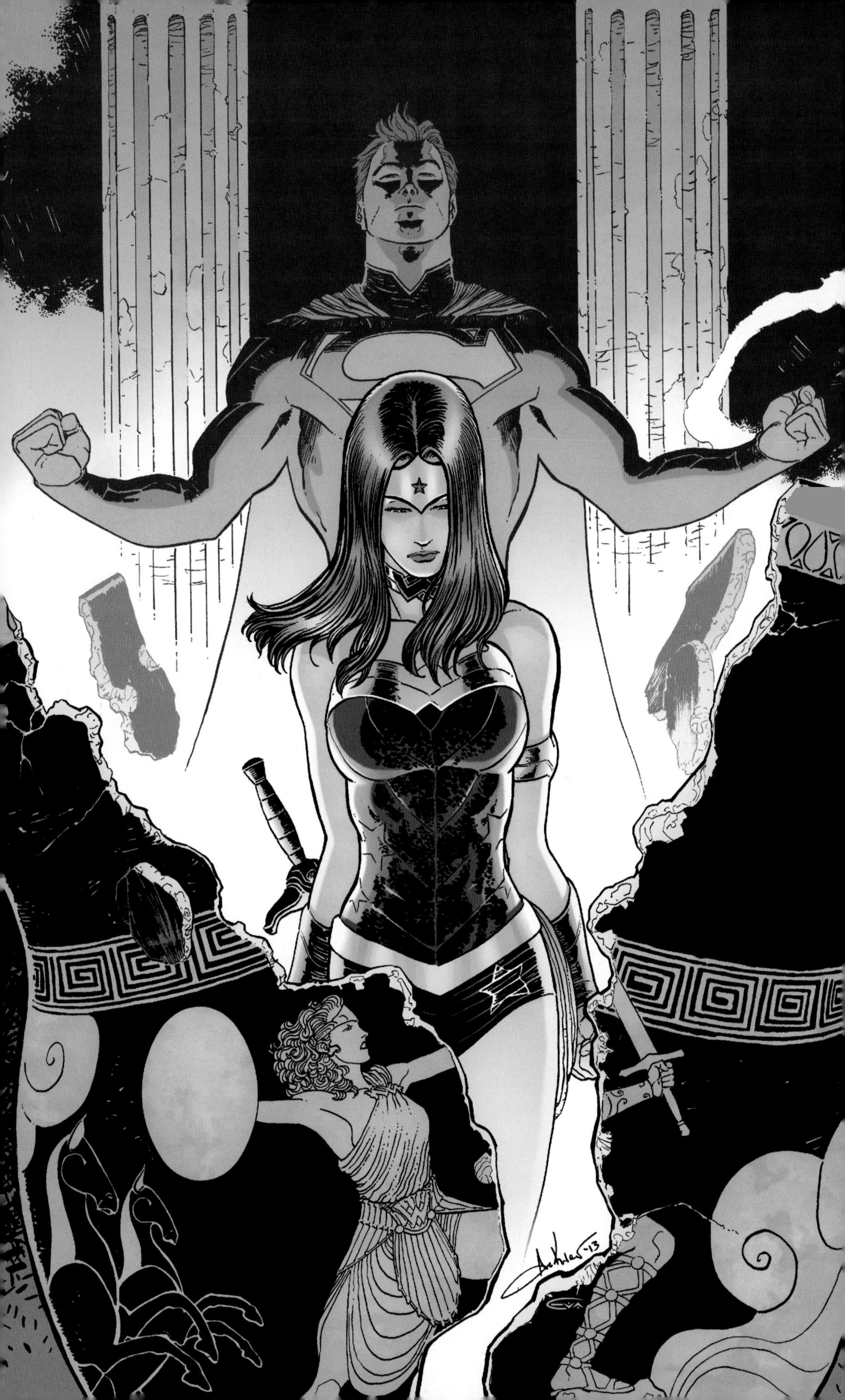

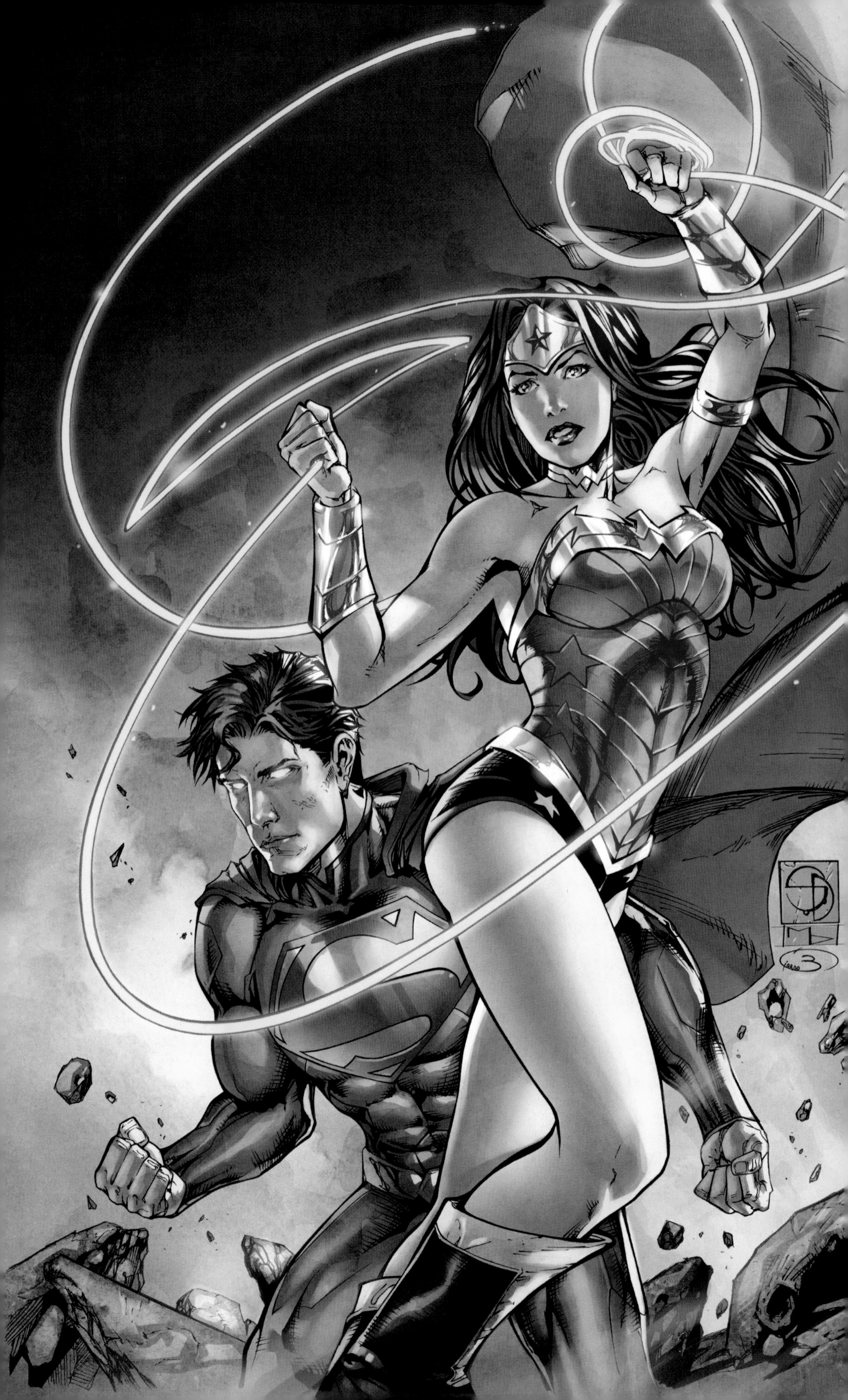

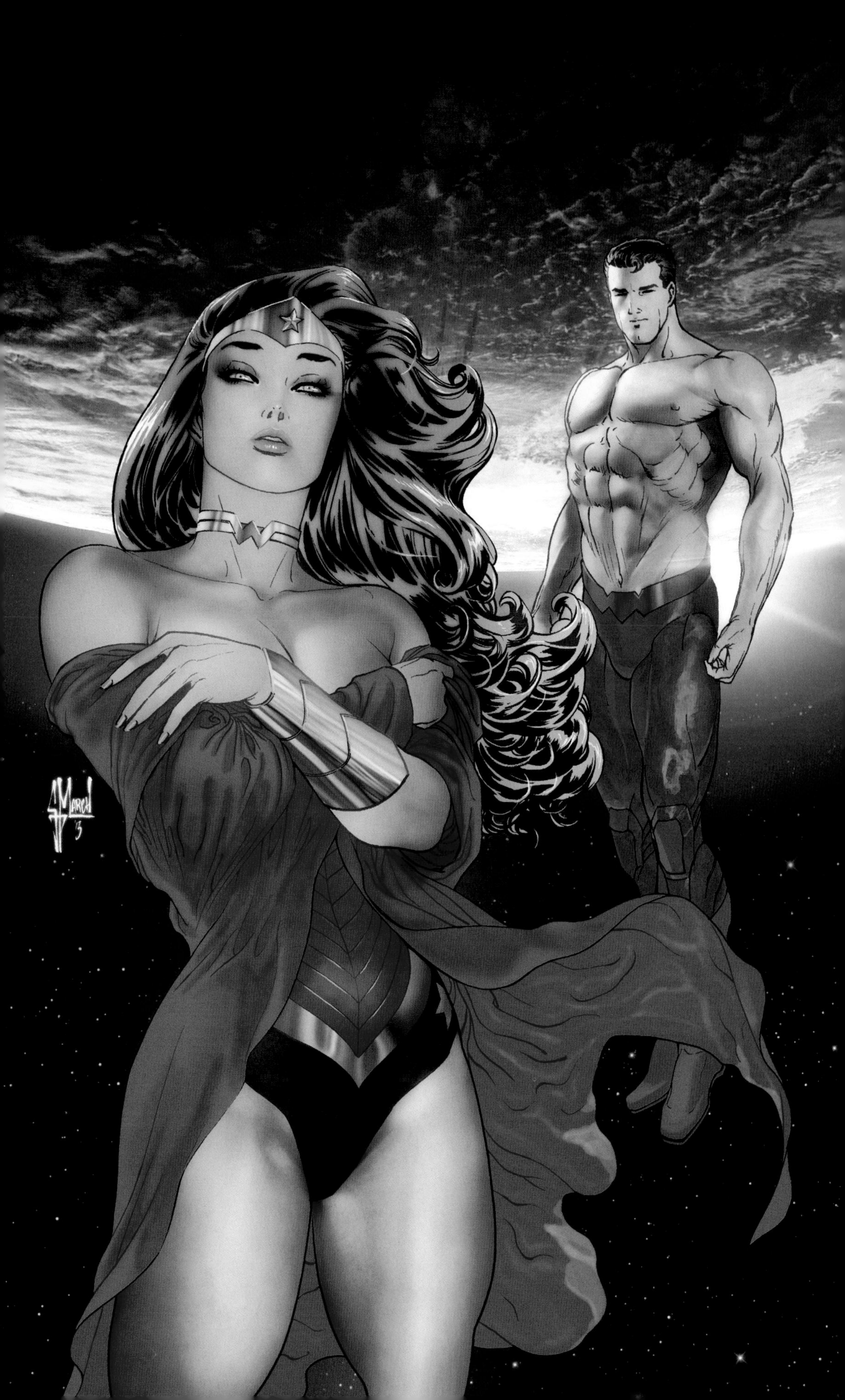

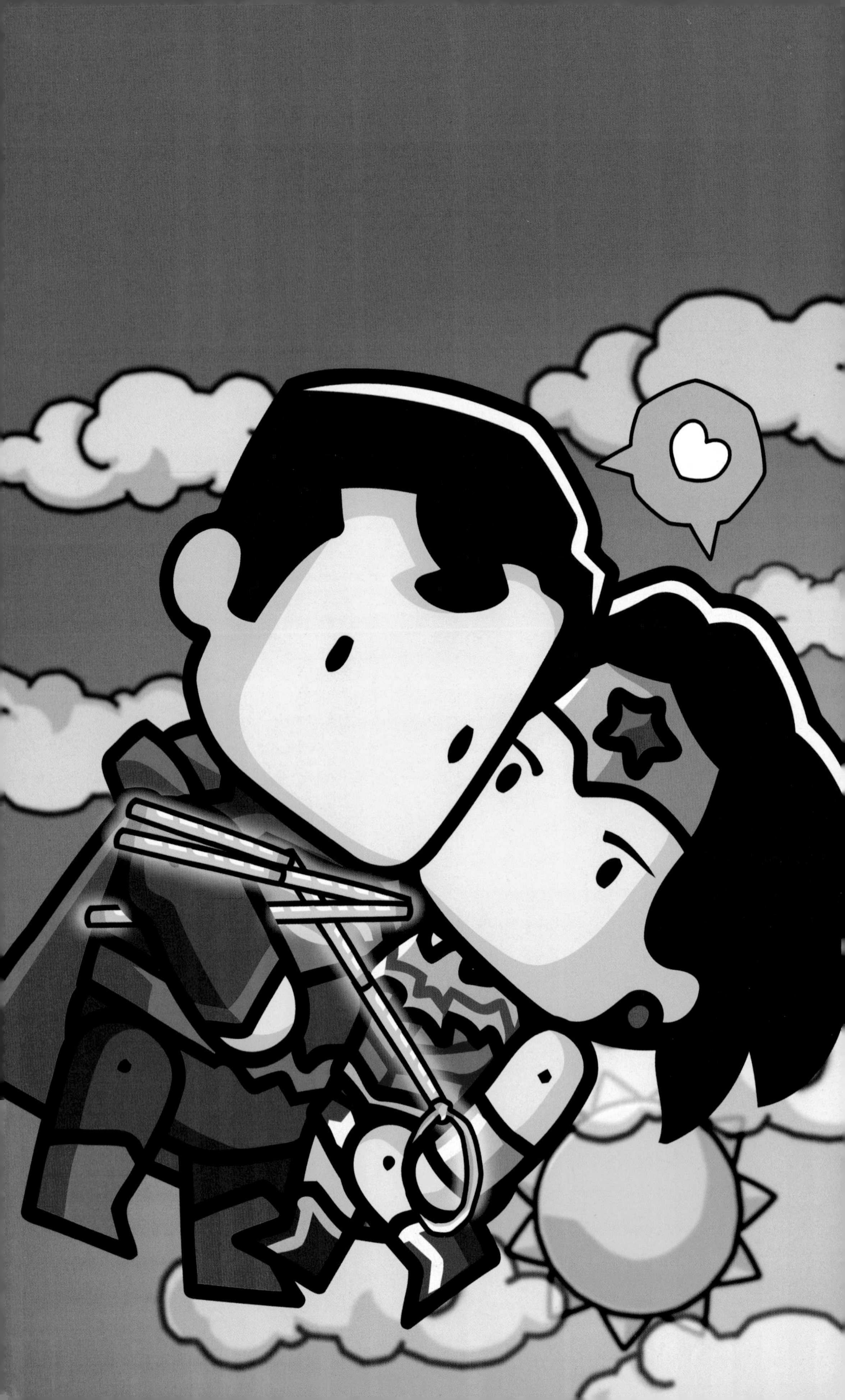

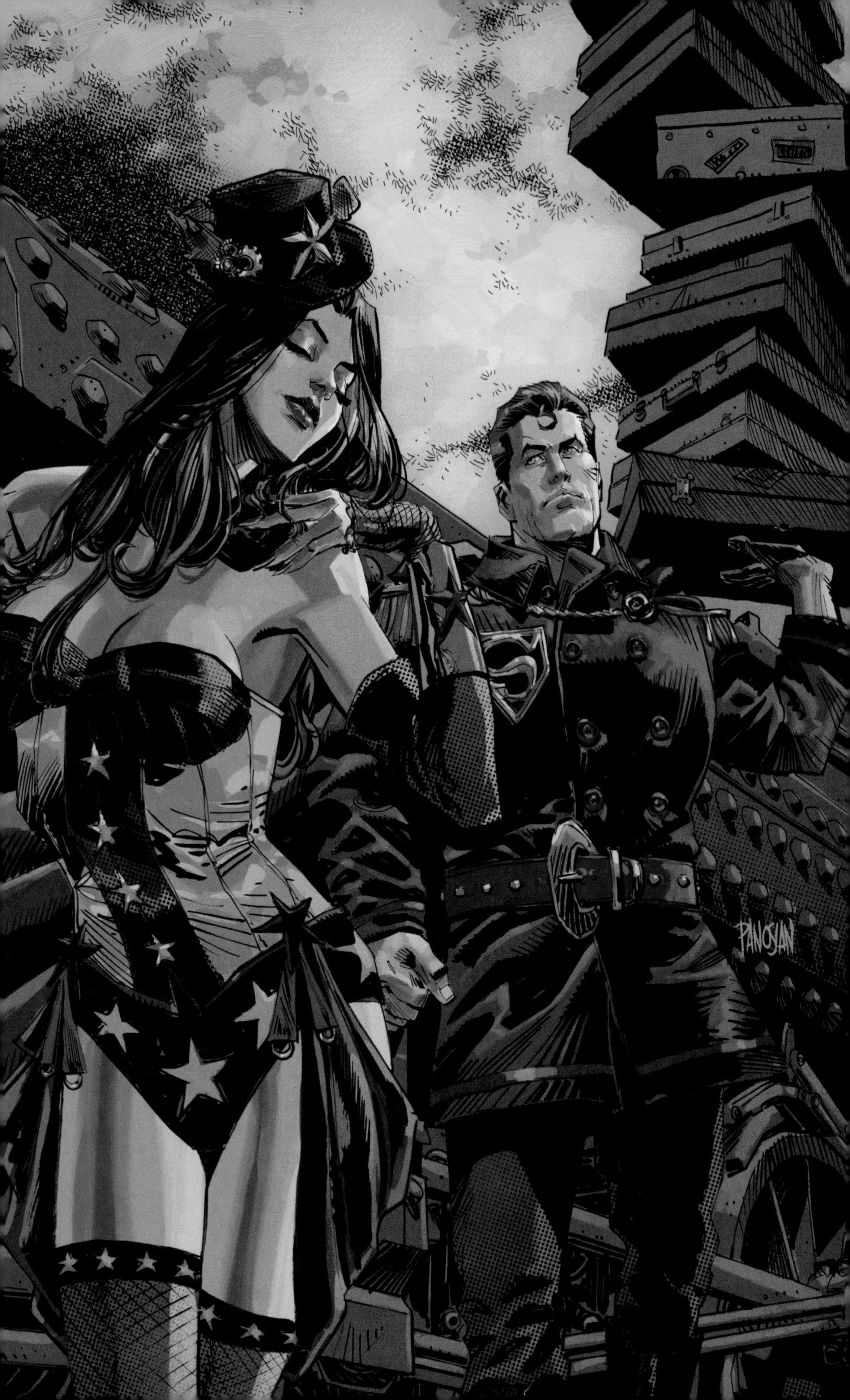
PANOSIAN

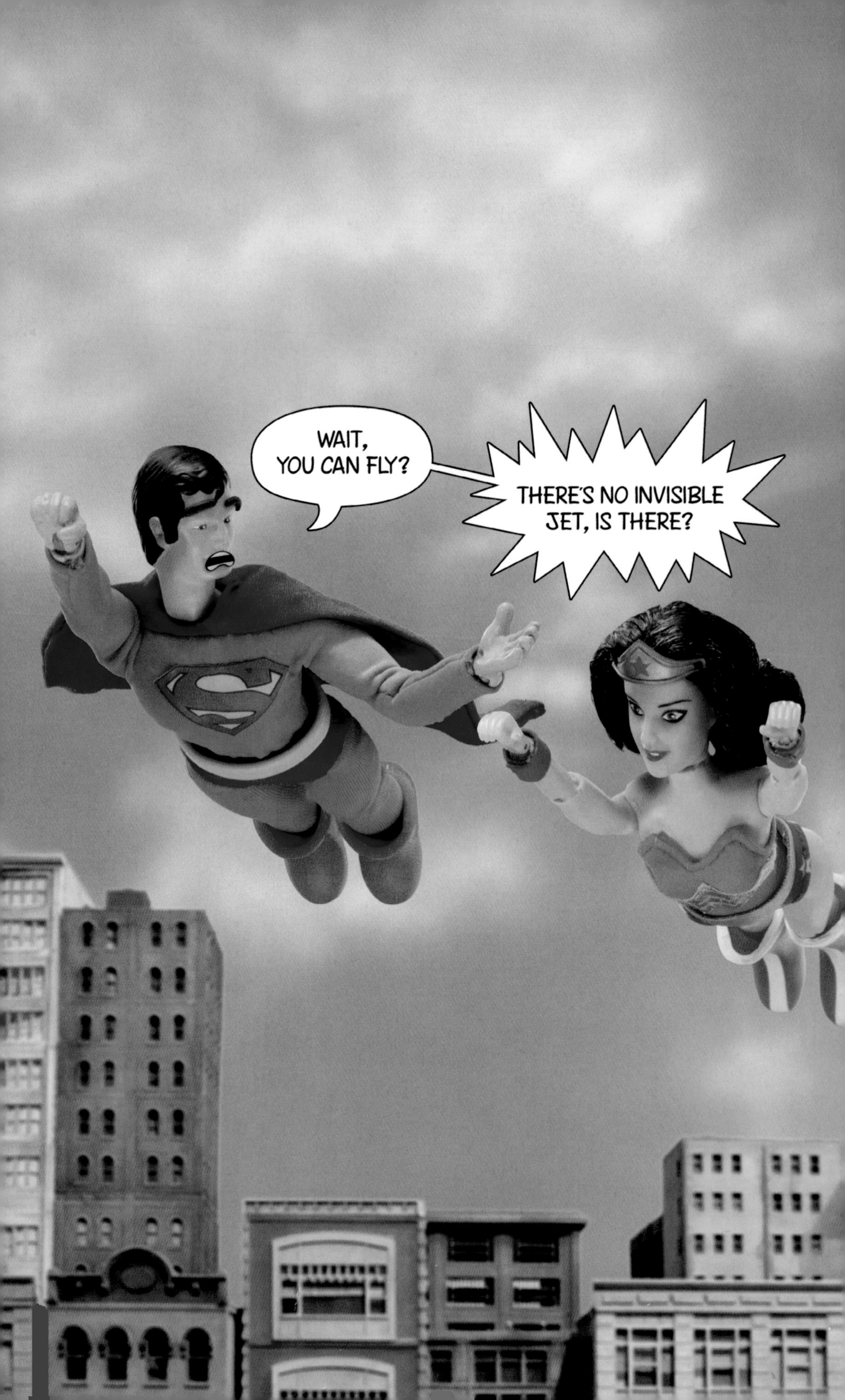
WAIT, YOU CAN FLY?
THERE'S NO INVISIBLE JET, IS THERE?

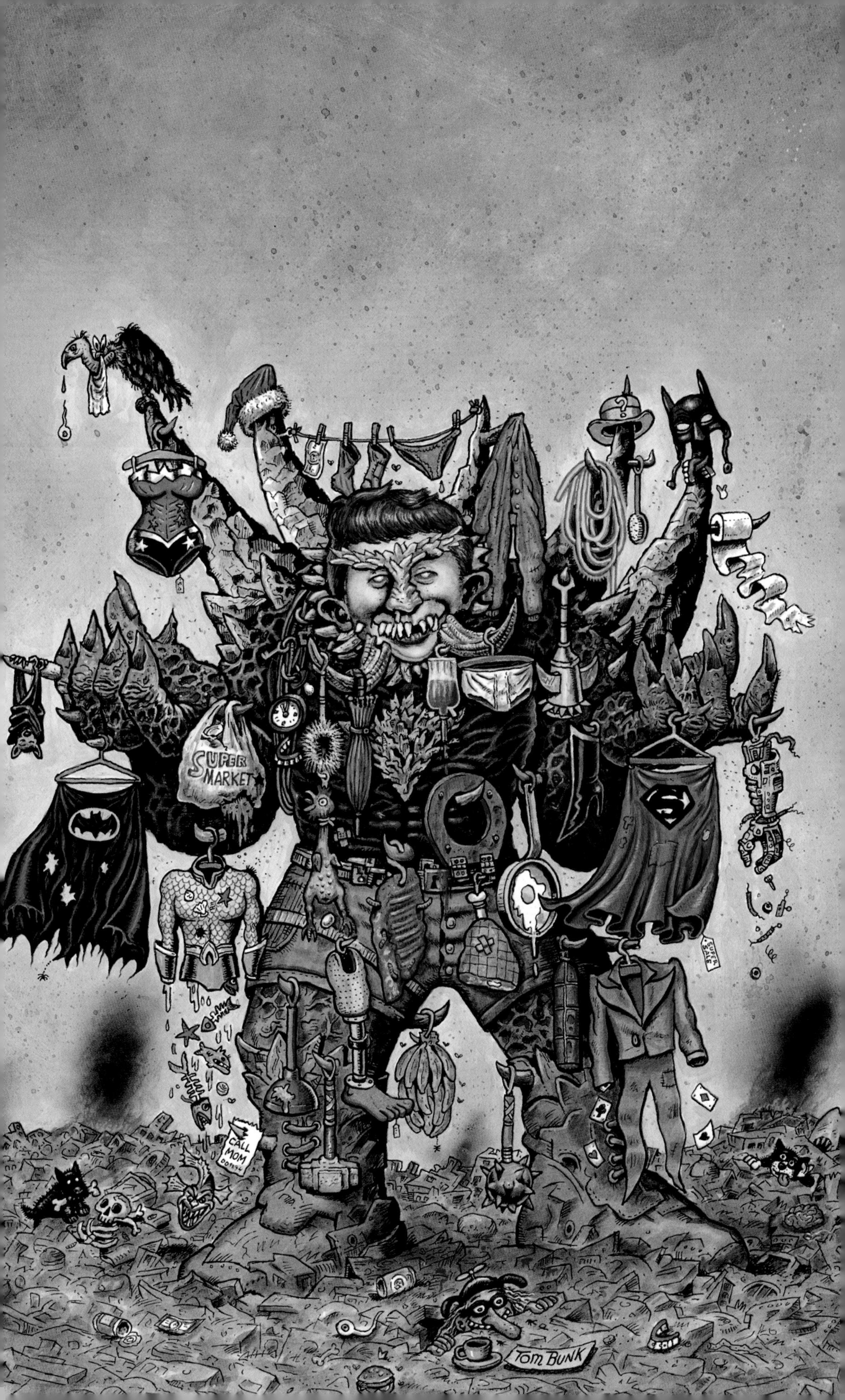
SUPER MARKET
CALL MOM
TOM BUNK

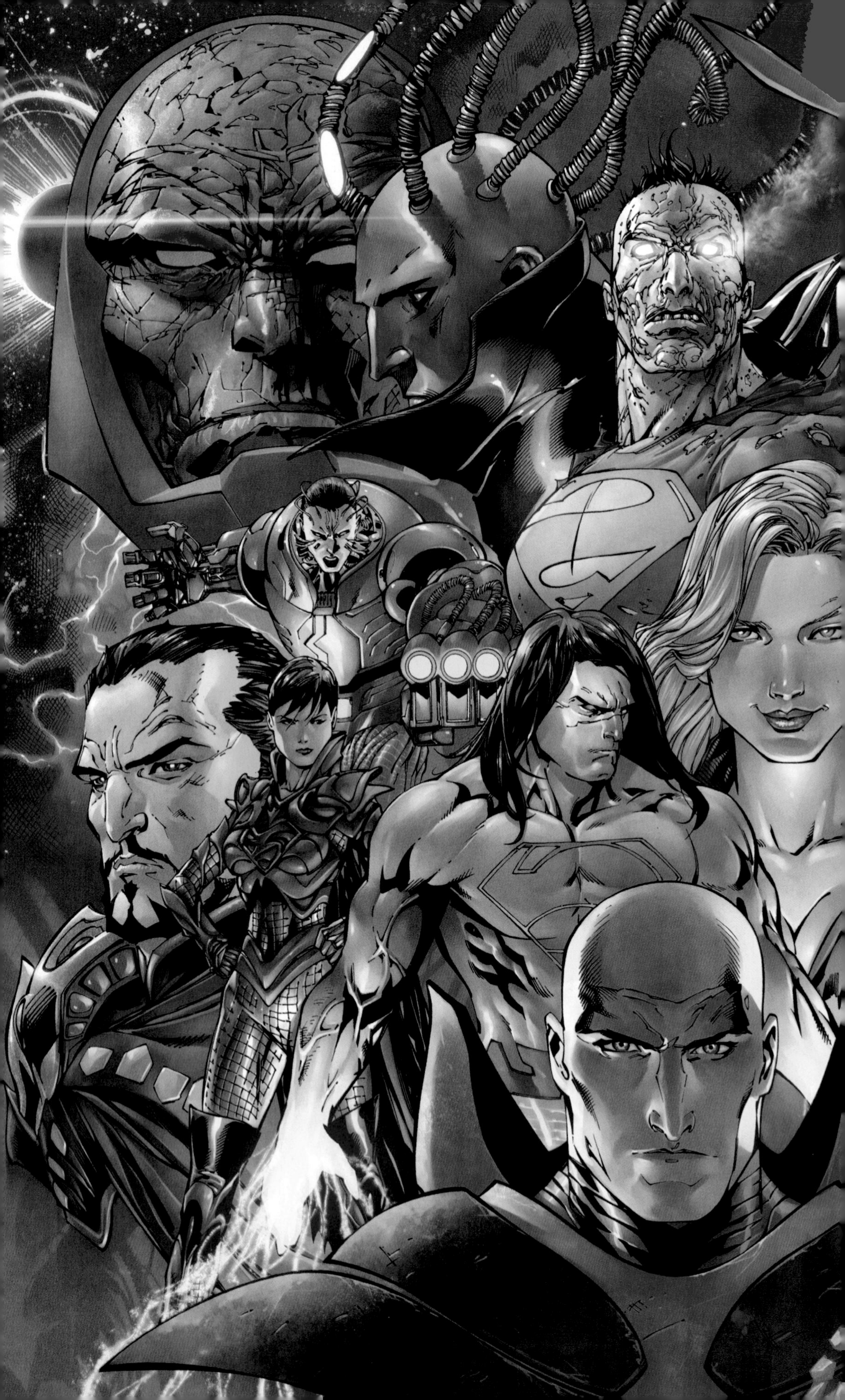

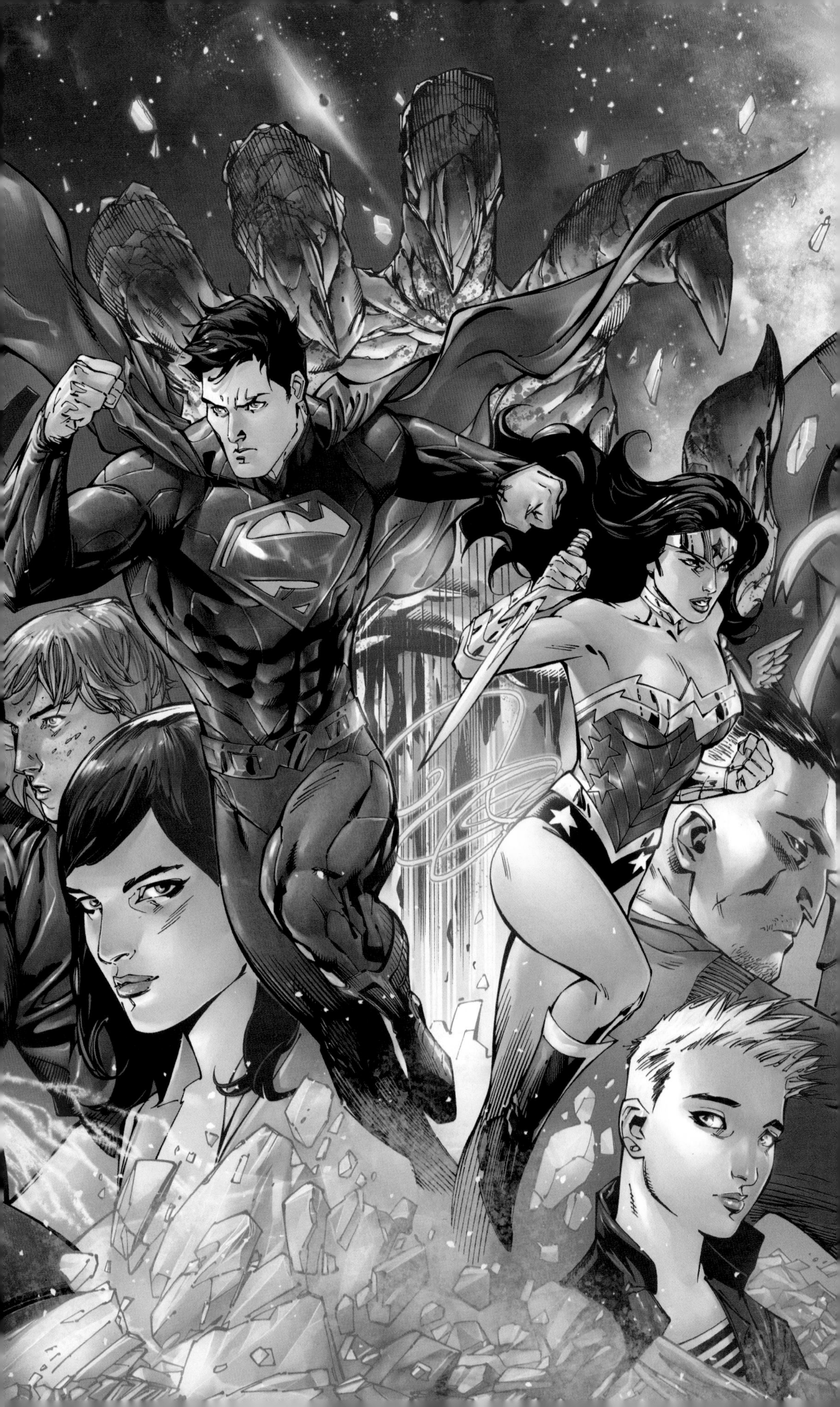

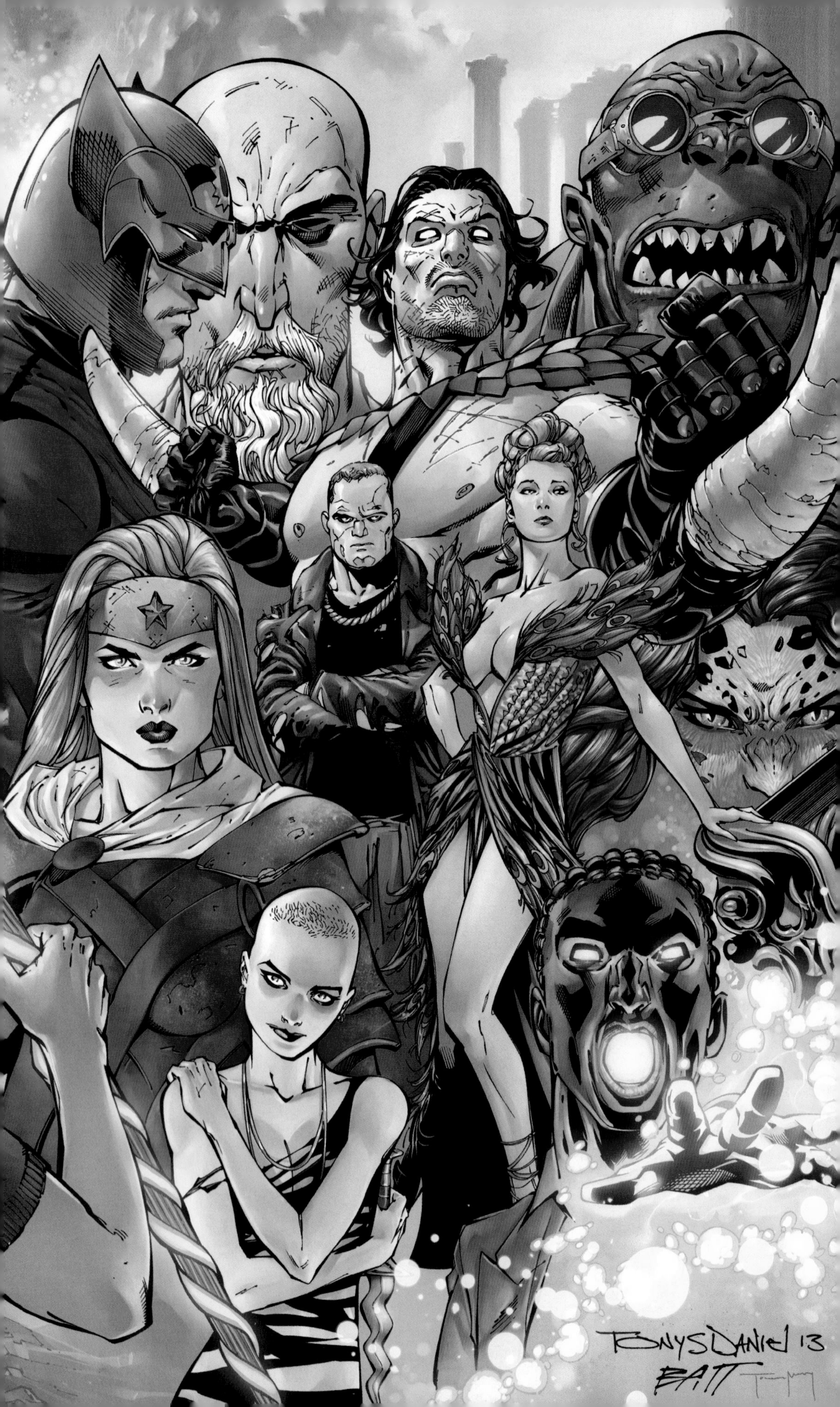
TONY S DANIEL 13
BATT

START AT THE BEGINNING!

SUPERMAN VOLUME 1:
WHAT PRICE TOMORROW?

**SUPERMAN VOL. 2:
SECRETS & LIES**

**SUPERMAN VOL. 3:
FURY AT WORLD'S
END**

**SUPERMAN:
H'EL ON EARTH**

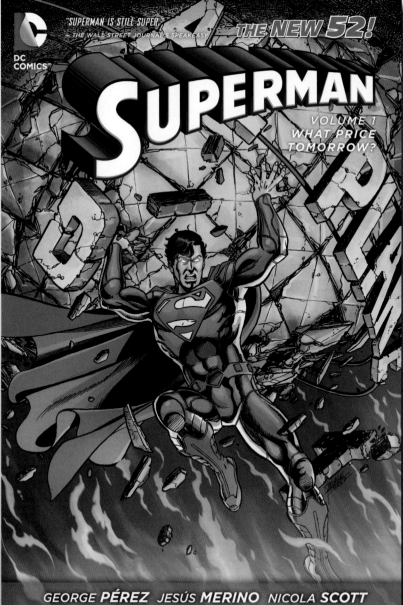

GEORGE **PÉREZ**   Jesús **MERINO**   Nicola **SCOTT**

"Clear storytelling at its best. It's an intriguing concept and easy to grasp."
—THE NEW YORK TIMES

"Azzarello is rebuilding the mythology of Wonder Woman."
-MAXIM

START AT THE BEGINNING!

WONDER WOMAN VOLUME 1: BLOOD

MR. TERRIFIC VOLUME 1: MIND GAMES

BLUE BEETLE VOLUME 1: METAMORPHOSIS

THE FURY OF FIRESTORM: THE NUCLEAR MEN VOLUME 1: GOD PARTICLE

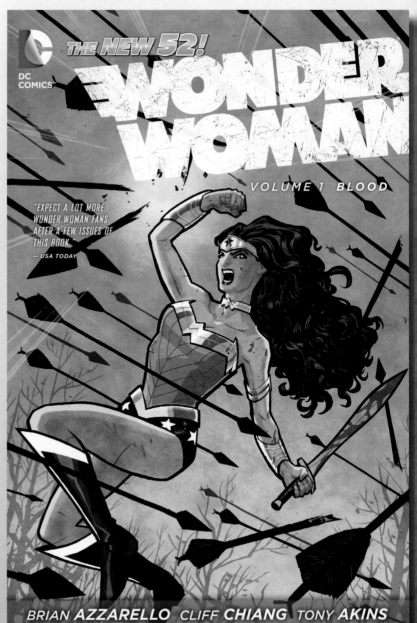

BRIAN **AZZARELLO** CLIFF **CHIANG** TONY **AKINS**

"Welcoming to new fans looking to get into superhero comics for the first time and old fans who gave up on the funny-books long ago."
—SCRIPPS HOWARD NEWS SERVICE

START AT THE BEGINNING!

JUSTICE LEAGUE VOLUME 1: ORIGIN

AQUAMAN VOLUME 1: THE TRENCH

THE SAVAGE HAWKMAN VOLUME 1: DARKNESS RISING

GREEN ARROW VOLUME 1: THE MIDAS TOUCH

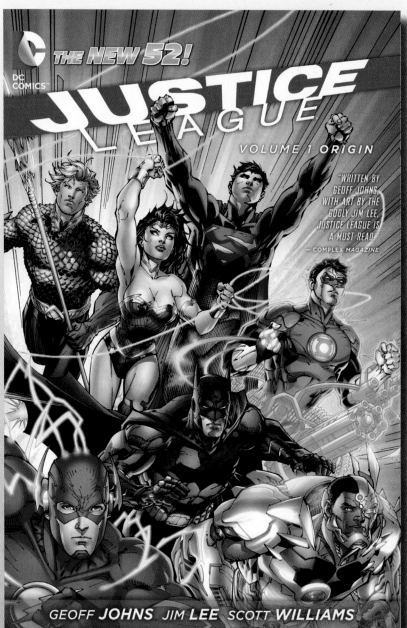

GEOFF **JOHNS** JIM **LEE** SCOTT **WILLIAMS**